# PAUL GERRARD

## THE CABIN BOY

## W. H. G. KINGSTON

1st WORLD
LIBRARY
Literary Society

# Paul Gerrard

## W. H. G. Kingston

© 1st World Library, 2007
PO Box 2211
Fairfield, IA 52556
www.1stworldlibrary.com
First Edition

LCCN: 2007934209

Softcover ISBN: 978-1-4218-9681-6
Hardcover ISBN: 978-1-4218-9781-3
eBook ISBN: 978-1-4218-9581-9

Purchase *"Paul Gerrard"*
as a traditional bound book at:
www.1stWorldLibrary.com/purchase.asp?ISBN=978-1-4218-9681-6

1st World Library is a literary, educational organization
dedicated to:

- Creating a free internet library of downloadable ebooks

- Hosting writing competitions and offering book publishing
scholarships.

Interested in more 1st World Library books? contact:
literacy@1stworldlibrary.com
Check us out at: www.1stworldlibrary.com

# 1ˢᵗ World Library Literary Society

## Giving Back to the World

"If you want to work on the core problem, it's early school literacy."

**- James Barksdale, former CEO of Netscape**

"No skill is more crucial to the future of a child, or to a democratic and prosperous society, than literacy."

**- Los Angeles Times**

"Literacy... means far more than learning how to read and write... The aim is to transmit... knowledge and promote social participation."

**- UNESCO**

"Literacy is not a luxury, it is a right and a responsibility. If our world is to meet the challenges of the twenty-first century we must harness the energy and creativity of all our citizens."

**- President Bill Clinton**

"Parents should be encouraged to read to their children, and teachers should be equipped with all available techniques for teaching literacy, so the varying needs and capacities of individual kids can be taken into account."

**- Hugh Mackay**

# CHAPTER ONE

Darkness had set in. The wind was blowing strong from the southwest, with a fine, wetting, penetrating rain, which even tarpaulins, or the thickest of Flushing coats, would scarcely resist. A heavy sea also was running, such as is often to be met with in the chops of the British Channel during the month of November, at which time of the year, in the latter part of the last century, a fine frigate was struggling with the elements, in a brave attempt to beat out into the open ocean. She was under close-reefed topsails; but even with this snug canvas she often heeled over to the blast, till her lee-ports were buried in the foaming waters. Now she rose to the summit of a white-crested sea; now she sunk into the yawning trough below; and ever and anon as she dashed onward in spite of all opposition, a mass of water would strike her bows with a clap like that of thunder, and rising over her bulwarks, would deluge her deck fore and aft, and appear as if about to overwhelm her altogether. A portion of the officers and crew stood at their posts on deck, now and then shaking the water from their hats and coats, after they had been covered with a thicker shower than usual of rain or spray, or looking up aloft at the straining canvas, or out over the dark expanse of ocean; but all of them taking matters very composedly, and wishing only that their watch were over, that they might enjoy such comforts as were to be found below, and take part in the conviviality which, in spite of the gale, was going forward.

It was Saturday night, and fore and aft the time-honoured toast of "sweethearts and wives" was being enthusiastically drunk,—nowhere more enthusiastically than in the midshipmen's berth; and not the less so probably, that few of its light-hearted inmates had in reality either one or the other. What cared they for the tumult which raged above their heads? They had a stout ship and trusted officers, and their heads and insides were well accustomed to every possible variety of lurching and pitching, in which their gallant frigate the *Cerberus* was at that moment indulging. The *Cerberus*, a fine 42-gun frigate, commanded by Captain Walford, had lately been put in commission, and many of her officers and midshipmen had only joined just before the ship sailed, and were thus comparatively strangers to each other. The frigate was now bound out to a distant station, where foes well worthy of her, it was hoped, would be encountered, and prize-money without stint be made.

The midshipmen's berth of the *Cerberus* was a compartment of somewhat limited dimensions,—now filled to overflowing with mates, midshipmen, masters'-assistants, assistant-surgeons, and captain's and purser's clerks,—some men with grey heads, and others boys scarcely in their teens, of all characters and dispositions, the sons of nobles of the proudest names, and the offspring of plebeians, who had little to boast of on that score, or on any other; but the boys might hope, notwithstanding, as many did, to gain fame and a name for themselves. The din of tongues and shouts of laughter which proceeded out of that narrow berth, rose even above the creaking of bulkheads, the howling of the wind, and the roar of the waves.

The atmosphere was somewhat dense and redolent of rum, and could scarcely be penetrated by the light of the three

W. H. G. Kingston

purser's dips which burned in some battered tin candlesticks, secured by lanyards to the table. At one end of the table over which he presided as caterer, sat Tony Noakes, an old mate, whose grog-blossomed nose and bloodshot eyes told of many a past debauch.

"Here's to my own true love, Sally Pounce," he shouted in a husky voice, lifting to his lips a stiff glass of grog, which was eyed wistfully by Tilly Blake, a young midshipman, from whose share of rum he had abstracted its contents.

"Mrs Noakes that is to be," cried out Tilly in a sharp tone. "But I say, she'll not stand having her grog drunk up."

"That remark smells of mutiny, youngster," exclaimed Noakes, with a fierce glance towards the audacious midshipman.

"By the piper, but it's true, though," put in Paddy O'Grady, who had also been deprived of the larger portion of his grog.

Most of the youngsters, on finding others inclined to stand up for their rights, made common cause with Blake and O'Grady. Enraged at this, Noakes threatened the malcontents with condign punishment.

"Yes, down with all mutiny and the rights of man or midshipmen," exclaimed in a somewhat sarcastic tone a good-looking youth, who himself wore the uniform of a midshipman.

"Well said, Devereux. We must support the rights and dignity of the oldsters, or the service will soon go to ruin," cried the old mate, whose voice grew thicker as he emptied glass after glass of his favourite liquor. "You show your sense, Devereux, and deserve your supper, but—there's no beef on the table. Here boy—boy Gerrard—bring the beef; be smart now—bring the beef. Don't stand staring there as if you saw a ghost."

The boy thus summoned was a fine lad of about fourteen, his shirt collar thrown back showing his neck, which supported a well-formed head, with a countenance intelligent and pleasant, but at that moment very pale, with an expression denoting unhappiness, and a feeling of dislike to, or dread of, those on whom he was waiting. A midshipmen's boy has seldom a pleasant time of it under any circumstances. Boy Gerrard, as he was called, did his best, though often unsuccessfully, to please his numerous masters.

"Why do you stand there, staring like a stuffed pig?" exclaimed Devereux, who was near the door. "It is the beef, not your calf's head we want. Away now, be smart about it."

The sally produced a hoarse laugh from all those sufficiently sober to understand a joke.

"The beef, sir; what beef?" asked boy Gerrard in a tone of alarm.

"Our beef," shouted old Noakes, heaving a biscuit at the boy's head. It was fortunate that no heavy missile was in his hand. "Take that to sharpen your wits."

Devereux laughed with others at the old mate's roughness. The boy gave an angry glance at him as he hurried off to the midshipmen's larder to execute the order.

Before long, boy Gerrard was seen staggering along the deck towards the berth with a huge piece of salt beef in his hands, and endeavouring to keep his legs as the frigate gave a heavy lurch or pitched forward, as she forced her way over the

W. H. G. Kingston

tumultuous seas. Boy Gerrard gazed at the berth of his many masters. He thought that he could reach it in another run. He made the attempt, but it was down hill, and before he could save himself he had shot the beef, though not the dish, into the very centre of the table, whence it bounded off and hit O'Grady, the Irish midshipman, a blow on the eye, which knocked him backward. Poor Gerrard stood gazing into the berth, and prepared for the speedy punishment which his past experience had taught him would follow.

"By the piper, but I'll teach you to keep a taughter gripe of the beef for the future, you spalpeen," exclaimed O'Grady, recovering himself, and about to hurl back the joint at the head of the unfortunate boy, when his arm was grasped by Devereux, who cried out, laughing,—"Preserve the beef and your temper, Paddy, and if boy Gerrard, after proper trial, shall be found to have purposely hurled the meat at your wise caput, he shall be forthwith delivered over to condign punishment."

"Oh, hang your sea-lawyer arguments; I'll break the chap's head, and listen to them afterwards," cried O'Grady, attempting to spring up to put his threat into execution.

Devereux again held him back, observing, "Break the boy's head if you like; I have no interest in preserving it, except that we may not find another boy to take his place; but you must listen to my arguments before you commence operations."

"Hear, hear! lawyer Devereux is about to open his mouth," cried several voices.

"Come, pass me the beef, and let me put some of it into my mouth, which is open already," exclaimed Peter Bruff, another of the older mates, who having just descended from the deck, and thrown off his dripping outer coat, had taken his seat at the table. His hair and whiskers were still wet with spray, his hands showed signs of service, and his fine open countenance—full of good-nature, and yet expressive of courage and determination, had a somewhat weather-worn appearance, though his crisp, curling, light hair showed that he was still in the early prime of manhood.

"Listen, gentlemen of the jury, and belay your jaw-tackles you who have no business in the matter, and Bruff being judge, I will plead boy Gerrard's cause against Paddy O'Grady, Esquire, midshipman of his Majesty's frigate *Cerberus*," cried Devereux, striking the table with his fist, a proceeding which obtained a momentary silence. "To commence, I must go back to first causes. You understand, gentlemen of the jury, that there is a strong wind blowing, which has kicked up a heavy sea, which is tossing about our stout ship in a way to make it difficult for a seaman, and much more for a ship's boy, to keep his legs, and therefore I suggest—"

"Belay all that, Master Long-tongue," shouted Noakes; "if the boy is to be cobbed, why let's cob him; if not, why let him fill the mustard-pot, for it's empty."

Others now joined in; some were for cobbing poor Gerrard forthwith; others, who had not had their supper, insisted on the mustard-pot being first replenished.

Devereux had gained his point in setting his messmates by the ears, and Peter Bruff seeing his object, sent off Gerrard for a supply of the required condiment. It was O'Grady's next watch on deck; and thus before Gerrard returned, he had been compelled to leave the berth. Devereux, however, immediately afterwards turned on Gerrard and scolded him harshly for not keeping steady while waiting at the door of

W. H. G. Kingston

the berth. At length the master-at-arms came round, the midshipmen were sent to their hammocks, and Paul Gerrard was allowed to turn into his. He felt very sick and very miserable. It was the commencement of his sea life, a life for which he had long and enthusiastically yearned, and this was what it proved to be. How different the reality from what he had expected! He could have cried aloud for very bitterness of heart, but that he was ashamed to allow his sobs to be heard.

"He treat me thus! he by birth my equal! to speak to me as if I was a slave! he who might have been in my place, had there been justice done us, while I should have been in his. A hard fate is mine; but yet I chose it, and I'll bear it."

With such thoughts passing through his mind, the young ship-boy fell asleep, and for a time forgot his cares and suffering. He dreamed of happier times, when he with his parents and brothers and sisters enjoyed all the luxuries which wealth could give, and he was a loved and petted child. Then came a lawsuit, the subject of which he could not comprehend. All he knew was, that it was with the Devereux family. It resulted in the loss to his father of his entire fortune, and Paul remembered hearing him say that they were beggars. "That is what I will not be," he had exclaimed; "I can work—we can all work—I will work."

Paul was to be tried severely. His father died broken-hearted. It seemed too probable that his mother would follow him ere long. Paul had always desired to go to sea. He could no longer hope to tread the quarter-deck as an officer, yet he still kept to his determination of following a life on the ocean.

"I will enter as a cabin-boy; I will work my way upwards. Many have done so, why should not I?" he exclaimed with enthusiasm; "I will win wealth to support you all, and honours for myself. 'Where there's a will there's a way.' I don't see the way very clearly just now; but that is the opening through which I am determined to work my way onward."

Paul's mother, though a well-educated and very excellent person, knew nothing whatever of the world. She would, indeed, have hesitated, had she known the real state of the case, and what he would have to go through, ere she allowed her son to enter before the mast on board a man-of-war; but she had no one on whom she could rely, to consult in the matter. Mrs Gerrard had retired to the humble cottage of a former servant in a retired village, where she hoped that the few pounds a year she had left her would enable her to support herself and her children, with the aid of such needlework as she might obtain. Little did she think, poor woman, to what trying difficulties she would be exposed. Not only must she support herself, but educate her children. She had saved a few books for this purpose, and some humble furniture for her little cottage; everything else had been sold to raise the small sum on the interest of which she was to live.

"Mother! mother! do let me at once go to sea!" exclaimed Paul, who understood tolerably well the state of affairs. "I can do nothing at home to help you, and only eat up what should feed others; if I go to sea, I shall get food and clothing, and pay and prize-money, and be able to send quantities of gold guineas home to you. Reuben Cole has been telling me all about it; and he showed me a purse full of great gold pieces, just the remains of what he came ashore with a few weeks ago. He was going to give most of it to his sister, who has a number of children, and then go away to sea again, and, dear mother, he promised to take me with him if you would let me go. Mary and Fred will help all the

W. H. G. Kingston

better, when I am away, to teach Sarah and John and Ann, and Fred is so fond of books that he is certain to get on some day, somehow or other."

What could the poor widow say to these appeals often repeated? What could she hope to do for her boy? There was a romance attached in those times to a sea life felt by all classes, which scarcely exists at the present day. She sent for Reuben Cole, who, though a rough sailor, seemed to have a kind heart. He promised to act the part of a father towards the boy to the best of his power, undertaking to find a good ship for him without delay. The widow yielded, and with many an earnest prayer for his safety, committed Paul to the charge of Reuben Cole. The honest sailor was as good as his word. He could scarcely have selected a better ship than the *Cerberus*. He volunteered to join, provided Paul was received on board; his terms were accepted, and he thought that he was doing well for his young charge when he got him the appointment of midshipmen's boy. The employment was very different from what Paul had expected, but he had determined to do his duty in whatever station he might be placed. The higher pay and perquisites would be of value to him, as he might thus send more money to his mother, and he hoped soon to become reconciled to his lot. One day, however, the name of a midshipman who had just joined struck his ear,—it was that of Devereux, the name of the family with whom his father had so long carried on the unsuccessful lawsuit.

From some remarks casually made by one of the other midshipmen while he was waiting in the berth, Paul was convinced that Gilbert Devereux was a son of the man who had, he conceived, been the cause of his father's ruin and death. Paul, had he been asked, would have acknowledged how he ought to feel towards young Devereux, but he at times allowed himself to regard him with bitterness and dislike, if not with downright hatred. He well knew that this feeling was wrong, and he had more than once tried to overcome the feeling when, perhaps, some careless expression let drop by Gilbert Devereux, or some order given by him, would once more arouse it. "I could bear it from another, but not from him," Paul over and over again had said to himself after each fresh cause of annoyance given by young Devereux, who all the time was himself utterly ignorant that he had offended the boy. Of course he did not suspect who Paul was; Paul had determined to keep his own secret, and had not divulged it even to Reuben. Reuben was somewhat disappointed with Paul. "I cannot make out what ails the lad," he said to himself, "he was merry and spirited enough on shore; I hope he's not going to be afraid of salt-water."

Poor Paul was undergoing a severe trial. It might prove for his benefit in the end. While the frigate was in harbour, he bore up tolerably well, but he had now for the first time in his life to contend with sea-sickness; while he was also at the beck and call of a dozen or more somewhat unreasonable masters. It was not, however, till that Saturday night that Paul began really to repent that he had come to sea. Where was the romance? As the serpent, into which Aaron's rod was changed, swallowed up the serpents of the Egyptian magicians, so the stern reality had devoured all the ideas of the romance of a sea life, which he had till now entertained.

Yet sleep, that blessed medicine for human woes, brought calm and comfort to his soul. He dreamed of happier days, when his father was alive, and as yet no cares had visited his home. He was surrounded by the comforts which wealth can give. He was preparing, as he had long hoped to do, for sea, with the expectation of being placed as a midshipman on the quarter-deck. His uniform with brass buttons, his dirk and gold-laced hat, lay on a table before him, with a bright quadrant and spy-glass; and there was his sea-chest ready to

　　　W. H. G. Kingston

be filled with his new wardrobe, and all sorts of little comforts which a fond mother and sisters were likely to have prepared for him. He heard the congratulations of friends, and the prophecies that he would some day emulate the deeds of England's greatest naval heroes. He dreamed on thus till the late events of his life again came into his thoughts, and he recollected that it was not his own, but the outfit of another lad about to go to sea which he had long ago inspected with such interest, and at length the poor ship-boy was awakened to the stern reality of his present condition by the hoarse voice of a boatswain's mate summoning all hands on deck. Paul felt so sea-sick and so utterly miserable that he thought that he would rather die where he lay in his hammock than turn out and dress. The ship was tumbling about more violently than ever; the noise was terrific; the loud voices of the men giving utterance to coarse oaths as they awoke from their sleep; their shouts and cries; the roaring of the wind as it found its way through the open hatches down below; the rattling of the blocks; the creaking of timbers and bulkheads, and the crash of the sea against the sides of the ship, made Paul suppose that she was about to sink into the depths of the ocean. "I'll die where I am," he thought to himself. "Oh, my dear mother and sisters, I shall never see you more!" But at that instant a kick and a blow inflicted by Sam Coulson, one of the boatswain's mates, made him spring up.

"What, skulking already, you young hedgehog," exclaimed the man; "on deck with your or your shoulders shall feel a taste of my colt."

Although Paul was as quick in his movements as his weak state would allow, a shower of blows descended on his back, which brought him on his knees, when, ordering him to pick himself up and follow, on pain of a further dose of the colt, Sam Coulson passed on. The sharp tattoo of a drum beaten rapidly sounded at the same time through the ship; but what it signified Paul in his ignorance could not tell, nor was there any one near him to ask. Bewildered and unable to see in the darkness, he tried in vain to gain the hatchway. He groped his way aft as fast as he could, for fear of encountering the boatswain's mate. "If the ship sinks I must go down with her; but anything is better than meeting him," he thought to himself. "Besides, I cannot be worse off than those on deck, I should think."

He worked his way aft till he found himself near the midshipmen's chests; there was a snug place between two of them in which he had more than once before ensconced himself when waiting to be summoned by his masters. "Here I'll wait till I find out what is happening," he said to himself as he sank down into the corner. The din continued, the frigate tumbled about as much as before, but he was very weary, and before long he forgot where he was, and fell fast asleep.

He was at length awoke by a crashing sound, as if the timbers were being rent apart. What could it be? He started up, scarcely knowing where he was. Had the ship struck on a rock, or could she be going down? There was then a loud report; another and another followed. The reports became louder; they were directly over his head. The main-deck guns were being fired. The ship must be engaged with an enemy, there could be no doubt about that. The light from a ship's lantern fell on the spot where he lay. The gunner and his crew were descending to the magazine. His duty he had been told would be in action to carry up powder to the crew; he ought to arouse himself. The surgeon and his assistants now came below to prepare the cockpit for the reception of the wounded. More lights appeared. The carpenter and his crew were going their rounds through the wings. Men were descending and ascending, carrying up shot from the lockers

W. H. G. Kingston

below. All were too busy to discover Paul. The sea had by this time gone down, and the ship was less tumbled about than before. Sleep, too, had somewhat restored his strength, and with it his spirits and courage.

"What am I about, skulking here? I ought to be ashamed of myself; have all my once brave thoughts and aspirations come to this? I will be up and do my duty, and not mind Sam Coulson, or the enemy's shot, or anything else." Such were the thoughts which rapidly passed through his mind; he sprang to his feet, and, as he hoped, unobserved reached the main-deck. He fortunately remembered that his friend Reuben Cole was captain of one of the main-deck guns, and that Reuben had told him that that was the gun he was to serve. The deck was well lighted up by the fighting-lanterns, and he had thus no difficulty in finding out his friend. The men, mostly stripped to their waists, stood grouped round their guns with the tackles in their hands, the captains holding the slow matches ready to fire. Paul ran up to Reuben, who was captain of his gun.

"What am I to do?" he asked; "you said you would tell me."

"So I will, lad; and I am glad to see you, for I was afraid that you had come to harm," answered Reuben, in a kind tone. "I said as how I was sure you wasn't one to skulk. Where was you, boy?"

Paul felt conscience-stricken, and he dared not answer; for utter a falsehood to excuse himself he would not. "Tell me what I am to do, and I'll try to do it," he said, at length.

"Why, then, do you go down with Tom Buckle to the powder-magazine with that tub there, and get it filled and come back and sit on it till we wants it," replied his friend, who possibly might have suspected the truth.

"Then I am about to take part in a real battle," thought Paul, as, accompanying the boy Tom Buckle, he ran down to the magazine. In a moment, sickness, fatigue, and fear were banished. He was the true-hearted English Boy, and he felt as brave as he could wish, and regardless of danger. Paul knew he was doing his duty. His tub was quickly filled, and he was soon again at Reuben's gun, behind which he was told to sit—one of a row of boys employed in the same manner. Many of his companions were laughing and joking, as if nothing unusual was occurring, or as if it was impossible that a shot could find them out.

Paul was now, for the first time, able to make inquiries as to the state of affairs. Reuben told him that, at about midnight, the lights of two ships had been seen. It was possible that they might be those of the look-out frigates of an enemy's squadron, at the same time as they might be British, and as Captain Walford had resolved that nothing should drive him back, the *Cerberus* was kept on her course. Whatever they were, the strangers seemed determined to become better acquainted. As they drew nearer, signals were exchanged; but those of the stranger's were not understood. The drum on this beat to quarters, and the ship was prepared for battle. The two ships approached, and soon gave the *Cerberus* a taste of their quality by pouring their broadsides into her; but, in consequence of the heavy sea which was then running, very few of their shot had taken effect. Two, however, which had struck her hull, had passed through the bulwarks and killed two of her men, whose bodies now lay stark and stiff on the main-deck, near where they had stood as their mates were now standing, full of life and manly strength. Paul's eyes fell on them. It was the first time he had seen death in its most hideous form. He shuddered and turned sick. Reuben observed the direction in which his glance was turned.

W. H. G. Kingston

"Paul, my lad, you mustn't think of them now," he cried out. "They've done their duty like men, and it's our business to try to do ours. We've got some pretty sharp work before us; but it's my belief that we'll beat off our enemies, or take one or both of them, maybe. Hurrah! lads. That's what we've got to do."

The crews of the guns within hearing uttered a cheerful response. "All ready!"

"Let 'em come on!"

"The more the merrier!"

"We'll give 'em more than we'll take!"

These, and similar expressions, were heard from the seamen, while now and then a broad joke or a loud laugh burst from the lips of the more excited among them. But there was no Dutch courage exhibited. One and all showed the most determined and coolest bravery. The officers whose duty it was to be on the main-deck kept going their rounds, to see that the men were at their stations, and that all were supplied with powder and shot and all things necessary. Then the first-lieutenant, Mr Order, came down.

"My lads," he exclaimed, "the captain sends to you to say that we have, perhaps, tough work before us; but that he is sure you all will do your duty like men, and will help him to thrash the enemy, as he hopes to do by daylight, when he can see them better."

A loud cheer rang out from the throats of the seamen, fore and aft. Mr Order felt satisfied that they were in the right temper for work. He returned again on deck. It was still very dark, and nothing could be seen through the open ports.

Every now and then, however, the crest of a sea washed in and deluged the decks, washing from side to side till it could escape through the scuppers. Any moment the order to fire might be heard, or the shot of the enemy might come crashing through the sides. It was a trying time for old salts, who had fought in many a previous battle; much more so for young hands. Paul sat composedly on his tub. Not far off from him stood Gilbert Devereux, in command of a division of guns.

"If a shot were to take his head off, there would be one of our enemies out of the way," thought Paul; but directly afterwards his conscience rebuked him. "No, no; that is a wicked feeling," it said; "I would rather be killed myself, if it were not for my poor mother and all at home—they would be so sorry."

Still, Paul could not help eyeing the aristocratic-looking young midshipman, who, with a firm, proud step, trod the deck, eager for the fight, and little aware that he was watched with so much interest by the humble ship's boy. Peter Bruff, who had the next division of guns under his charge, came up to Gilbert.

"Well, Devereux, how do you like this fun?" he asked. "Have you ever before been engaged?"

"Never; but I like the idea of the sport well enough to wish to begin," answered Devereux. "Where are our enemies?"

"Not far off, and they will not disappoint us," answered Bruff. "We shall have pretty tough work of it, depend on that."

"The tougher the better," answered Devereux, in a somewhat affected tone. "I've never been in a battle, and I really want

W. H. G. Kingston

to see what it is like."

"He's wonderfully cool," thought Paul. "He hasn't seen the dead men there, forward. It would be some satisfaction if he would show himself to be a coward, after all. I could throw it in his teeth when he attempts to tyrannise over me."

Paul's feelings were very far from right; but they were natural, unfortunately. Gilbert's firm step and light laugh showed that there was little chance of Paul's wishes being realised. Now a rumour spread from gun to gun that the enemy were again drawing near. The men took a firmer hold of the gun-tackles, hitched up their trousers, drew their belts tighter round their waists, or gave some similar sign of preparation for the coming struggle.

"Silence, fore and aft!" cried the officer in command of the deck.

He was repeating the order which the captain had just given above. The frigate plunged on heavily through the seas. The awful moment was approaching. There was neither jest nor laughter now. The men were eagerly looking through the ports. The lights from two ships were seen on the weather beam. In smooth water the enemy having the weather-gauge would have been to the disadvantage of the *Cerberus*; but with the heavy sea which then ran it mattered, fortunately, less.

"Starboard guns! Fire! fire!" was shouted by the officers.

"Hurrah, lads! We have the first of it this time, and it's my belief we hit the mounseer," cried Reuben Cole, as he discharged his gun.

Scarcely had the smoke cleared off from the deck when the

roar of the enemy's guns was heard, and several shot came crashing against the side. One, coming through a port, passed close above Paul's head, and though it sent the splinters flying about in every direction, no one was hurt.

"I've an idea there'll be work for the carpenters, to plug the shot-holes," cried Reuben, as the guns, being rapidly run in, loaded, and run out again, he stood ready for the command to fire.

It soon came, and the whole broadside of the *Cerberus* was poured, with good aim, into the bows of the leading Frenchman, which had attempted to pay her the same compliment. For a few moments at a time Paul could catch sight of the lights of the enemy's ships through the ports; but the smoke from their own guns quickly again shut out all objects, except the men standing close to him. Paul had plenty to do; jumping up to deliver the powder, and running down to the magazine for more when his tub was empty. He discovered that, small as he was, he was taking a very active part in the battle, and doing considerably more than the midshipmen, who had to stand still, or only occasionally to run about with orders. This gave him infinite satisfaction.

"After all, I am doing as much as he is," he thought, looking towards Devereux.

The firing became very rapid, and the enemy were close to the frigate; for not only round-shot flew on board, but the rattle of musketry was heard, and bullets came pattering through the ports. Such a game could not be played without loss. Fore and aft the men were struck down,—some never to rise again; cut in two, or with their heads knocked off. Others were carried below; and others, binding up their wounds, returned eagerly to their guns. Now there was a cessation of firing. The smoke cleared off. There stood Devereux,

W. H. G. Kingston

unharmed, and as cool as at the commencement of the action, though smoke-begrimed as the rest of the crew; but as Paul glanced round and saw the gleam of the lanterns on the blood-stained decks, and the pale faces of the dead, and the bandaged heads and limbs of the wounded, he again turned sick, and wished, as many a person has wished before, that there was no such thing as fighting and slaughtering one's fellow-creatures.

It was supposed that the enemy had hauled off to repair damages. The crew of the *Cerberus* were accordingly called away from their guns to repair those she had received, as far as could be done in the darkness. Not much time was allowed them. Again their enemies returned to the attack. Each ship was pronounced to be equal in size to the *Cerberus*, if not larger than it. She had already suffered severely; the men were again ordered to their quarters. The suspense before the firing should recommence was trying,—the very silence itself was awful. This time it was broken by the enemy, but their fire was speedily returned by a broadside from the *Cerberus*. Now, as rapidly as the guns on both sides could be loaded, they were run out and fired, for the British had an enemy on either beam, and each man knew that he must exert himself to the utmost to gain the victory. When did English sailors ever fail to do that? There could be no doubt, however, that the *Cerberus* was hard pressed.

Dreadful was the scene of havoc and carnage; the thunder of the guns; the rattle of the musketry; the crashing of the enemy's shot as they tore the stout planks asunder; the roar of the seas as they dashed against the sides, and the cries of the wounded, while the shouts of the men, who, as the fight grew more bloody, were more and more excited, became louder and louder; bright flashes, and wreaths of dark smoke, and splinters flying about, and men falling, and blood starting from their wounds, made up that horrid picture. Paul had seen old Noakes carried below; O'Grady followed, badly hurt; others of his masters were killed or wounded. Devereux seemed to bear a charmed life. No! no man's life is charmed. One moment he was standing full of life, encouraging his men; the next he lay wounded and bleeding on the wet and slippery deck. As he saw the handsome youth carried writhing in agony below, Paul's feelings of animosity instantly vanished. He would have sprung forward to help him, but he had his own duty to attend to, and he knew that he must not neglect it, even though it was only to sit on a tub.

From the exclamations of the men, Paul thought that the battle was going against them; still the crew fought on as bravely as at first. "Fire! fire!" What dreadful cry is that? "The ship is on fire!"

"All is lost!" No; the firemen leave their guns and run forward to where some hay is blazing. The enemy have discovered what has occurred and redouble their efforts. The fire must be got under in spite of shot and bullets. The men rush up to the flames fearlessly. Buckets upon buckets of water are thrown on them; the burning fragments of timber are hove overboard. The fire is reported to be got under. The British seamen cheer, and good reason have they to do so now, for flames are seen bursting from the ports and hatchways of their most determined opponent. Still all three ships tear on over the foaming ocean. Thus closes that fearful night, and so must we our first chapter.

W. H. G. Kingston

# CHAPTER TWO

The *Cerberus*, stout frigate that she was, plunged onward across the foam-covered ocean. On one side was the burning ship, at which not a shot had been fired since her condition was discovered; on the other was a still active enemy. With the latter, broadside after broadside was rapidly exchanged, but without much damage being sustained. From the burning ship a few shots continued for a short time to be fired, but as the fire increased, the crew must have deserted their guns, and as the flames gained the mastery, they burned through the ropes and attacked the sails, and the ship fell off and rolled helplessly in the trough of the sea, where the two combatants soon left her far astern.

"I wish as how we could heave-to and send a boat to help them poor fellows," cried Reuben Cole, looking at the burning ship.

"To my mind, the mounseer out there would be doing better if he was to cry, Peccavi, and then go and look after his countrymen, instead of getting himself knocked to pieces, as he will be if he keeps on long at this game."

The sentiment was highly applauded by his hearers. There was not a man indeed on board the frigate who was not eager to save the lives of the hapless crew of the burning ship, which they had till now striven so hard to destroy.

The firing had ceased; the grey dawn broke over the waste of waters; astern was seen the smoke from the burning ship, with bright flashes below it, and away to leeward their other antagonist making all sail to escape. The battle was over, though the victor could boast but of a barren conquest. The guns were run in and secured, and the weary crew instantly set to work to repair damages. As the wind had fallen and the sea had considerably gone down, the work was performed without much difficulty. Captain Walford had narrowly watched his flying foe, in the hopes that she might go to the assistance of her late consort. Her royals had not long sunk below the horizon when once more the *Cerberus* was in a condition to make sail.

Captain Walford considered whether he should go in pursuit of the enemy, or attempt to save the lives of the unfortunate people from the burning ship. In the first case he might possibly capture an enemy's ship, but ought he for the chance of so doing to leave his fellow-creatures to perish miserably?

"No, I will risk all consequences," he said to his first-lieutenant after a turn on deck. And the *Cerberus* stood towards the wreck.

The wind had fallen so much that her progress was very slow. The English now wished for more wind, for every moment might be of vital consequence to their late enemies. Not a man on board felt the least enmity towards them; even the wounded and dying when told of their condition looked on them as brothers in misfortune.

War is sad work, sad for those at home, sad for those engaged in it, and the only way to mitigate its horrors is to treat the fallen or the defeated foe as we should ourselves

　　　　　　　W. H. G. Kingston

wish to be treated.

While the frigate sailed on, the crew were repairing as far as possible the damages she had received; for at that season of the year it was probable that another gale might spring up, which she was as yet ill-prepared to encounter. The men were nearly dropping with fatigue, but they worked on bravely, as true-hearted seamen always do work when necessity demands their exertions.

Meantime Paul was summoned below. The midshipmen who were not required on deck were again assembled in the berth; but the places of several were vacant. They were eating a hurried meal which Paul had placed on the table, and discussing the events of the fight. One or two of the youngsters were rather graver than usual, but Paul thought that the rest took matters with wonderful indifference. He was anxious to know what had happened to Devereux, whom he had seen carried below badly wounded. Nobody mentioned him; perhaps he was dead; and he did not feel sorry at the thought. After a time, though, he had some compunctions of conscience. He was thinking that he would find his way towards the sick bay, where the wounded midshipmen and other junior officers were placed, when one of the assistant-surgeons came towards the berth.

"Here, boy Gerrard, I can trust you, I think," he exclaimed. "I want you to stay by Mr Devereux, and to keep continually moistening his lips, fomenting his wound as I shall direct. He is very feverish, and his life may depend on your attention."

Paul felt as he had never felt before, proud and happy at being thus spoken to, and selected by the surgeon to perform a responsible office, even though it was for one whom he had taught himself to look upon in the light of an enemy. He was soon by the side of the sufferer. The sight which met his eyes was sufficient to disarm all hostility. The young midshipman, lately so joyous, with the flush of health on his cheeks, lay pale as death, groaning piteously; his side had been torn open, and a splinter had taken part of the scalp from his head. The assistant-surgeon showed him what to do, and then hurried away, for he had many wounded to attend to, as the chief surgeon had been killed by a shot which came through one of the lower ports.

Gerrard felt greatly touched at Devereux's sufferings. "Poor fellow! he cannot possibly live with those dreadful wounds, and yet I am sure when the fight began that he had not an idea that he was to be killed, or even hurt," he said to himself more than once. Paul was unwearied in following the surgeon's directions. Devereux, however, was totally unconscious, and unaware who was attending on him. He spoke now and then, but incoherently, generally about the home he had lately left. Once Paul heard him utter the name of Gerrard.

"We beat them, though they kept us long out of our fortune, and now they are beggars as they deserve. Hard for the young ones, though, I think; but it cannot be helped—must not think about them."

Such expressions dropped at intervals from the lips of Devereux. How he came to utter them at that time Paul could not guess. Did he know him, or in any way associate his name with the family of whom he was speaking?

"He has some sympathy, at all events, poor fellow, with our misfortunes," thought Paul. "I wish that I had not thought so ill of him. I hope he won't die. I will pray that God will spare his life; even if he were my enemy I should do that."

The surgeon, when he came his rounds, expressed his

W. H. G. Kingston

approval of the way Paul had managed his patient.

"Will he live, sir?" asked Paul, in a trembling voice.

"That is more than the wisest of us can say," was the answer.

Paul was at length relieved from his charge by a marine who acted as Devereux's servant. He was, however, very unwilling to quit his post. He was feeling more interest in the wounded midshipman than he could have supposed possible.

Paul, as soon as he could, made his way on deck. He wanted to know what had become of the burning ship. He looked around; she was nowhere to be seen. He inquired what had happened to her. She had blown up; and probably nearly all on board had sunk beneath the waves. There were men aloft, however, looking out, and now they were pointing in the direction of where the burning ship had gone down. A speck on the ocean was observed; it was probably part of the wreck, and perhaps some of the crew might be clinging to it. The captain ordered a boat to be lowered, for the wind was so light that the frigate would take a much longer time than it would to reach the spot. The boat pulled away; the men in the rigging and all on deck eagerly watched her progress. It seemed, however, doubtful whether any one of their late foes had escaped destruction. The crew in the boat made no sign that they saw any one. At length, however, they reached the spot towards which they were rowing.

"Anyhow, they've got something," cried a topman.

The boat made a wide circuit round the fatal spot. After some time she was seen returning to the ship.

"They have got a man, I do believe," exclaimed one of the men.

"No; to my mind it is only a mounseer midshipmite," observed Reuben Cole, looking down from his work into the boat.

"They've picked up a few other things, though, but it's a poor haul, I fear."

When the boat came alongside, a fine young boy in a French uniform was handed up and placed on the deck. He looked around with a bewildered air, as if not knowing where he was. Captain Walford then took him kindly by the hand, and told him that he should be well cared for, and that he would find friends instead of those he had lost. The boy sighed.

"What! are all, all gone?" he asked in French.

"I fear so," answered the captain. "But you are cold and wet, and you must go below to the surgeon, who will attend to you."

The poor young stranger was, however, very unwilling to leave the deck, and kept looking up into the countenances of the bystanders as if in search of some of his missing friends. Paul watched him with interest.

"Poor boy!" he said to himself; "I thought that I was very forlorn and miserable; but I have Reuben Cole and others who are kind to me, and he has no one here who can care for him. How fortunate that I learned French, because now I can talk to him and be useful to him."

When the humane Captain Walford found that all the rest of the hapless crew of his late antagonist were lost, he ordered all the sail to be made which the frigate in her present crippled state could carry, in chase of his other opponent, having noted carefully the direction in which she was

W. H. G. Kingston

steering when last seen.

"I thought that we had done with fighting for the present," said Paul to Reuben Cole, who told him that they were looking out for the other frigate.

"No, boy, that we haven't, and what's more, I expect we shan't, as long as the flag of an enemy of old England flies over the salt sea. You'll live, I hope, Paul, to help thrash many of them. I liked the way in which you behaved in the action just now. You was cool and active, which is just what you should be. It won't be my fault if you don't make a first-rate seaman some day."

Paul was again much pleased with Reuben's commendations. He was sure that he would keep his promise, and he resolved to profit by his instructions, as far as his duties in the midshipmen's berth would allow him. Before long, the young Frenchman made his appearance on deck, dressed in the uniform of an English midshipman who had been killed. He lifted his hat in the politest manner to the captain and officers, and thanked them for the courtesy they had shown him. He was in the middle of his speech, which was very pathetic, when his eye fell on some of the articles which had been picked up and had not been taken below. Among them was a long narrow case. He sprang towards it with a shout of joy.

"C'est a moi! c'est a moi!" he exclaimed, as he produced a key from a lanyard round his neck. He opened the case and drew forth a violin and bow. The case had been well made and water-tight; he applied the instrument to his chin. At first, only slow melancholy sounds were elicited; but by degrees, as the strings got dry, the performer's arms moved more rapidly, and he at last struck up a right merry tune.

The effect was curious and powerful. The captain

unconsciously began to move his feet, the officers to shuffle, and the men, catching the infection, commenced a rapid hornpipe, which Mr Order, the first-lieutenant, in vain attempted to stop. The young Frenchman, delighted at finding that his music was appreciated, played faster and faster, till everybody on deck was moving about in a fashion seldom seen on the deck of a man-of-war.

"Stop, stop!" shouted the first-lieutenant; "knock off that nonsense, men; stop your fiddling, I say, youngster—stop your fiddling, I say."

The discipline of the ship was very nearly upset; the men, however, heard and obeyed; but the young Frenchman, not comprehending a word, and delighted moreover to get back his beloved violin, continued playing away as eagerly as at first, till Mr Order, losing patience, seized his arm, and by a significant gesture, ordered him to desist. His musical talent, and his apparent good-nature, gained for the French lad the goodwill of the crew, and of most of the officers also.

"What is your name, my young friend?" asked Captain Walford.

"Alphonse Montauban," was the answer.

"Very well; you will be more at your ease in the midshipmen's berth, I suspect. Take him below, Mr Bruff, and say that I beg the young gentlemen will accommodate him and treat him with kindness. You'll get a hammock slung for him."

"Ay, ay, sir," answered Bruff, taking Alphonse by the hand. "Come along, youngster."

Bruff was anxious to say something kind to the poor boy, but

W. H. G. Kingston

there was a bar to this, as neither understood each other's language. Paul followed, guessing this, and hoping that his knowledge of French might be put into requisition. Alphonse, with his fiddle tucked under his arm, entered the berth.

"Here's a young chap who is a first-rate hand with the catgut, and if any of you can tell him that he is welcome in his own lingo, I wish you would, mates," said Bruff.

"Mounseer, you are mucho welcomo to our bertho," exclaimed Blake. "Here's to your healtho, Mounseer. I hope, Bruff, this is first-rate French."

"It doesn't sound like it, but maybe he understands you, for he's bowing to you in return," answered Bruff.

Similar attempts at speaking French were made; but, as may be supposed, the young foreigner was as unable as at first to understand what was said.

"How very ignorant they are," thought Paul. "I wish that they would let me speak to him."

The young Frenchman, who was of an excitable disposition, at last thinking that the English boys were laughing at him, began to lose temper, and so did they, at what they considered his unexampled stupidity.

Paul, who was standing near the door, mustering courage, at length interpreted what was said into very fair French. The young stranger, with a pleased smile, asked—

"What! can a poor boy like you speak my dear language?"

"Yes, I learned it of my sisters at home," answered Paul.

"Then we must be friends, for you can sympathise with me more than can these," said Alphonse.

"Do not say so to them," observed Paul; "they may not like it. I am but a poor ship's boy and their servant."

"Misfortune makes all people equal, and your tone of voice and the way you speak French, convince me that you are of gentle birth," said Alphonse.

It is possible that the midshipmen might have looked at Paul with more respect from hearing him speak a language of which they were ignorant, though some sneered at him for talking the Frenchman's lingo.

Paul, as soon as he could leave the berth, hurried to the side of Devereux. He found the surgeon there.

"Ah! come to look after your patient, boy?" said Mr Lancet. "You have performed your duty so well, that I have begged Mr Order to relieve you from your attendance on the young gentlemen, and to give you to me altogether."

Paul thanked Mr Lancet, but told him frankly, that though he was very glad to be of service to Mr Devereux, or to any other wounded shipmate, he wished to learn to be a sailor, and therefore that he would rather be employed on deck; still he was gratified at what Mr Lancet had said.

He devoted himself, however, to Devereux, by whose side he spent every moment not absolutely required for sleep or for his meals. Mr Order sent another boy, Tom Buckle, to attend on the young gentlemen, who came to the conclusion that he was a perfect lout after Paul.

"There is something in that youngster after all," observed

Bruff, who resolved to try what he was really worth, and to befriend him accordingly.

Meantime, the *Cerberus* continued in chase of the French frigate, which Alphonse told Captain Walford was the *Alerte*, and perhaps to induce him to give up the chase, he remarked that she was very powerfully armed and strongly manned, and would prove a dangerous antagonist. Captain Walford laughed.

"It is not a reason for abandoning the chase which would weigh much with any one on board this ship, I hope, though it will make them the more eager to come up with her," he answered.

Alphonse also let drop that the two frigates were bound out to the West Indies with important despatches. It was most probable, therefore, that the *Alerte*, in obedience to orders, would make the best of her way there. Captain Walford resolved to follow in that direction.

The *Alerte* had probably not received as much injury in her rigging as was supposed, and as Alphonse said that she was very fast, there was little expectation on board the *Cerberus* that they would come up with her before she got to her destination. Still, Captain Walford was not a man to abandon an object as long as there remained a possibility of success. He was a good specimen of a British naval officer. Brave, kind, and considerate, his men adored him; and there was no deed of daring which he would not venture to undertake, because he knew that his crew would follow wherever he would lead. He never swore at or abused those under him, or even had to speak roughly to them. Every officer who did his duty knew that he had in him a sincere friend; and his men looked upon him in the light of a kind and wise father, who would always do them justice, and overlook even their faults, if possible.

Mr Lancet took an opportunity of speaking to the captain of the boy Gerrard, and remarked that he was far better educated than were lads generally of his class.

"I will keep my eye on the lad, and if he proves worthy, will serve him if I can," was the answer.

Devereux continued in great danger; the surgeon would not assert that he would recover. It was some time before he remarked Paul's attention to him.

"You are boy Gerrard, I see," he observed faintly. "You are very good to me, and more than I deserve from you; but I never meant you ill, and I got you off a cobbing once. I have done very few good things in the world, and now I am going to die, I am afraid. You'll forgive me, Gerrard, won't you?"

"Oh, yes, yes, sir!" answered Paul, with tears in his eyes; "even if you had wronged me much more than you have done; but it wasn't you, it was your father and those about him."

"My father! What do you mean, boy; who are you?" exclaimed Devereux, in a tone of astonishment, starting up for a moment, though he immediately sank back exhausted; while he muttered to himself,—"Gerrard! Gerrard! can it be possible?" He then asked quietly—

"Where do you come from, boy?"

"No matter, sir," answered Paul, afraid of agitating Devereux. "I will tell you another time, for I hope that you will get well soon, and then you may be able to listen to what I have to say; but the doctor says that at present you must  be kept perfectly quiet, and talk as little as possible."

Devereux, who was still very weak, did not persist in questioning Paul, who had time to reflect how far it would be wise to say anything about himself. He was not compelled to be communicative; and he considered that Devereux ill, and expecting to die, and Devereux well, might possibly be two very different characters. "If I were to tell him, he might bestow on me a sort of hypocritical compassion, and I could not stand that," he thought to himself. Whatever were Paul's feelings, he did not relax in his care of Devereux.

Day after day came, and the first question asked of the morning watch was, "Is there anything like the *Alerte* yet ahead?" All day, too, a bright look-out was kept from the mast-heads for her; but in vain, and some began to think that she must have altered her course and returned to the coast of France.

Paul was not sorry when he heard this, for he had seen enough of the effects of fighting to believe that it was not a desirable occupation; and he, moreover, felt for young Alphonse, who naturally earnestly hoped that the *Cerberus* would not fall in with the *Alerte*.

No one rejoiced more than did Paul when one day Mr Lancet pronounced Devereux to be out of danger, and that all he required was care and attention. Paul redoubled his efforts to be of use. Alphonse missed him very much from the berth, as he was the only person who could interpret for him, and whenever he wanted anything he had to find him out and to get him to explain what he required. Before long, therefore, the young Frenchman found his way to the sick bay, where Devereux and others lay. Devereux was the only midshipman who could speak French, though not so well as Paul.

The ship had now reached a southern latitude, and the balmy air coming through an open port contributed to restore health and strength to the sick and wounded. When Devereux heard Alphonse addressing Paul, and the latter replying in French, he lifted up his head.

"What, boy Gerrard, where did you learn French?" he asked.

"At home, sir," answered Paul, quietly.

"Yes, he speaks very good French, and is a very good boy," remarked Alphonse.

"And you, monsieur, you speak French also?"

Devereux replied that he did a little.

"That is very nice, indeed," said the young Frenchman. "We will talk together, and I shall no longer fear dying of *ennui*."

After this, Alphonse was constantly with Devereux, and when the latter was better, he brought his fiddle and played many a merry tune to him. Indeed, the young Frenchman, by his light-hearted gaiety, his gentleness, and desire to please, became a general favourite fore and aft.

"Ah, mounseer, if there was many like you aboard the frigate which went down, I for one am sorry that I had a hand in sending her there," exclaimed Reuben Cole one day, in a fit of affectionate enthusiasm.

Alphonse, who understood him, sighed. "There were many, many; but it was the fortune of war."

"But, suppose, Reuben, we come up with the other, and have to treat her in the same way, what will you say then?"

asked Paul.

"Why, you see, Paul, the truth is this: if the captain says we must fight and sink her, it must be done, even if every one on us had a mother's son aboard. I stick up for discipline, come what may of it."

The ship was within one or two days' sail of the West Indies, when, as Paul was on deck, he heard the man at the mast-head shout out, "A sail on the lee-bow standing for the westward."

"It is the *Alerte*," thought Paul, "and we shall have more fighting." Others were of the same opinion. Instantly all sail was made in chase. The crew of the *Cerberus* had been somewhat dull of late, except when the little Mounseer, as they called Alphonse, scraped his fiddle. They were animated enough at present. Even the sick and wounded were eager to come on deck. Devereux especially insisted that he was able to return to his duty. Mr Lancet said that he might not suffer much, but that he had better remain out of harm's way, as even a slight wound might prove fatal. He would listen to no such reasoning, and getting Paul to help him on with his uniform, he crawled on deck.

"Gerrard," he said as he was dressing, "if I am killed, you are to be my heir as regards my personal effects. I have written it down, and given the paper to Mr Lancet, witnessed by Mr Bruff, so it's all right. I have an idea who you are, though you never told me."

Captain Walford was surprised at seeing Devereux on deck, and though he applauded his zeal, he told him that he had better have remained below.

As soon as the stranger discovered the *Cerberus*, she made

all sail to escape. It was questioned whether or not she was the *Alerte*, but one thing was certain, that the *Cerberus* was overhauling her, and had soon got near enough to see her hull from aloft. It was now seen, that though she was a large ship, she was certainly not a frigate; it was doubted, indeed, whether she was French. The opinion of Alphonse was asked.

"She is not the *Alerte*, she is a merchantman and French; she will become your prize. I am sorry for my poor countrymen, but it is the fortune of war," he answered as he turned away with a sigh.

A calm, of frequent occurrence in those latitudes, came on, and there lay the two ships, rolling their sides into the water, and unable to approach each other.

"If the stranger gets a breeze before us she may yet escape," observed the captain. "Out boats, we must attack her with them."

The sort of work proposed has always been popular among seamen. There was no lack of volunteers. The boats were speedily manned; the second-lieutenant went in one boat; old Noakes, though badly wounded, was sufficiently recovered to take charge of another; Peter Bruff had a third. Paul was seized with a strong desire to go also. In the hurry of lowering the boats, he was able to slip into the bows of the last mentioned, and to hide himself under a sail thrown in by chance. Reuben Cole went in the same boat. Devereux watched them away, wishing that he could have gone also. The boats glided rapidly over the smooth, shining ocean. Their crews were eager to be up with their expected prize. The sun beat down on their heads, the water shone like polished silver, not a breath of air came to cool the heated atmosphere; but they cared not for the heat or fatigue, all

W. H. G. Kingston

they thought of was the prize before them. Paul lay snugly under his shelter, wondering when they would reach the enemy's side. He soon began to repent of his freak; he could hear the remarks of the men as they pulled on. The ship was from her appearance a letter of marque or a privateer, and such was not likely to yield without a severe struggle, he heard. Paul could endure the suspense no longer, and creeping from under his covering, he looked out over the bows.

"Hillo, youngster, what brings you here?" sung out Mr Bruff. "If you come off with a whole skin, as I hope you will, you must expect a taste of the cat to remind you that you are not to play such a trick again."

The reprimand from the kind-hearted mate might have been longer, but it was cut short by a shot from the enemy, which almost took the ends off the blades of the oars of his boat. The men cheered and dashed forward. At the same moment eight ports on a side were exposed, and a hot fire opened on the boats from as many guns, and from swivels and muskets. Hot as was the fire, it did not for a moment stop the boats. Paul wished that he had remained on board. The deck of the enemy seemed crowded with men.

"Hurrah, lads!" cried Peter Bruff when he saw this, "they'll only hamper each other and give us an easier victory."

The boats dashed alongside. Langrage and grape and round-shot were discharged at them, and boarding-pikes, muskets, and pistols were seen protruding through the ports ready for their reception. The boats hooked on, and, in spite of all opposition, the British seamen began to climb up the side. Some were driven back and hurled into the boats, wounded, too often mortally; the rest persevered. Again and again the attempt was made, the deck was gained, a desperate hand-to-hand combat began. It could have but one termination, the defeat of the attackers or the attacked. Paul climbed up with the rest of his shipmates. It is surprising that human beings could have faced the bristling mass of weapons which the British seamen had to encounter. Paul followed close behind Reuben, who kept abreast of Mr Noakes. Pistols were fired in their faces, cutlasses were clashing, as the seamen were slashing and cutting and lunging at their opponents. In spite of all opposition the deck was gained; the enemy, however, still fought bravely. Mr Larcom, the second-lieutenant of the *Cerberus*, fell shot through the head. Several men near him were killed or badly wounded; it seemed likely that after all the boarders would be driven back. Old Noakes saw the danger; there was still plenty of British pluck in him in spite of the pains he took to wash away all feeling; the day must be retrieved. "On, lads, on!" he shouted, throwing himself furiously on the enemy; "follow me! death or victory!"

Again the Frenchmen gave way; at first inch by inch they retreated, then more rapidly, leaving many of their number wounded on the deck. Bruff had faced about and driven the enemy aft; Noakes and Reuben still pushed forward. Paul, following close at their heels with an officer's sword which he had picked up, observed, fallen on the deck, a man, apparently a lieutenant, whose eye was fixed on Noakes, and whose hand held a pistol; he was taking a steady aim at Noakes's head. Paul sprang forward, and giving a cut at the man's arm, the muzzle of the pistol dropping, the contents entered the deck.

"Thanks, boy, you've saved my life, I'll not forget you," cried Noakes. "On, on, on!"

"Well done, Gerrard, well done!" exclaimed Reuben. "You've saved your hide, boy."

The Frenchmen, finding that all was lost, leaped down the

fore-hatchway, most of them singing out for quarter. A few madly and treacherously fired up from below, which so exasperated the seamen, that nearly half of them were killed before their flag was hauled down and the rest overpowered. The frigate was by this time bringing up a breeze to the prize.

"It's a pity it didn't come a little sooner; it might have saved the lives of many fine fellows," observed Bruff, as he glanced round on the blood-stained deck.

"It's an ill wind that blows no one good," remarked Noakes, looking at Mr Larcom's body. "If he had been alive, I shouldn't have gained my promotion, which I am now pretty sure of for this morning's work, besides the command of the prize."

"'There's many a slip between the cup and the lip.' I've found it so, and so have you, mate, I suspect," said Bruff; "yet, old fellow, I hope you'll get what you deserve."

There was no jealousy in honest Bruff's composition. He put his old messmate's gallantry in so bright a light privately before Captain Walford, that the captain felt himself bound to recommend Noakes for promotion to the Admiralty, and to place him in charge of the prize to take home. She was the *Aigle*, privateer, mounting sixteen guns, evidently very fast, but very low, with taut masts, square yards, and seemingly very crank. Most of the prisoners were removed, and Mr Noakes got leave to pick a crew. He chose, among others, Reuben Cole and Paul Gerrard. The surgeon advised that Devereux and O'Grady should go home, and Alphonse Montauban was allowed a passage, that he might be exchanged on the first opportunity.

"Be careful of your spars, Noakes," observed Mr Order, as

he looked up at the *Aigle's* lofty masts, "remember that you are short-handed."

"Ay, ay, sir," answered the old mate as he went down the side, adding to himself, "I should think that I know how to sail a craft by this time; I'm no sucking baby to require a nurse."

Paul was very glad to find himself with Devereux and Alphonse, as also with Reuben, on board the prize. Mr Noakes did not forget the service he had rendered him, and was as kind as could well be. He called him aft one day.

"Gerrard, my boy, you want to be a seaman, and though I can't give you silver and gold, I can make you that, if you will keep your wits about you, and I'll teach you navigation myself. You are a gentleman by birth, and that's more than some of us can boast of being; but I don't advise you to aspire to the quarter-deck. Without money or friends, you may repent being placed on it, as I have often done; that's no reason, however, that you shouldn't become fit to take command of a ship; a privateer or a merchantman may fall in your way; at all events, learn all you can."

Paul resolved to follow his new friend's advice. A course was shaped for Plymouth, and the *Aigle* proceeded merrily on her way.

Noakes could give good advice to others, but he did not follow after wisdom himself. He had a great failing, from the effects of which he had often suffered. Drink was his bane, as it is that of thousands. Several casks of prime claret were found on board; it would not have done much harm by itself, but there were some casks of brandy also. By mixing the two with some sugar, Noakes concocted a beverage very much to his taste. He kept his word with Paul as long as he was able, and lost no opportunity in giving him instruction in seamanship and navigation; but in time the attractions of his claret-cup were so great, that he was seldom in a condition to understand anything clearly himself, much less to explain it to another. Devereux and O'Grady expostulated in vain. He grew angry and only drank harder. The prisoners observed matters with inward satisfaction. They might have entertained hopes of regaining their ship. Alphonse warned Devereux.

"They have not spoken to me, or I could not say this to you, but they may, so be prepared," he observed one day as they were on deck together, no one else being near.

Noakes was compelled to keep watch. He always carried on more than either of his companions ventured to do. It was night, and very dark; the first watch was nearly over; the weather, hitherto fine, gave signs of changing. Devereux, who had charge of the deck, was about to shorten sail, when Noakes came up to relieve him.

"Hold all fast," he sung out, adding, "Nonsense, Devereux, your wounds have made you weak and timid. We've a slashing breeze, and let's take advantage of it to reach the shores of old England."

"Too much haste the worst speed," observed Reuben to Paul; "our sticks are bending terribly, they'll be whipping over the sides presently, or will capsize the craft altogether. I don't like the look of things, that I don't, I tell you." Scarcely had he spoken, when a blast, fiercer than its predecessor, struck the ship.

"Let fly of all," shouted Noakes, sobered somewhat.

The crew ran to obey the orders, but it came too late. Over

went the tall ship; down, down, the raging tempest pressed her.

"Axes, axes, cut, cut," was heard from several mouths.

"Follow me, Paul, and then cling on for your life," cried Reuben Cole, climbing through a weather port; "it's too late to save the ship."

# CHAPTER THREE

"What are we to do now?" asked Paul, after he had secured his hold in the main-chains.

"Hold on, Jack, where you are, while I will go and try to help some of our shipmates," answered Reuben. "There's Mr Devereux, who can't do much to help himself; and the young Mounseer, I should like to save him."

Several men had already got to the upper side of the ship, some in the main, and others in the mizen-chains, while others were in the rigging. As the ship was light, she still floated high out of the water. Many might possibly, therefore, be alive below. Reuben had not been gone long, when he put his head through the port, singing out—

"Here, Paul, lend a hand and help up Mr Devereux."

Devereux had been partially stunned, but had happily clung to a stanchion, where Reuben had found him. Paul hauled him up, while Reuben again dived in search of some one else. He was gone for some time, and Paul began to fear that some accident had happened to him. At length his voice was again heard.

"Hurrah, Paul, here he is; and what is more, he has his fiddle, too, all safe and sound."

Sure enough, there was Alphonse and his beloved fiddle in its case, which he had contrived to get up from below at no little risk of being drowned himself.

"Ah! I would not part from this," he exclaimed, as he made himself secure in the chains. "It is my own dear friend; shall I play you a tune now?"

"No, thank ye, Mounseer, it might chance to get wet, and may be there are more poor fellows to help up here," answered Reuben.

"Ah! truly, I forgot what had happened," said Alphonse in a dreamy tone, showing that his mind was wandering, overcome by the sudden catastrophe. It was no time for laughter, or Paul would have laughed at the oddness of the young Frenchman's remark. Still, awful as was the scene, he felt very little sensation of fear. The night was very dark, the wind howled, the rain fell in torrents, the sea dashed over the wreck, nearly washing off those who clung to it, while vivid flashes of lightning darted from the clouds and went hissing along like fiery serpents over the summits of the waves. The party in the main-chains spoke but little. It seemed too probable that none of them would ever see another day. Indeed, even should the ship not go down, Paul feared that Devereux could scarcely endure the hardships of their situation. He asked Reuben if nothing could be done.

"If we could get at the axes, we might cut away the masts and the ship might right," answered Reuben. "But, you see, we want daylight and the officers to give the order, so that all may act together."

While he was speaking, a voice was heard apparently from

the mizen rigging, shouting, "Cut, I say, all of you; cut, I say, and cut together."

It was that of Mr Noakes. Directly after, a flash of lightning revealed him standing in the mizen-top, holding on with one hand, while he waved the other wildly around. His nervous system had been completely weakened by drinking, and it was evident that he had lost his senses. He continued to shout louder and louder, and then to abuse the crew for not obeying his orders. Flash after flash of lightning revealed him still waving his arm; his hat had fallen off, and his long grizzly hair flew wildly about his head. He seemed unaware of the danger of his position and indifferent to the seas which frequently dashed over him. He was thus seen standing, when a sea rose high above the half-submerged hull, and rolling over the after part, struck the mizen-top. A loud shriek was heard, and by the glare of a flash of forked lightning, the unhappy officer, the victim of hard drinking, was seen borne away amid its foaming waters. In vain he stretched out his arms to catch at floating ropes; in vain he struck out boldly towards the ship, and shouted to his men to help him. His strength was as nothing, no aid could be given, and in another instant the waves closed for ever over his head. O'Grady was the only other officer not accounted for. He had been below, and it was to be hoped had got to the upper side and had thus escaped being drowned. While his messmates were inquiring for him, his voice was heard shouting for help. He had clambered up through a hatchway, scarcely knowing what had occurred. Reuben Cole and Paul helped him up to the main-chains. Devereux and Alphonse bore up wonderfully well. The former especially showed what spirit and courage ran do under difficulties and hardships.

"I wish that the day were come," said Paul more than once.

"It's what many have wished before, boy, and if has come in

good time," answered Reuben.

"There's just only one thing for it, and that's patience, as Sandy McPherson, an old shipmate of mine, used to say whenever he was in trouble."

The dawn did come at last, but it was very grey and very cold; but the wind and sea had gone down and the ship was still afloat. Whether she could be saved was the first question asked by all. Devereux was now senior officer, but his experience was very limited.

"I wish that I had attended more to this sort of thing," he observed to O'Grady. "I never thought of the possibility of this happening to myself."

"Faith, I can't say that I ever thought much about it either," answered the other midshipman. "But I think that we couldn't do better than to follow old Noakes's last order, to cut away the masts. If the ship keeps on her side much longer, she'll go down, that's pretty certain."

"It's very well to give the order, but where are the axes to cut with?" asked Devereux.

"Well, to be sure, I didn't think about that," answered O'Grady. "But I'll volunteer to go and search for them, and probably others will come and help me."

"I will, sir," exclaimed Paul, who overheard the conversation.

"And so will I," said Reuben Cole; "and what is more, even if the ship does not go down, we shall starve if we don't, for there isn't a scrap of food among any of us."

W. H. G. Kingston

Alphonse also expressed his readiness to go on the expedition, but O'Grady begged that he would remain and take care of Devereux. No time was to be lost. As soon as there was sufficient light for them to see, securing themselves by ropes, they slipped through a port and disappeared. Devereux, who was unfit for any exertion, remained in the chains. Some minutes passed. He became at last very anxious about his companions. He shouted to them, but no one replied. It appeared to him that the ship was turning over more, and settling deeper than before in the water.

"They have only gone a short time before me," he thought. "It matters but little, yet how unfit I am to die. But I must not yield without a struggle. People in our circumstances have formed rafts and escaped; why should not we? Though without food, or water, or compass, or chart, we shall be badly off." He proposed his plan to Alphonse and the people near him. All promised to obey his directions. They were on the point of climbing along the masts to get at the lighter spars, when Paul poked his head through a port, flourishing above it an axe.

"We've found them, we've found them," he shouted; "but there's no time to be lost, for the water is already making its way through the hatches."

The rest of the party appearing, corroborated this statement. Devereux roused up his energies and distributed his crew, some at the masts, and the rest at the shrouds.

"Cut off all, and cut together!" he shouted. In a minute every shroud and stay and mast was cut through. The effect was instantaneous. The ship rolled up on an even keel so rapidly, that Devereux and those with him could with difficulty climb over the bulwarks to regain the deck. Their condition was but little improved, for so much water had got down below, that it seemed improbable the ship could swim long, and there she lay a dismasted wreck in the middle of the wide Atlantic. The young commander's first wish was to endeavour to clear the ship of water, but the pumps were choked, and long before the water could be bailed out, another gale might spring up and the ship go down, even supposing there was no leak. It was probable, however, that from the quantity of water in her she had already sprung a serious leak. Every boat on board had been washed away or destroyed when the ship went over. Blank dismay was visible on the countenances of even some of the boldest of the crew. The masts and spars were, however, still hanging by the lee rigging alongside.

"We could make a stout raft anyhow," observed Reuben.

The idea was taken up by the rest. There was a chance of life. Devereux gave orders that a raft should be formed.

"But we'll be starving entirely, if we don't get up some provisions," observed O'Grady.

"May I go and collect them?" asked Paul. "Stronger people than I can be working at the raft."

"And I will go too," said Alphonse, when Paul had obtained the permission asked.

They found, however, that most of the casks and jars in the officers' cabins had been upset and their contents washed away, while there was already so much water in the hold, that they could not get up anything from it. A cheese, some bottles of spirits, and a small cask of wet biscuit, were all they could collect. While groping about in the hold, it appeared to them that the water was rising; if so, the ship must have sprung a serious leak. With the scanty supply of provisions they had obtained, they hurried on deck to report what they had remarked. Considerable progress had been made with the raft, but without food and water it could only tend to prolong their misery. Reuben, with three other men, were therefore ordered below, to get up any more provisions which they could find. They very soon returned with the only things they could reach,—a small cask of pork, another of biscuit, and a keg of butter. Water was, however, most required, and it was not to be obtained. It was evident, too, that the ship was settling down more and more, and that no time must be lost in getting the raft finished. All hands now worked with the knowledge that their lives depended on their exertions, rapidly passing the numerous lashings in a way of which sailors alone are capable. Even before it was completed, the small amount of provisions which had been collected were placed on it, for all knew that at any moment it might prove their only ark of safety.

Devereux had no occasion to urge his men to increased exertion. A sail and spars for a mast, and yards and rudder were got ready. At length all the preparations were concluded.

"To the raft! to the raft!" was the cry, for the ship had sunk so low that the water was already running through the scuppers. Gradually she went down; the raft was slightly agitated by the vortex formed as the waters closed over her, and then it floated calmly on the wide ocean.

The crew looked at each other for some time without speaking. Devereux was very young to be placed in so trying a position, still he saw that he must maintain discipline among those under his command, and prevent them from sinking into a state of despondency. There was much to be done; the mast to be rigged, the sail to be fitted, and a rudder formed. It was necessary also to secure the articles on the raft, and all being done, he steered a course for the west, hoping to reach one of the West India Islands.

Paul had often when at home pictured such a scene as that in which he was now taking a part, but how far short did the scene he had drawn come of the reality! Scarcely had the ship disappeared than the wind fell and the sea became like glass, while the sun shone with intense heat on the unprotected heads of the seamen.

"Reuben, can I ask for a mug of water, do you think? I am dreadfully thirsty," said Paul.

Reuben looked at him with compassion. "Every drop of water we've got is worth its weight in gold and many times more," he answered. "It will be served out to us in thimblefuls, and each officer and man will share alike. It will be well for us if it even thus lasts till we make the land or get picked up."

Not a mouthful of food had been eaten since the previous evening.

"It's mighty like starving we are," observed O'Grady; "we had better begin to eat a little, or we shall grow so ravenous, that it will be no small allowance will satisfy us."

"You are right, Paddy," said Devereux, rousing himself up. "Ascertain what quantity we have, and calculate how long it will last."

O'Grady commenced the examination as directed. He soon reported that there was enough food to support life for eight, or perhaps, ten days.

"And water?" asked Devereux.

W. H. G. Kingston

"Not for eight," was the answer.

"Heaven preserve us!" ejaculated Devereux. "It will take us double that time to reach the land!"

The provisions were served out with the greatest care and in equal portions. The people on the raft suffered more from heat than from any other cause. The sea remained perfectly calm, the sun sank down, and darkness reigned over the ocean. It was their first night on the raft. Who could say how many more they might have to spend on it? Devereux did his best to keep up the courage of his men, but in spite of all he could say, the spirits of many sank low. He encouraged them to tell stories, to narrate their adventures, to sing songs, and he himself took every opportunity of talking of the future, and spoke confidently of what he would do when they should reach the shore. Paul felt very unhappy. He was hungry and thirsty, and that alone lowers the spirits. The men were grouped round their officers in the centre of the raft. Paul was sitting near Reuben.

"I don't think that I shall ever live through this," he said, taking his friend's hand. "You are strong, Reuben, and you may weather it out. If you do, you'll go and tell my poor mother and sisters how it all happened and what became of me. Tell them that if I had lived I might, perhaps, have been placed on the quarter-deck and become a captain or an admiral; but that dream is all over now."

"As to that being a dream, a dream it is, Paul," said Reuben; "but as to your living and turning out a good seaman, I've no fear about that, my boy," he added cheerfully. "You see, there's One above cares for us, and if we pray to Him He'll send us help."

The night passed on, the stars shone brightly down from the

pure sky, the waters flashed with phosphorescence, the inhabitants of the deep came up to the surface to breathe, while not a breath of air ruffled the face of the ocean. Except two appointed to keep watch, all on the raft soon sank into a deep sleep. They were awoke by the hot sun beating down on their heads; then they again wished for night. As the rays of the sun came down with fiercer force their thirst increased, but no one asked for more than his small share of water. Those only who have endured thirst know the intensity of the suffering it causes. Devereux had no more able supporter than Alphonse, who had saved his well-beloved violin. The moment the young Frenchman saw that the spirits of the people were sinking, he pulled it from its case, and putting it to his chin, began scraping away with right good will; now a merry, now a pathetic air. The excitable state of the nerves of the seamen was shown by the effect he produced. On hearing the merry tunes they burst into shouts of laughter; with the pathetic, even the roughest melted into tears. Alphonse played on till his arm ached, and scarcely was he rested before they begged him to go on again. Before the day closed, however, several of the party appeared to be sinking into a state of apathy, scarcely knowing where they were, or what they were saying. Some clamoured loudly for food, but Devereux mildly but firmly refused to allow any one to have more than his allotted share. Paul looked at him with a respect he had never before felt. He seemed so cool and collected, so different from the careless, thoughtless midshipman he had appeared on board the frigate. He had evidently risen to the difficulties of his position. He well knew, indeed, that the lives of all the party would depend in a great measure on his firmness and decision; at the same time, he knew that all he could do might avail them nothing. He also felt compassion for Paul, who was the youngest person on the raft. He had brought him away from the frigate, and it was very probable that he would be one of the first to sink under the hardships to which they were exposed. Paul was not aware that Devereux, when serving out the food, gave him a portion of his own scanty share, in the hopes that his strength might be thus better supported and his life prolonged. Another night passed by, and when the sun rose, it shone as before on a glassy sea. There was no sign of a breeze, and without a breeze no ship could approach the raft, nor could the raft make progress towards the land. Still Devereux persevered as before in endeavouring to keep up the spirits of his men. Alphonse and his fiddle were in constant requisition, and in spite of his own suffering, as long as he could keep his bow moving, he played on with right good will. When Alphonse grew weary, Devereux called for a tale; now for a song; now he told one of his own adventures, or some adventure he had heard.

"Come, O'Grady, you used to be one of the best singers in the berth till the Frenchman's shot knocked you over; try what you can do now!" he exclaimed, so that all might hear. "Never mind the tune, only let it be something comic, for a change," he added in a whisper; "you and I must not let the rest know what we feel."

"I'll do my best, though, faith, it's heavy work to sing with an empty stomach," answered O'Grady. "However, here goes:—

"'Twas on November, the second day,
The Admiral he bore away,
Intending for his native shore;
The wind at south-south-west did roar,
There likewise was a terrible sky,
Which made the sea to run mountains high.

"The tide of ebb not being done,
But quickly to the west did run,
Which put us all in dreadful fear,
Because there was not room to wear;

The wind and weather increased sore.
Which drove ten sail of us ashore.

"Ashore went the *Northumberland*,
The *Harwich* and the *Cumberland*,
The *Cloister* and the *Lion*, too;
But the *Elizabeth*, she had most to rue,
She ran stem on and her *Lion* broke,
And sunk the *Cambridge* at one stroke.

"But the worst is what I have to tell,
The greatest ships had the greatest fall;
The brave '*Crounation*' and all her men,
Was lost and drownded every one,
Except a little midshipman and eighteen more
Who in the long-boat comed ashore.

"And thus they lost their precious lives,
But the greatest loss was unto their wives,
Who, with their children, left ashore,
Their husbands' watery death deplore;
And weep their fate with many of tears,
But grief endureth not for years.

"Now you who've a mind to go to sea,
Pray take a useful hint from me;
Oh! stay at home and be content
With what kind Providence has sent;
For these were punish'd unto their deeds,
For grumbling when they had no needs.

"Now may Heaven bless our worthy King,
Likewise his ministers we sing,
And may they ever steer a course,
To make things better 'stead of worse;
And England's flag triumphant fly,

W. H. G. Kingston

The dread of every enemy."

O'Grady's song, though often heard before, was received with no less applause in consequence. Other songs followed, but the effort was greater than many of the seamen could make. Several attempted to tell stories or their own adventures, but the former had no ending, and they very soon lost the thread of their adventures. Then they wandered strangely; some stopped altogether; others laughed and cried alternately. Even Devereux could with difficulty keep command of his own senses. Food and a few drops of precious water were distributed among the sufferers; without it, few could have survived another night. That night came, however, and that night passed, though some on the raft had passed away from life when another sun arose.

Paul more than once asked himself, "Why did I come to sea?"

Reuben overheard him. "To my mind, Paul, when a person has done what he believes is for the best and because he thinks it is right, he has no cause to grumble or to be unhappy," he observed in his quiet way. "Don't you fear, all will turn out right at last."

Paul felt weaker than he had ever done before, and his eye was dim and his voice sounded hollow, and yet his thoughts flowed as freely as ever. He was fully aware that death might be approaching, yet he had no fear of death. He thought of home and of his mother and sisters, and he prayed for them, and that they might not grieve very much at his loss. He was but a poor young ship-boy, but he knew that his mother would mourn for him as much as would the mother of Devereux, or any other high-born midshipman on board.

The sun rose higher and higher in the sky: its rays struck

down as hotly as on the day before. "Water! water! water!" was the cry from all on the raft; still discipline prevailed, though only a young midshipman was the chief, and not a man attempted to take more than his share. At about noon Paul was feeling that he could not endure many more hours of such thirst, when he saw Reuben's eyes directed to the north-east.

"Yes! yes! it is! it is!" exclaimed Reuben at length.

"What! a ship?" asked Paul, almost breathless with eagerness.

"No, but a breeze," cried his friend. "It may carry us to land; it may send us rain! it may bring up a ship to our rescue."

All eyes were now turned in the direction from which the breeze was supposed to be coming. At the edge of the hitherto unvarying expanse of molten silver, a dark blue line was seen; broader and broader it grew. With such strength as they possessed the seamen hoisted their sail. It bulged out and again flattened against the mast; now again it filled, and the raft began to glide slowly over the ocean. A faint cheer burst from the throats of the hitherto despairing crew; yet how many long leagues must be passed over before that raft could reach the land! How many of those now living on it would set foot on that land? Too probably not one—not one. Day after day the raft glided on, but each day death claimed a victim. Still, Devereux and O'Grady and Alphonse kept up their spirits in a way which appealed wonderful to Paul, till he found that he was himself equally resolved to bear up to the last. There was still some food; still a few drops of water. Rain might come; the wind was increasing; clouds were gathering in the sky; the sea was getting up, and the raft, though still progressing, was tossed about in a way which made those on it feel the risk they ran of being thrown or

W. H. G. Kingston

washed off it. They secured themselves with lashings. Again the water was served out. A mouthful was given to Paul.

"Poor boy! let him have it," he heard Devereux say; "it is the last drop."

Now more than ever was rain prayed for. Without rain, should no succour come, in a few days the sufferings of all the party would be over. Faster and faster the raft drove on. It was well constructed, or it would not have held together. Still they dared not lessen their sail. Land might be reached at last if they would persevere. Now they rose to the summit of a foaming sea, now they sank into the deep trough. It seemed every instant that the next must see the destruction of the raft, yet, like hope in a young bosom, it still floated buoyantly over the raging billows. Now dark clouds were gathering. Eagerly they were watched by the seamen with upturned eyes. A few drops fell. They were welcomed with a cry of joy. More came, and then the rain fell in torrents. Their parched throats were moistened, but unless they could spread their sail to collect the precious fluid, they could save but little for the future. Still, life is sweet, and they might obtain enough to preserve their lives for another day. As they dared not lower their sail, they stretched out their jackets and shirts, and wrung them as they were saturated with fresh water into the only cask they had saved. Before it was a quarter full the rain ceased. They watched with jealous eyes the clouds driving away below the horizon, while the sun shone forth as brightly as before on their unguarded heads. Still the raft tumbled furiously about, and with the utmost difficulty the seamen retained their hold of it. Night returned; it was a night of horror. Their provisions were exhausted. When the morning at length broke, two who had been among the strongest were missing. They must have let go their hold while sleeping and been washed away.

"It may be our lot soon," observed Paul, whose strength was failing.

"The same hand which has hitherto preserved us few still alive on this raft is strong to preserve us to the end," said James Croxton, an old seaman, who, even on ordinary occasions said but little, and had only spoken since the ship went down to utter a few words of encouragement to his companions. He was known on board the frigate as Jim the Methodist, but was respected by the greater number of his shipmates. "Never fear, mates, help will come if we pray for it, though we don't see the Hand which sends it. Let us pray."

Jim's words and example had a great effect. It was followed by all, and the united prayers of the seamen, acknowledging their own utter helplessness, ascended together on high. One and all seemed to gain a strength they had not before felt. The raft continued to be tossed about as before, and the hot wind blew, and the sun shone on their unsheltered heads. The sun rose higher and higher and then descended, watched anxiously by the seamen till it dipped below the horizon. Could any of them expect to see another sun arise? They seldom spoke to each other during the night. The voice of Jim Croxton was now most frequently heard, exhorting his companions to repentance, and to put their faith in the loving and merciful One. When the morning broke they were all alive, and the voice of Reuben, who had dragged himself upright by the mast, was heard crying, "A sail! a sail! standing towards us!"

The information was received in various ways by the people on the raft; some laughed, others wept, a few prayed, and others groaned, declaring that they should not be seen, and that the ship would pass them by. Old Croxton, however, who had simply poured forth his heart in a few words of thanksgiving, kept his eyes steadily on the approaching ship.

W. H. G. Kingston

"She is nearing us! she is nearing us!" he uttered slowly every now and then.

Paul gasped his breath, and felt as if he should faint away altogether, as he saw that the ship was a British man-of-war, and that the raft was evidently perceived by those on board. She drew nearer and nearer, and, heaving to, lowered two boats, which rapidly approached the raft. In that tumbling sea there was no small difficulty in getting close enough to the raft to take off the people. Paul, as the youngest, was the first to be transferred by his companions to the nearest boat. Even at that moment he was struck by the expression of the countenances of most of the crew. No one smiled; no one seemed pleased at the work of mercy they were performing.

"You think, youngster, that you'll be changing for the better, getting off your raft aboard that frigate there?" growled out one of the men, as Paul was passed along forward. "You've got out of the frying-pan into the fire, let me tell you. It's a perfect hell afloat, and to my mind the captain's the—"

"Silence there, forward!" shouted the officer in command of the boat. "Back in again."

One by one the people were taken off the raft. Devereux insisted on remaining to the last, and he was taken off in the second boat. No sooner had he been placed in her than several of her crew leaped on to the raft.

"Better run the chance of a watery grave than live aboard there," shouted one of the men, attempting to hoist the sail which had been lowered. "Hurrah, lads! for the coast of America and freedom!"

"Back into the boat: back, you mutinous scoundrels!" shouted the officer in command. "What foolery are you about? If you were to go, and small loss you would be, you would all of you be dead before a week was over. Back, I say."

In vain the men tried to hoist the sail. The mast gave way, throwing one of them into the sea. He made an attempt to save himself, but sank in sight of his shipmates. The boat was soon again dropped alongside the raft, and the men with sulky indifference returned on board. Very little was said by anybody as the boats pulled back to the frigate. The officers, indeed, saw that those they had taken off the raft were in no condition to answer questions. Devereux and his companions were lifted up on deck, and from thence at once transferred to the sick bay below under the doctor's care. Paul, after a sound sleep, recovered his senses, and very soon perceived, that although there was strict discipline maintained on board, each person went about his duty in a dull, mechanical way. Reuben was, however, on foot before Paul. He came to the side of the hammock in which the latter still lay unable to move.

"I am thankful, Reuben, that we are safe off that dreadful raft," said Paul.

"No reason to call it dreadful, boy. It was our ark of safety, as Jim Croxton says, rightly, and we should be grateful that we were allowed to be saved by it. There's many here, as you saw, would rather be on that raft than aboard this fine frigate," answered Reuben.

"Why? what is the matter with the ship?" asked Paul.

"Why, just this," answered his friend; "the captain is a tyrant; many of the officers imitate him, and altogether the men's lives are miserable. The ship is a complete hell afloat."

Several days passed by; the frigate was steering for the West Indies, which were sighted soon after Paul had managed to creep on deck. He saw the men casting wistful glances at the land.

"If once I set my foot ashore, it will take a dozen red coats to carry me aboard again!" exclaimed a seaman near him.

"Ay, Bill, it's a dog's life we lead; but there's a way to free ourselves if we were men enough to use it," said another.

"It's not the first time that has been thought of," observed a third. "But hush, mates, that boy may hear; he looks like a sharp one."

The men were silent till Paul walked farther aft, where he saw them still earnestly engaged in talking together. He considered what he ought to do. Should he tell Devereux what he had heard? Perhaps, after all, it meant nothing. He could trust Reuben; that is to say, Reuben would not betray him; but he might take part with the men. He would consult Croxton. He found old Jim after some time, but had no opportunity of speaking to him alone. There was an ominous scowl on the countenances of all the men, which confirmed his suspicions that something was wrong. Below they gathered together more in knots than usual, speaking in subdued voices. Whenever an officer approached, they were silent, and generally dispersed with an appearance of indifference. Thus two or three more days passed, and Paul felt as well able as ever to do his duty. It was the forenoon watch; the men were summoned to divisions. It was perfectly calm; no land was in sight; the sun struck down fiercely on their heads.

"There's work in hand for us to-day," exclaimed a topman, as he sprang on deck.

In a little time the order to furl sails was given. The men flew aloft.

"Reef topsails," cried the first-lieutenant.

The men appeared to do the work slowly. Oaths and curses were hurled at them by the officers on duty. Paul took the opportunity of going down to see Devereux, who, with O'Grady and Alphonse, was still too weak to go on deck. He told him that he was afraid something was wrong. Devereux answered—

"I fear that the men are dissatisfied, but they dare do nothing. I pity them, though, poor fellows."

The words were overheard by some of the idlers, as they are called below. While Paul was speaking to Devereux, Croxton came in. He also heard what had been said.

"Man is born to suffer," he remarked. "He must submit, and leave the righting in the hands of Providence. He cannot right himself."

His remarks were scarcely understood by those who heard him, even by Devereux, who, however, remembered them. After a time, Paul returned on deck. The captain was still exercising the men at furling sails. With watch in hand he stood on the quarter-deck, his rage increasing as he found that they could not or would not accomplish the work in the time he desired. At length he shouted in a voice which made the blood run cold in Paul's veins—

"The last men in off the yards shall get four dozen for their pains. Remember that, ye scoundrels! Away aloft!"

Again the men ascended the rigging. The sails were furled.

Two active young topmen on the mizen-yard made an attempt to spring over the backs of the rest. They missed their hold. With a fearful crash they fell together on the deck.

"Throw the lubbers overboard!" exclaimed the captain, kicking contemptuously their mangled remains.

These words were the signal of his own destruction. The men, regardless of his threats, sprang below.

"Vengeance! vengeance!" was the cry.

The first-lieutenant who ventured among them was cut down, and while yet breathing, hove overboard. Others who appeared met with the same fate. The mutineers then rushed to the captain's cabin. He stood fiercely at bay, but in vain. Bleeding from countless wounds, he was forced through the stern port. His last words were, "Vengeance! vengeance! vengeance!" Fearfully it was paid.

# CHAPTER FOUR

The deed of blood was not yet completed, although we would fain avoid entering more minutely than is necessary into the horrible details of the massacre which followed the death of the captain. It is a proof of the evil passions which dwell within the bosoms of men, and shows how those passions may be worked up by tyranny and injustice to make men commit deeds at which, in their calmer moments, their minds would revolt. Many of the victims struggled manfully for their lives. Among the officers was a young midshipman. He was fighting bravely by the side of one of the lieutenants, who was at length cut down.

"Will you swear not to utter a word of what you have seen done to-day?" exclaimed Nol Hargraves, a quartermaster, who was one of the leaders of the mutineers, if any could be called leaders, where all seemed suddenly inspired by the same mad revengeful spirit. The brave boy, as he stood leaning on his sword, looked undaunted at Hargraves and at those standing round him.

"Swear—no!" he exclaimed. "If I live to see you brought to justice, as you will be some day, I will say that you were cowardly murderers of your officers; that you killed sleeping men; that you threw others, still alive, overboard, and that you murdered the surgeons who had cured the wounded, and

W. H. G. Kingston

tended the sick like brothers. I'll say that you butchered one of my helpless messmates—a poor boy younger than myself; I'll—!"

"Overboard with him—overboard!" exclaimed Hargraves, who had just cut down the lieutenant, and seemed like a tiger, which having once tasted blood, thirsts for more.

The midshipman, already fatigued and wounded, raised his weapon to defend himself. Hargraves rushed at the boy, who in an instant afterwards lay writhing at his feet.

"Heave the carcase overboard. It is the way some of us have been treated, you know that, mates," he exclaimed, throwing the yet palpitating form of the boy into the sea, when it was eagerly seized on by the ravenous sharks, waiting for their prey supplied by the savage cruelty of man. Many even of the mutineers cried, "Shame! shame!" Hargraves turned fiercely round on them—

"Ye none of you cried shame when the captain did the same—cowards! why did ye not do it then? Were the lives of our brave fellows of less value than the life of that young cub?"

The men were silenced, but the eyes of many were opened, and they began from that moment bitterly to repent the cruel deed of which they had been guilty. Oh! if they could have recalled the dead, how gladly would they have done so,—their officers, who, if they had sometimes acted harshly, were brave men and countrymen; even the captain, tyrant as he was, they wished that they could see once more on his quarter-deck, with the dreadful scene which had been enacted wiped away; but the deed had been done—no power could obliterate it. They had been participators in the bloody work. It stood recorded against them in the imperishable books of Heaven. Blood had been spilt, and blood was to cry out against them and to demand a dreadful retribution.

The mutinous crew stood gazing stupidly at each other; the helm had been deserted, the wind had fallen, the sails were flapping lazily against the masts, and the ship's head was going slowly round and round towards the different points of the compass. Hargraves and others felt that something must be done; there was no safety for them while their frigate floated on the broad ocean. What if they should fall in with another British man-of-war? What account could they give of themselves? Some were for scuttling her and saying that she had foundered, while they had escaped in the boats, but the boats would not hold them all, and could they trust each other? What likelihood that all would adhere to the same tale? Was it probable that all the crew should have escaped, and not an officer with them? The boats might separate, to be sure, but to what lands could they direct their different courses? On what shore, inhabited by countrymen, dared they place their feet without fear of detection? Discussions loud and long took place. It was agreed that the ship should be carried to a Spanish port; sold, if the sale could be effected, and with the proceeds and with such valuables as the murdered officers possessed, they would separate in various directions, and by changing their names, avoid all chance of discovery.

But while these dreadful events were occurring, what had become of those who had been so lately rescued from a terrible fate on the raft? Had they suffered one still more terrible by the hands of their own countrymen? Paul Gerrard was asleep in his hammock when he heard a voice calling him. It was that of old James Croxton.

"Turn out, Paul," he said, "there is some fearful work going forward on deck, and I know not who may be the sufferers. We may save some of them, though."

Paul was on his feet and dressed in an instant.

"What is to be done?" he asked.

"Mr Devereux is in danger; we might save him," said the old man. "The people are gone mad. Come along."

Paul followed Croxton to the sick bay. Devereux had heard the disturbance, and from the expressions uttered by the men as they passed, feared that an attack was being made on the officers of the ship. He was endeavouring to get up for the purpose of joining the officers, and sharing their fate, whatever that might be. O'Grady was still asleep. Croxton guessed what Devereux was about to do.

"It's of no use, sir—they'll only murder you with the rest," he whispered: "you must keep out of their way till they're cool. Rouse up Mr O'Grady, Paul, and come along."

Saying this, the old man, with a strength scarcely to be expected, lifted up Devereux, and carried, rather than led him, down to the hold. Paul, meantime, had awakened O'Grady, who, though not comprehending what had occurred, followed him mechanically. The two midshipmen found themselves stowed away in total darkness among chests and casks containing stores of various sorts.

"The crew have mutinied, there's no doubt about that," answered old Jim to an inquiry made by Devereux; "but we will go and face them, they will not harm either the boy or me. Don't you speak, though, or make the slightest sound; they'll think that you are hove overboard with the rest."

These words confirmed the midshipmen's worst apprehensions. They had no time to ask questions, before the old man, taking Paul by the hand, hurried away. Paul and his companion reached the deck unobserved. The mutineers were all too eager in the desperate work in which they had engaged to remark them. At that moment Paul saw his friends Reuben Cole and the young Frenchman, Alphonse, with some of the inferior and petty officers, dragged forward by the mutineers. Hargraves was the chief speaker.

"What is to be done with these?" he asked, turning round to his companions in crime.

"Serve them like the rest," shouted some.

"Dead men tell no tales," muttered others.

"We've had enough of that sort of work," cried the greater number. "No more bloodshed! Let them swear to hold their tongues and do as we bid them."

"You hear what is proposed," said Hargraves, gruffly. "Will you fellows take your lives on these terms?"

"Not I, for one, ye murderous villains," exclaimed Reuben Cole, doubling his fists and confronting the mutineers. "I'll take nothing at your hands, but I'm very certain that there are plenty of men aboard here who'll not stand idly by and see me butchered on that account. As to peaching on you, I'm not going to do that, but you'll not get another word out of me about the matter."

Had Hargraves had his way, it would have fared ill with honest Reuben; but the latter had not wrongly estimated the support he was likely to receive from his new shipmates, whose goodwill he knew that he had gained.

"Reuben Cole is not the man to peach, even if he has the chance," shouted several of them.

"No fear; he'll prove true to us, and so will the little Mounseer there; won't you?" asked one, turning to Alphonse. "We couldn't afford to lose you and your fiddle, especially just now, when we shall want something to keep up our spirits."

Alphonse, not comprehending what was said, made no reply. His silence was construed into contumacy, and some of Hargraves' adherents laid hands on him, and appeared as if they were about to throw him overboard, when Paul shouted out to him in French what was said. Alphonse very naturally had no scruples to overcome. He could only look on the fate of the captain as a just retribution on his tyranny.

"Oh, yes, yes! I play the fiddle," he exclaimed; "I go get it—I play for you all."

Not waiting for an answer, he ran towards the nearest hatchway, and passing near Paul, inquired for Devereux and O'Grady.

"Safe," whispered Paul, and the young Frenchman dived below.

He speedily returned with his faithful violin, and without waiting to be asked, began to play. The hearts of all his hearers were too heavy to allow them to be influenced as under other circumstances they would have been by the music, but it served in a degree to calm their fierce passions, and to turn them from their evil intentions. Of the principal officers of the ship the master alone had hitherto escaped destruction. He was no coward. He had seen with horror the murder of his messmates and captain, but life was sweet, and when offered to him, even on terms degrading, undoub- tedly—that he would navigate the ship into an enemy's port—he accepted them. The few warrant and petty officers who had escaped being killed, at once declared their intention of acting as the master had done.

"It's fortunate for you, mates, that you don't belong to the brood who grow into captains," exclaimed Hargraves, fiercely. "I, for one, would never have consented to let you live if you had."

Paul trembled for the fate of his friends when he heard these expressions, for Hargraves looked like a man who would put any threats he might utter into execution. Order was somewhat restored, officers were appointed to keep watch, and the ship was put on the course for the port to which it was proposed she should be carried. The crew had once been accustomed to keep a sharp look-out for an enemy; they now kept a still more anxious watch to avoid any British cruiser which might approach them. Day and night they were haunted with the dread of meeting their countrymen. Paul overheard some of the ringleaders consulting together.

"There are only two things to be done; if we can't run from them, to fight it out to the last, or to kill all those who won't swear to be staunch, and to declare that they died of fever," said one of them in a low, determined voice.

"Ay, that's the only thing for it," growled out another; "I'm not going to swing for nothing, I've made up my mind."

"Swing! who talks of swinging? None of that, Tom," exclaimed a third, in uneasy tones.

"It's what one and all of us will do, mates, if we don't look out what we're about," said Hargraves, who was waiting for an opportunity of pressing his plans on his companions. "We have let too many of them live as it is, and it's my opinion there's no safety for any of us as long as one of them breathes. I've heard tell what the old pirates used to do to make men faithful. They didn't trust to oaths—not they—but they made those who said they were ready to join them shoot their shipmates who refused. That's what we must do, mates; it's the only secure way, you may depend on't."

Paul was convinced that the men spoke in earnest, and afraid of being discovered should he remain, he crept stealthily away. He searched about till he found Croxton and Reuben, and told them at once what he had heard and feared.

"There's little doubt but that you are right, Paul," said old Croxton, after meditating for some time. "We thought that we were fortunate in getting on board this ship, and now, to my mind, we shall be fortunate to get out of her. I'm afraid for poor Mr Devereux and Mr O'Grady. It will go hard with them if they're discovered."

"I have it," said Reuben, after thinking for some time— speaking in a low voice—"We must leave this cursed ship and carry off the two young gentlemen. I'd sooner be on the raft out in the Atlantic, than aboard of her."

"Ay, lads, 'Better is a dry crust with contentment,'" remarked old Jim. "But how to leave the ship, so as to escape without being followed—there's the difficulty."

"'Where there's a will there's a way,'" said Reuben. "If it must be done, it can be done."

"Right, lad," said Croxton; "it must be done, for we deserve the fate of villains if we consort with them longer than we can help; though I'll not say that all on board this unhappy ship are equally bad. There are many who would be glad to escape from her if they had but the chance."

"It must be done," repeated Reuben. "We may make off with a boat some dark night. The young Frenchman and our own fellows will be sure to join, and I think that there's three or four others—maybe more—who'll be glad to get away at any risk."

"We must run the risk, and it isn't a small one," said Croxton. "If they were to catch us, they'd kill us. There's no doubt about that."

The whole plan was soon settled—who were to be got to join—the boat to be taken—the way she was to be lowered. Devereux and O'Grady were to be told of it when all was ready, and were to be brought up on deck as soon as it was dark, and stowed away in the boat herself till the moment of escape had arrived. Paul was usually employed to carry food to the midshipmen. Sometimes, however, Croxton went, sometimes Reuben, to lessen the risk of his object being suspected. Paul waited till night—the time he visited his friends—and hiding a lantern under his jacket, carefully groped his way down to them. They highly approved of the plan proposed for escaping from the ship, and were eager for the moment for putting it into execution. O'Grady, especially, was heartily weary of his confinement.

"I doubt if my two legs will ever be able to stretch themselves out straight again, after being cramped up so long, like herrings in a cask," he exclaimed, in the low tone in which it was necessary to speak. "We owe you a heavy debt, Gerrard, and if you succeed in getting us out of this, it will be a huge deal greater."

"If it were not for old Jim and Reuben Cole, I could be but of little use, so say nothing about that, Mr O'Grady," answered Paul. "I am going to try and find out on the charts, when the master is working his day's work, exactly where we are, and if there's land near, we may, perhaps, get away to-morrow."

Paul felt far from comfortable all the next day. He could not help fancying that the mutineers suspected him, and that he should suddenly find himself seized and thrown overboard. What he dreaded most was the ultimate failure of the undertaking. His two friends had in the meantime sounded those they hoped might join them, but whether all were favourable to the plan he could not ascertain. His eye was constantly on the master, who at length, seeing him near, sent him for his quadrant and tables. This was just what Paul wanted. He stood by while the observations were being taken, and then, carrying the instrument, followed the master to the cabin. Paul brought out the chart, and placed it before him, watching anxiously the movements of his companion as he measured off the distance run since the previous day.

More than once the master glanced round the cabin, and sighed deeply. "In five or six days my disgraceful task will be done," he muttered, as he moved the compasses towards the coast of the Spanish main. "Then what remains for me in life? If I escape an ignominious death, I must ever be suspected of having consented to the murder of my brother officers. I would rather that the ship had gone down, and the whole history of the butchery been hid from mortal knowledge. Yet God knows it, and it may teach officers for the future the dreadful consequences of tyranny and cruelty."

He continued on in the same strain, not aware, it seemed, that Paul was listening. Paul retired to a distance. "Shall I ask the master to join us?" he thought to himself. "No, it will not do. It would greatly increase the risk of our being caught." He waited till the master was silent. He went back to the table. "Shall I put up the charts?" he asked. "But before I do so, will you, sir, kindly show me where we are?"

Since the outbreak the poor master had not been treated with so much respect. He showed Paul the exact position of the ship, the neighbouring lands, and remarked on the prevailing currents and winds. Paul rolled up the chart, and put it in its place. He fancied that the master must have suspected his thoughts. Paul soon after met his friends, and told them of all he had learned.

It was agreed that they would wait till it was the master's watch, for so few of the mutineers could take command of a watch, that he was compelled constantly to be on deck. It was suspected that he had at times given way to intemperance, and Paul had observed more than once that when he came on deck he appeared to have been drinking, and that he frequently dropped asleep when sitting on a gun or leaning against the side of the ship. Many of the seamen who had free access to the spirit-room were also constantly tipsy at night, though the chief mutineers, from necessity, kept sober. The once well-ordered man-of-war soon became like a lawless buccaneer. The men rolled about the decks half tipsy, some were playing cards and dice between the guns, some were fighting, and others were sleeping in any shady place they could find.

Paul passed old Croxton on deck. "We shall have little difficulty in accomplishing our object if this goes on," he whispered.

"Yes, Paul, what is lost by fools is gained by wise men," he answered. "Ay, and there is one who will gain more than all by the work done on board this ship. He will soon leave his poor dupes to wish that they had never been born."

Paul and his friends waited anxiously for night: they had resolved no longer to delay their attempt.

W. H. G. Kingston

"I'll take care that they don't follow us," said Reuben.

"What do you mean?" asked Paul.

"I'll tell you, lad," was the answer; and he whispered something into his companion's ear.

Paul felt that there was a great deal to be done, and longed for the moment of action. He observed with satisfaction that frequent visits were made to the spirit-room, and that even the master was taking more than his usual share of grog. The ship sailed steadily over the calm sea—night drew on. Paul's heart beat unusually fast. He waited till he was sure that he was not perceived, and then he climbed into one of the boats. He was there for some time, and then descending he got into another; and so he visited all in succession. Again he slunk down below.

At length the master came on deck to keep his watch. The night, for those latitudes, was unusually dark, but the sea was smooth. The ship glided calmly on, the ripple made by her stem as she drove her way through the water showing, however, that a fair breeze filled her sails. The master leaned against a gun-carriage, and gradually sunk down on it, resting his head on his hands. The helmsman stood at his post, now gazing at the broad spread of canvas above him, and then mechanically at the compass, with its light shining in the binnacle before him, but looking neither to the right hand nor to the left. The rest of the watch placed themselves at their ease between the guns, and were soon, whatever might have been their intention, fast asleep. One by one others now stole on deck towards the boat Paul had last visited. Not a word was spoken. At length two men appeared bearing two slight figures on their backs. The latter were carefully deposited in the boat, which was quickly lowered. The whole manoeuvre was executed with the greatest rapidity and in the most perfect silence. Even the helmsman, who, though drowsy, could not have been entirely asleep, took no notice of them. In another instant, had anybody been looking over the side, a dark object might have been seen dropping astern. It was a boat, which contained Paul Gerrard and his companions, who had thus made their perilous escape from the blood-stained ship. Not till they were far astern did any one venture to speak. Devereux at last drew a deep sigh. "Thank Heaven, we are free of them!" he exclaimed.

"Amen!" said old Croxton, in a deep voice. "We have reason to rejoice and be thankful. Sad will be the end of all those wretched men. Their victims are more to be envied than they."

As soon as it was deemed safe the oars were got out, a lantern was lighted to throw its light on the compass, and the boat was steered towards the north-west. The wind soon dropped to a perfect calm.

"We are safe now," exclaimed Paul. "Even if they were to miss us they could not follow, for there is not a boat on board which can swim or an oar to pull with. Some I dropped overboard, and others I cut nearly through just above the blades, and I bored holes in all the boats where they could not be seen till the boats were in the water."

"Well done, Gerrard. If we get clear off, we shall owe our escape to your judgment; but you ran a great risk of losing your life. The mutineers would have murdered you if they had discovered what you were about."

"I knew that, sir; but I knew also that nothing can be done without danger and trouble."

W. H. G. Kingston

"Ay, boy, and that no danger or trouble is too great, so that we may escape from the company of sinners," remarked old Croxton. "Think of that, young gentleman. If you consent to remain with them because you are too lazy to flee, you will soon fall into their ways, and become one of them."

Some of his hearers remembered those words in after years. All night long the oars were kept going, and when morning dawned the ship was nowhere to be seen.

"Now let us turn to and have some breakfast," exclaimed O'Grady. "It will be the first for many a day that you and I have eaten in sunlight, Devereux, and I see good reason that we should be thankful. Then we'll have a tune from Alphonse, for I'll warrant that he has brought his fiddle."

"Ah, dat I have," cried the young Frenchman, exhibiting his beloved instrument. "But, mes amis, ve vill mange first. De arm vil not move vidout de oil!"

Alphonse had greatly improved in his knowledge of English.

A good supply of provisions had been collected, but as it was uncertain when they should make the land, it was necessary to be economical in their use. A very good breakfast, however, was made, and the spirits of the party rose as their hunger was appeased, and they thought of their happy escape. As the sun, however, arose in the blue sky, its rays struck down on their unprotected heads, and they would gladly have got under shelter, but there was no shelter for them out on the glassy shining sea. Still they rowed on. To remain where they were was to die by inches. Devereux did his best, as he had done on the raft, to keep up the spirits of his men, and, weak as he was, he would have taken his spell at the oar if they had let him.

"No, no, sir; you just take your trick at the helm, if you think proper," exclaimed Croxton. "But just let us do the hard work. It's your head guides us, and without that we should be badly off."

Devereux saw the wisdom of this remark. They knew that they had five, and perhaps six days' hard rowing before they could hope to reach Dominica, the nearest island they supposed belonged to Great Britain, according to the information Paul had gained from the master. They were, however, far better off than when they had been on the raft, for they had food, were in a well-found boat, and knew tolerably well their position. Still they were not in good spirits, which is not surprising, considering the scenes they had witnessed, the dangers they had endured, and the uncertainty of the future.

Dominica was an English possession, but it had once been taken by the French, and might have been again; and Alphonse fancied that he had heard that it was proposed to make a descent on the island, in which case they would fall among enemies instead of friends.

"Ah! but your countrymen would surely treat us who come to them in distress as friends," observed O'Grady.

"Ah, dat dey vould!" exclaimed Alphonse, warmly.

"Well, mounseer, there is good and there is bad among 'em, of that there's no doubt," observed Reuben, taking his quid out of his mouth, and looking the young Frenchman in the face; "but do ye see I'd rather not try lest we should fall among the bad, and there's a precious lot on 'em."

Notwithstanding these doubts Devereux continued his course for Dominica. As the sun rose higher in the sky, the heat became greater and greater, till it was almost insupportable. A sail spread over the boat afforded some shelter from its rays, but they pierced through it as easily as a mosquito's sting does through a kid glove, till the air under it became even more stifling than that above.

All the time in turns they continued to row on—night and day there was to be no cessation. Reversing the usual order, they longed for the night, when the air would be cooler, and their heads would escape the frying process going on while the sun was above them.

"Och, but this is hot," cried O'Grady for the hundredth time. "If this goes on much longer, we'll all be turned into real black ebony niggers, and the Christians on shore will be after putting us to work at the sugar-canes, and be swearing we've just come straight across from Africa. As to our tongues, there'll be no safety for us through them, and they'll swear we've made off with the uniforms from some ship of war or other, and perhaps be tricing us up as thieves and murderers. Did you ever hear tell of the Irishman—a sweet countryman of mine,—who once came out from the Emerald Isle to these parts—to Demerara, I believe? As soon as the ship which brought him entered the harbour, she was boarded by a boat full of niggers.

"'Will yer honour have your duds carried ashore now?' asks one, stepping up to him. 'It's myself will see ye all comfortable in a jiffy, if ye'll trust me, at Mother Flannigan's.'"

"My countryman looked at him very hard."

"'What's your name now?' he asks with some trepidation."

"'Pat O'Dwyer, yer honour,' says the nigger."

"'Pat, how long have ye been here?' asks my countryman, solemnly."

"'Faith, about two years, yer honour,' says the nigger."

"'Two years, did ye say—two years only to turn a white Irishman into a nigger?' exclaimed my countryman with no little alarm. 'Then faith the sooner I get away back from out of this black-burning country the better—or my own mither down in Ballyshannon won't be after knowing her own beautiful boy again at all, and my father would be after disowning me, and my sisters and brothers to boot, and Father O'Roony would be declaring that it was a white Christian he made of me, and that I couldn't be the same anyhow. Take my duds on shore. No. Take 'em below, and I'll go there too, and remain there too till the ship sails and I'm out of this nigger-making land.' My countryman kept to his intention, and from that day till the ship sailed, never set foot on shore. You'll understand that no small number of Irishmen go out to that country, and that the nigger boy had learnt his English from them—for he wasn't a real Irishman after all, but that my countryman did not find out till he got back to auld Ireland again."

"Och, they are broths of boys the Paddies, but they do make curious mistakes somehow or other, it must be allowed."

"I was one day dining at the mess of some soldier officers, when one of them, a Captain O'Rourke, positively declared on his faith as a gentleman that 'he had seen anchovies growing on the walls at Gibraltar.'"

"Most of the party opened their eyes, but said nothing, for O'Rourke was not a man whose word a quietly-disposed person would wish in his sober moments to call in question."

W. H. G. Kingston

"Unfortunately, there was present an Englishman, a Lieutenant Brown, into whose head the fumes of the tawny port and ruby claret had already mounted."

"'Anchovies growing on a wall?' he blurted out. 'That's a cram if ever there was one.'"

"O'Rourke was on his feet in a moment,—"

"'What, sir—it's not you who mean to say that you don't believe me, I hope?' he exclaimed, in a voice which meant mischief."

"'Believe you! I should think I don't, or any man who can talk such gammon,' answered Brown, in a tone of defiance."

"As may be supposed, there was only one way in which such a matter could end. Preliminaries were soon settled. The affair would have come off that evening, but it would have broken up the party too soon, and besides it wouldn't have been fair, as Brown's hand was not as steady as it might have been. So it was put off till the next morning soon after daylight, when there was a good gathering to see the fun. The English generally took Brown's side. I of course stood by O'Rourke, not that I was quite sure he was in the right, by-the-by."

"It was very evident that Brown had no notion of handling his pistol."

"'I'll just wing him to teach the spalpeen better manners,' whispered O'Rourke to his second. 'He's unworthy game for my weapon.'"

"The word was given to fire. Brown's bullet flew up among some trees away to the right, not a little frightening the young in a nest of birds, who popped out their heads to see what was the matter. It was now our friend's turn.

He smiled as he sent his ball through Brown's trousers, cruelly grazing his leg, whereon he began to skip about in the most comical way possible with the pain.

"'By—, you've made that fellow cut capers at all events,' observed O'Rourke's second."

"'Cut capers, did ye say?' exclaimed O'Rourke. 'Them's the very things I saw growing on the wall, and not anchovies at all, at all.' And rushing up to poor Brown, who had fallen on the ground, he took his hand, greatly to the surprise of the wounded man, crying out,—'It's myself made the trifle of a mistake, my dear fellow, it's capers, it's capers, grows on walls, so get up and don't think anything more about the matter.'"

"Poor Brown went limping about for many a day afterwards, and didn't seem to consider the matter half as good a joke as the rest of us."

O'Grady's stories amused the party, though Croxton very properly remarked that duelling was a wicked heathen custom, and that he wondered people who called themselves Christians could ever indulge in it. Other stories were told, but their interest flagged, for people are not generally in a talkative mood with the thermometer above a hundred, and with a small supply of water. Alphonse, however, from time to time kept his fiddlestick going, both to his own satisfaction, and that of his hearers. Still he, on account of the heat, was often compelled to put it down, and to declare that he could play no longer.

Great and unusual, however, as was the heat, it did not

W. H. G. Kingston

appear to cause any apprehension of danger in the mind of Devereux. The night came on, and though the air even then was hot, the weary crew were refreshed by sleep. The sun rose, and the air was hotter than ever, notwithstanding a dense mist, which gradually filled the atmosphere, while soon a lurid glare spread over it. Croxton, as he watched the change, looked even graver than before. "You've not been in these seas before, Mr Devereux, sir?" he observed.

"No; and if the weather is always as broiling as it is at present, I don't wish to come to them again in a hurry," answered Devereux. "But one thing is fortunate—they are calm enough to please any old ladies who might venture on them."

"Don't count too much on that, sir, if an old man who has cruised for many a long year out here in every part may venture to give you advice," said Croxton, in an earnest tone. "The weather here is often like a passionate man—calm one moment, and raging furiously the next. I tell you, sir, I don't like its look at present, and I fear, before long, that we shall have a job to keep the boat afloat."

"What do you mean, Croxton?" said Devereux. "The boat is the strongest and best-built belonging to the frigate."

"I mean, sir, that a hurricane is about to burst over us, and that the strongest and best-built boat can scarcely live through it," was the answer.

"I fear that you are right," replied Devereux. "We'll prepare the boat as best we can for what is coming."

No time was to be lost. The staves of a cask knocked to pieces were nailed round the sides of the boat, and to these a sail, cut into broad strips, was nailed, so that the water might the better be kept out. The men were also ordered to rest and to take some food, and then calmly they waited the expected event. They were not kept long in suspense.

"Here it comes," cried Croxton. "Our only chance is to run before it." He pointed as he spoke astern, where a long line of snow-white foam was seen rolling on over the leaden ocean, the sky above it being even darker than before.

"Out oars, and pull for your lives, lads!" cried Devereux.

Scarcely had the boat gathered full away before the hurricane overtook her, and she was surrounded by a seething mass of foam; every instant the seas growing higher and higher, and rolling up with fierce roars, as if to overwhelm her. It seemed impossible that an open boat could live in such tumultuous waters, yet still she kept afloat, flying on before the tempest. Devereux firmly grasped the helm. He knew that any careless steering would cause the destruction of the boat and all in her. The crew looked at each other. No wonder that many a cheek was pale. Who could tell how soon they might be struggling helplessly amid the foam, while their boat was sinking down below their feet? It was impossible to say also where they might drive to.

On flew the boat. As the hurricane increased in strength and gained greater and greater power over the water, the seas increased in height and came rolling and tumbling on, foaming, hissing, and roaring—threatening every instant to engulph her. So great was the force of the wind, that the oars were almost blown out of the men's hands, their efforts being expended solely in keeping the boat running before the sea. Those not rowing were employed in baling, for, in spite of all their efforts, the water washed in in such abundance as to require all their exertions to heave it out again.

W. H. G. Kingston

Paul, as he laboured away with the rest, thought a great deal of home and the dear ones he had left there. He believed, and had good reason for believing, that he should never see them again, for by what possible means could he and his companions escape destruction, unless the hurricane was suddenly to cease, and it had as yet not gained its height. Even as it was, the boat could scarcely be kept afloat. Night, too, would soon arrive, and then the difficulty of steering before the sea would be greatly increased. Still the boat floated. Now a sea higher than its predecessors came roaring on—the foam blown from its summit half filled the boat. With difficulty she could be freed of water before another came following with a still more threatening aspect. The voice of old Croxton was heard raised in prayer. Each one believed that his last hour was come. It turned suddenly aside, and the boat still floated. Again and again they were threatened and escaped. Darkness, however, was now rapidly coming on and increasing the terrific aspect of the tempest. Devereux, aided by Reuben Cole, sat steering the boat. Not a word was spoken. The roar of the waves increased.

"Breakers ahead!" cried old Croxton, in a deep solemn voice. "The Lord have mercy on our souls!"

The boat was lifted higher than before amid the tumultuous hissing cauldron of foaming waters, and then down she came with a fearful crash on a coral reef.

# CHAPTER FIVE

The shrieks and cries and shouts of Paul's companions rang in his ears as he found himself with them struggling in the foaming water amid the fragments of their boat. His great desire was to preserve his presence of mind. He struck out with hands and feet, not for the purpose of making way through the water, but that he might keep himself afloat till he could ascertain in which direction the sea was driving him. That some of his companions were yet alive, he could tell by hearing their voices, though already it seemed at some distance from each other. He felt that, though now swimming bravely, his strength must soon fail him. Something struck him. He stretched out his hands and grasped an oar. He found himself carried along, even more rapidly than before, amid the hissing foam. He judged by the sensation that he was lifted to the summit of a wave; it rolled triumphantly on with him, and it seemed as if he was thrown forward by it a considerable distance, for he dropped, as it were, into comparatively smooth water. He did not stop, but he was borne on and on till he felt his feet, for the first time, touch for an instant something hard. It might have been the top of a rock, and he would be again in deep water; but no—he stretched out one leg. It met the sand—a hard beach. Directly after, he was wading, and rapidly rising higher out of the water. He found some difficulty in withstanding the waters as they receded, but they did not seem to run back with the

W. H. G. Kingston

force they frequently do; and struggling manfully, he at length worked his way up till he was completely beyond their power. Then exhausted nature gave way, and he sank down in a state of half-stupor on the ground. The hurricane howled over his head; the waves roared around him; he had the feeling that they would come up and claim him as their prey, and yet he had no power to drag himself farther away. He had consciousness enough left to show that he was on a wild sea beach, and to believe that his last moments were approaching. At length he fell asleep, and probably slept for some hours, for when he awoke he felt greatly refreshed. It was still dark. He tried to stand up, that he might ascertain the nature of the country on which he had been thrown; he could see no trees, and he fancied that he could distinguish the foam-covered waves leaping up on the other side of the land. It might be a point of land, or it might be some small sandy islet; it had, at all events, a very desolate appearance. Was he its sole occupant? He scarcely dared to shout out an inquiry, lest the sea-bird's shriek should be the only reply he might receive—or, what would be worse, no responding voice should answer him. He sat down again, wishing that day would come. He felt very sad—very forlorn. He could scarcely refrain from crying bitterly, and almost wished that he had been swallowed up by the foaming sea. He sat on, wishing that the night would come to an end. How long it seemed! Hour after hour passed by; he could not sleep, and yet he would gladly have lost all recollection of his past sufferings, and thoughts of those which were to come. He watched the hurricane decreasing; the wind grew less and less in strength; the waves lashed the island shores with diminished fury; and the foam no longer flew, as heretofore, in dense showers over him. Dawn at last broke, and before long the sun himself rose up out of his ocean bed. Paul started to his feet, and looked about him. Along the beach, at no great distance, his eye fell on two figures. He rushed towards them. They did not see him, for they were sitting down, looking the other way. He shouted for joy on recognising Devereux and O'Grady. On hearing his voice they turned their heads, and the latter, jumping up, ran to meet him. The greeting was warm, for both looked on each other as rescued from the grave. Poor Devereux, however, did not move; and as Paul got nearer to him he saw that he was very pale.

"I'm so glad that you have escaped, Gerrard, both for your sake and ours," exclaimed O'Grady, shaking hands with Paul, and forgetting all about their supposed difference in rank: "I do believe that with your help Devereux may recover. He and I, you see, were thrown on shore near here, and as his feet were hurt I managed to drag him up here; but, had my life depended on it, I could not have dragged him up an inch further. We can manage to get some shelter for him from the heat of the sun, and while one stays by him, the other can go in search of food."

"Oh! my good fellow, it will be all right," said Devereux, scarcely able to restrain a deep groan. "I am sure Gerrard will be a great help, and we ought to be thankful; but I can't help mourning for the poor fellows who have gone. There's Alphonse, and his fiddle too—I didn't know how much I liked the poor fellow."

"Yes, he was a merry little chap; and then that honest fellow, Reuben Cole, and old Croxton too, in spite of his sermons— they were not very long, and he had good reason for them," chimed in O'Grady with a sigh, which sounded strange from his lips. "It seems a wonder that any of us are alive. But I am getting terribly hungry, and it doesn't seem as if there were many fruits or vegetables to be procured on this island; however, I will go in search of what is to be found, though I suspect we shall have to make up our minds to live on shell-fish and sea-weed. In the meantime, Gerrard, do you look after Mr Devereux."

"I will do as you order, sir; but perhaps I know more about getting shell-fish out of the crevices in the rocks than you do, and a person may easily slip in and be drowned: so if you will let me I will go," observed Gerrard.

"No, no, I'll go," said O'Grady; "lend me your knife—I shall want it to scrape the shells off the rocks. And now I'm off."

"Look out for fresh water on your way," said Devereux, as O'Grady was moving off; "I am already fearfully thirsty."

Devereux and Paul watched O'Grady for some time as he walked along the beach, where, as there were no rocks, he vainly searched for shell-fish. At length he was lost to sight in the distance.

"This is, I fear, a barren spot we are on, Gerrard; still, we must never give in while we are alive," observed Devereux. "I say this, because I feel that I am not long for this world; and when you and O'Grady are left alone, you may fall into despair. Remember, struggle on till the last moment, for you do not know when help may come."

"Oh! don't speak in that way, Mr Devereux," cried Paul, taking the other's hand; "you are not acting as you advise us to act. We may find food and water too. The island seems much larger than I at first thought it was."

"I have no wish to die, but still I do not feel as if I should recover," answered Devereux, in a feeble voice. "If I do not, and you should get home, I wish you to go to my father and mother and sisters, and to tell them that my earnest prayer was, that those who have the right to it should have the fortune, and that I said I would rather dig or plough all my days than enjoy what is not my own."

Paul had little doubt as to what Devereux was thinking of; still he did not like to ask him to be more explicit, so he replied—

"I am afraid that I should not be believed if I took such a message, so pray do not ask me to convey it."

Devereux made no reply, and for some time seemed very unwilling to converse. Paul earnestly wished that O'Grady would return, or that Devereux would give him leave to go in search of fresh water, which he thought might be found further in the interior. Devereux, whose eyes had been shut, at last looked up.

"Oh, for a glass of water, Gerrard! None but those who have been placed as we are know its true value," he whispered.

"Let me go and try to find some, sir," said Paul. "I see a large shell a few yards off; it will carry as much as you can drink. And now that the light is stronger, I observe in the distance some shrubs or low trees, and I cannot but hope that water will be found near them."

"Then go," said Devereux; "but take care that you can find me again."

Paul looked about, and saw a small spar floating on to the beach. Without hesitation, he ran into the water to bring it out. He seized the prize, and was dragging it on shore, when a large monster darted towards him. He struck out the spar with all his force in the direction of the creature. It was almost torn from his grasp, and he was nearly dragged, with his face down, into the water; but he held on manfully, and sprang back. He just saw a pair of fierce eyes, two rows of sharp teeth, and a glance of white skin, convincing him that he had narrowly escaped from the jaws of a ravenous shark. He felt also that he had additional cause for thankfulness at having escaped the sharks when he and his companions had been so long helplessly tumbled about in the waves during the night. "Poor Alphonse and the rest! what has been their fate?" he thought. He did not tell Devereux of his narrow escape; but planting the pole in the sand, with a handkerchief tied to the top of it, he set off towards the spot where he hoped to find water. Devereux wished him good speed.

"You will easily find me again," he said, as Paul left him. Paul hurried on. The ground was composed of sand and rock, with scarcely any vegetation. The spot where he had left Devereux was the summit of a bank; the space he was traversing looked as if it had been recently covered by the sea. The trees were much farther off than he had fancied. The heat of the sun increased; he felt very weak and hungry, and it was with difficulty that he could make his way through the deep sand.

"If I do not go on, poor Mr Devereux will die of thirst, and water must be found," he said to himself whenever he found his resolution flagging. A famous word is that *must*. We *must* do what has to be done. We *must* not do what ought not to be done. Paul struggled on in spite of the heat, and thirst, and hunger, and weariness, and the strange creatures which crawled out from the crevices in the rocks, and ran along the hot sand. He had no time to examine them. At length he found that he was rising on the side of another bank, and what had seemed mere shrubs in the distance, now assumed the appearance of a group of tall cocoa-nut trees. "Should there be no water below, I shall find what will be almost as refreshing," thought Paul, as he hurried on, almost forgetting his fatigue in his eagerness to reach the spot. The sand, however, seemed deeper and hotter than any he had before traversed. Below the cocoa-nut trees there were low shrubs and some herbage. These indicated water without doubt. He ran on. He stopped and hesitated. There was a long, low building, capable of holding a number of persons. If it was at present occupied, what reception could he expect to meet from its inmates? He had read about savage Caribs, and buccaneers, and pirates, and he thought that, possibly, the people in the hut might be one or the other. He advanced cautiously, expecting every moment to see some one come out of the hut. "I am but a boy, and however bad they may be, they will not hurt me; and I must have the water at all events—for water there must be, or the hut would not have been built on that spot." Saying this, he hurried on, treading lightly, "The people may be asleep, and I may get the water and be away without any one seeing me," he thought. He passed the door of the hut. Before him appeared a tank cut in the coral rock, with the pure clear water bubbling up in the middle of it. Stooping down, he quickly washed out his shell, and then took a long, delicious draught. He felt as if he could never take enough. He did not forget his companions; and while he was considering how little the shell could carry, his eye fell on an iron pot by the side of the tank. He stooped down and filled it, and was carrying it off, when the door of the hut opened, and a woolly head with a hideous black face popped out, and a voice which sounded like a peal of thunder, the roll of a muffled drum, and the squeak of a bagpipe, mingled in one, shouted out to him in a language he could not understand. Instead of running away, Paul turned round and asked the negro what he wanted. The latter only continued growling as before, and making hideous faces, while his eye glanced at the can. Paul made signs that he was only borrowing it, and would bring it back. He, however, did not venture within grasp of the unattractive-looking negro, who showed no inclination to follow him. The reason was soon apparent, for, as the black came rather more out of the doorway, Paul perceived that he had lost both his legs, and

W. H. G. Kingston

stood upon two wooden stumps. No one else appeared to be moving inside the hut, and Paul concluded, therefore, that the black was its only inmate. To avoid that unprepossessing individual, he had made a circuit, and as he looked about to ascertain the direction he was to take, he discovered that he was near the head of a long narrow lagoon, or gulf, which ran up from the sea. He had no time to examine it, as he was anxious to get back to Devereux. He ran on as fast as he could without spilling the water. He thought that he knew the way. He stopped. He feared that he had mistaken it. He looked back at the tall cocoa-nut trees, and wished that he had brought some of the fruit with him; but then he remembered that alone he could not have got it, and that the black, might possibly not have chosen to give him any. Again and again he stopped, fearing that he must be going in a wrong direction. The flagstaff could nowhere be seen. "Poor Mr Devereux! what will become of him should I miss him?" he said frequently to himself, as he worked his way on through the heavy sand. At last the looked-for signal appeared above the top of a bank. Devereux was lying where he had left him, but seemed unconscious of his approach. "Was he asleep—or, dreadful thought! could he be dead?" He ran on, nearly spilling the precious water in his eagerness. He called. Devereux did not answer. He knelt down by his side. His eyes were closed, and his arms were helplessly stretched out like those of the dead. Paul moistened his lips, and by degrees got them far enough apart to pour some water down his throat. At length, to Paul's great joy, Devereux opened his eyes.

"Where is O'Grady?" he asked, and then continued—"Ah! Gerrard, is that you? Where did you get the water? It is delicious! delicious!"

In a short time Devereux appeared to be sufficiently recovered to understand what was said to him; and while

Paul was giving him an account of his adventures, O'Grady was seen running towards them. He arrived almost breathless, with his arms full of shell-fish, which he threw before them on the ground.

"I have had hard work to get them, but there is no lack of more on the lee side of the island, so we shall not starve," he exclaimed. "But set to and eat, for it won't do to wait for cooking, as we have no means of kindling a fire. When we have broken our fast, I will tell you what I have seen."

Although raw fish and cold water was not luxurious fare, the party were much strengthened by it, and after a time Devereux declared that he felt able to accompany his companions either to the spring, or in the direction O'Grady had been. They came to the conclusion that the island was inhabited; for O'Grady had seen some objects moving, which he took for people, on a rock at some little distance from the shore, and he supposed that they had gone there in a canoe for the purpose of fishing. It was finally agreed that they would go towards the rock, and endeavour to gain some information as to the island on which they had been cast, which they were not likely to obtain from the black Paul had seen at the hut. Devereux had much difficulty in walking, though with the help of his shipmates he got on faster than could have been expected. They made a shorter cut than O'Grady had taken, and were soon opposite the rock on which he fancied that he had seen some people.

"There are two men and a boy," exclaimed Paul, whose eyesight was the keenest of the party. "Who can they be?"

The three lads hurried on, as fast as Devereux's weakness would allow, to the beach.

"I thought so. There can be no doubt about it," cried Paul.

W. H. G. Kingston

"They see us. They are making signs to us. There is Alphonse, and Reuben Cole, and old Croxton. How can they get to us?"

Devereux and O'Grady were soon convinced that they were their shipmates. O'Grady proposed swimming to them, as the distance was not great; but Paul remembered the shark from which he had so narrowly escaped in the morning, and urged him not to make the attempt. It was then agreed that they must either hollow out a canoe or build a raft.

"But where is the tree from which the canoe is to be formed, and the axes with which it is to be cut down?" asked Paul. "There are no trees nearer than the fountain."

The midshipmen had in their eagerness overlooked that consideration, and there did not seem much greater probability of their finding materials for the raft. Still, something must be done to rescue their shipmates, and that speedily, or they would die of thirst if not of hunger. Paul recollected the spar he had stuck up, and which had some rope attached to it, and O'Grady had observed some driftwood on the beach. They had passed some low shrubs, with thick stems, of a bamboo character, and they would assist to make the platform for the raft if a framework could be formed. The rope, by being unlaid, would serve to bind the raft together. No time was to be lost. Paul set off for the spar, while the other two, making signals to their friends that they would try to help them, went along the shore to collect what wood they could find. There was plenty of driftwood fit for burning, but too small for their object. At last they found a plank, and not far off a spar, and then another plank. Their spirits rose.

"What is one man's poison is another man's meat," cried O'Grady, as he found several planks together. "Some craft has been lost hereabouts, and probably all hands with her, and we are likely to benefit by her remains."

They had now, they fancied, got enough wood, with the aid of the shrubs, to form a raft, on which they might ferry themselves across to the rock. They accordingly began to drag them towards the spot where they had parted from Paul. It was a work, however, of no little labour, as they could draw only one plank at a time over the heavy sands. They had made, three trips, and still Paul did not appear. They began to fear some accident might have happened to him, and, now that they had found so large a supply of wood, to regret that they had sent him for the spar. They had brought together all they had found; and while Devereux began to form the framework, O'Grady cut down with his knife branches from the shrubs near at hand. They had little doubt that their friends on the rock knew what they were about. While thus employed, a shout made them turn their heads, and, looking up, they saw Paul, with the spar on his shoulder, running towards them. When he came up, he had an extraordinary tale to tell. The spar, which had been left planted in the sand, had been removed. He had hunted about for it in every direction, and had almost given up the search, when he saw it lying on the ground in the direction of the hut. It was a sign that there must be somebody on the island besides the black, as with his wooden stumps he could scarcely have got as far and back again without having been seen. Paul reported also that he had seen a vessel a long way to leeward, but that she appeared to be beating up towards the island. However, all their thoughts were required for the construction of their raft. The rope had not been removed from the spar, and this was a great assistance in strengthening it. The raft, however, without the means of guiding it, would be of little use. They had, therefore, to construct a couple of paddles and a rudder, and they then found that, with the help of two small spars, they could form a makeshift mast and yard, their shirts and pocket-handkerchiefs fastened together forming a sail. This would carry them to the rock, as the wind was off the shore, and they must trust to the assistance of their friends to get back. What was their disappointment, on stepping on the raft, to find that it would only well support two people, and that although a third could be carried on it, a fourth would most certainly upset it, and bring it under water. The two midshipmen, therefore, agreed to go, and to leave Paul on shore, much to his disappointment. "Shove us off," cried O'Grady to Paul, as he let fall the sail, to which their neck-handkerchiefs and stockings served as sheets.

Devereux steered with the long spar, which had a piece of board fastened to the end of it, and O'Grady tended the sail with one hand, aided by his teeth, and paddled with the other. They made fair progress, but Paul watched them anxiously, for the raft was difficult to steer, and it was very possible that they might miss the rock, and, if so, have hard work to save themselves from being carried out to sea. The people on the rock waved their hands to encourage them. The wind came somewhat more on the quarter, and they had to paddle hard to keep the raft on its proper course.

Paul was eagerly watching their progress, when he was startled by a loud guttural sound behind him, and looking round there, he saw the hideous black standing on what might be literally called four wooden legs—for besides his two timber extremities, he supported his shoulders on a pair of crutches with flat boards at the bottom, which accounted for his being able to move on so rapidly over the soft sand. Paul could not escape from him except into the sea, so he wisely stood still. There was something very terrific in the black's countenance, increased by the grimaces he made in his endeavours to speak. He pointed to the iron pot, which Paul had slung by his side. Paul at first thought that he was accusing him of stealing it. "If he catches hold of me, I do not know what he may do; but at the same time, as he has no weapon in his hand, I do not suppose that he intends to hurt me," he thought. "I will boldly go up to him and give him the cup, and if he looks as if he would grab me, I can easily spring out of his way."

Paul forgot that the black's crutch would make a very formidable and far-reaching weapon. He advanced slowly, but was much reassured when the black, pointing to the rock, made signs of drinking. "After all, he is come as a friend to help us. He is not so ugly as I thought," he said to himself, as he handed the can to the black. No sooner did the black receive it, than away he went at a great rate over the sand.

Meantime the raft had been making good progress. The great fear was, lest it might meet with some current which would sweep it out of its course. Paul had no selfish feelings—he dreaded any accident as much as if he had been himself on the raft. O'Grady seemed to be paddling harder than ever. Devereux was too weak, he feared, to do much. "I wish that I had gone," he said more than once to himself. Now the raft was again making direct for the rock; the sail was lowered. One of the men caught it as it was being driven round the rock by the surge of the sea, and while they steadied it Alphonse was placed upon it, and immediately it began to return to the shore. Alphonse had taken a paddle, and he and O'Grady worked away manfully. They made good progress, and in a short time reached the beach. Alphonse was sitting on a box. It was the case of his beloved fiddle. He put it under his arm as he stepped on shore, and shook Paul warmly by the hand.

"Ah! this has been the means of saving my life," he said; "I clung to it when I had nothing else to support me, and was washed, with the wreck of the boat to which Croxton and Cole were hanging on, up to the rock, though how we got on to it I do not know, nor do my companions, I believe."

Alphonse looked very pale, and complained of hunger and thirst. While he was speaking, the black was seen coming over the sand at a great rate on his four legs. To one of his arms was slung the can of water. It showed that he had good instead of evil intentions towards the shipwrecked seamen. He made signs for Alphonse to drink, which he thankfully did.

Paul was eager to go off for the rest, and obtained leave to take Devereux's place. The negro seemed to take an interest in their proceedings, and both Devereux and Alphonse expressed their belief that he wished to be friendly.

When O'Grady and Paul arrived at the rock, they found old Croxton and Reuben disputing who should remain to the last.

"The old before the young," cried Reuben.

"Ay, but the old should have the choice of the post of honour," said Croxton.

However, he was at last induced to step on to the raft. It was not a time to stand on ceremony, for the sky gave indications that the weather was about to change, and it was very evident that, should the sea get up, the rock would no longer be tenable. The raft felt the weight of the old man, and the two boys found it much more difficult to paddle to the shore.

They had not got far when Paul observed a dark triangular-shaped object above the water; then he saw a pair of fierce eyes fixed on him. It was a huge shark—large enough to upset the raft with a whisk of his tail. He did not tell his companions, but paddled steadily on. What did the appearance of the monster portend? He had heard of the instinct of sharks. Did the creature follow in the expectation of obtaining a victim?

On this trip the shark was to be disappointed, for they reached the shore in safety, and landing the old man, who was suffering much from thirst, and was therefore doubly grateful for the supply of water brought by the black, they for the last time shoved off. Both the lads felt greatly fatigued, and though they set their sail, they had to paddle hard to keep the raft on a right course. The sea had been getting up, and every moment made Reuben's situation on the rock more insecure. Even if he could have swum across the channel, the monster Paul had seen would have taken good care that he should never have reached the shore. The knowledge of this, as well as their own safety, made them exert themselves to the utmost. Already more than one sea had dashed over the rock, and Reuben had to grasp it tightly to prevent himself from being washed off. A huge foaming billow was seen rolling in. It must sweep over the reef, and perhaps come thundering down on the raft.

The boys had just lowered their sail, and were paddling in. Reuben saw the roller coming. Making a sign to them to paddle back, he sprang into the water and struck out towards them. On came the billow—roaring, foaming. The rock was hidden from view by a mass of spray as the wave curled over it.

"Oh, he has gone! he has gone!" cried Paul, as, looking back, he could nowhere see his friend.

It was but for a moment. He had been concealed by the swelling water. Again he appeared.

"Your hand! your hand!" cried Reuben.

Paul stretched out his hand with terror at heart, for at that moment he saw the dark fin of a shark on the surface of the water. He seized Reuben's hand, and dragged with all his might. The wave rushed on, dashing over the raft, and almost sweeping O'Grady and Paul from off it; but they held on, and it served the purpose of lifting Reuben on to it at the moment that a pair of ravenous jaws appeared opening in an attempt to seize him. The same sea, lifting the raft, drove it rapidly towards the shore—and another following, the boys paddling at the same time, sent it high up on the beach; but even then the receding waters would have carried it off, had not the negro and old Croxton rushed towards them, the former planting his crutches against it, and the latter grasping it tightly. Even thus they could not hold it long, but they gave time to the boys and Reuben to spring on shore, and then it was carried off, and soon shattered to pieces.

The black now made signs to all the party to accompany him to his hut, which, as may be supposed, they gladly did.

"Faith, Mr Charcoal is better than he looks," observed O'Grady, as he bade them enter.

The inside offered a strong contrast to the outside. There was a large table and chairs, and several bed-places, with coverlids to the beds of rich damask, and there were numerous chests and articles of ships' furniture in corners and ranged along the wall. The black, too, produced from a chest several silver and richly-embossed plates, dishes, and other utensils, into which having emptied a rich stew from an iron pot, he placed them before his guests, and made them a sign to fall to. This they were not slack to obey, for all were desperately hungry. No one inquired of what it was composed, though a qualm came over the feelings of Devereux, who was likely to be the most particular, as he hooked up what certainly looked very like the body and feet of a lizard. However, he said nothing, and minced up the remainder of his portion before he examined it. O'Grady made some queer faces at some of the things which caught his eye in the pot, but he said nothing, as he was too hungry to be particular.

When the whole party were satisfied, the good-natured black pointed to the couches, and signified that they might rest on them—a permission of which they did not fail immediately to avail themselves, and in a few minutes all were fast asleep. The black, meantime, in spite of the warmth of the weather, sat down by the side of the fire at which he had been cooking, and gave himself up to contemplation. How completely at that moment were all his guests in his power! Who could tell what injuries he had to avenge on the white men? Whatever were his feelings, he gave them no cause for suspicion.

Having waited till they were so sound asleep that a great gun fired close to their ears would scarcely have awakened them, he took his crutches and stumped out of the hut. Some hours passed away. Paul was the first to open his eyes; no one besides his friends were in the hut. He did not like to rouse them up, though, in a short time, hunger—the same cause which had awoke him—made them also awake. They had consumed all the food the negro had given them in the morning, and they could find nothing more to eat in the hut. O'Grady proposed that they should climb the trees, and get some cocoanuts.

It was, however, more easy to propose than to execute the achievement. He himself first tried to get up a tree, and then Paul made the experiment; but, sailors as they were, they could not manage to grasp the stem with sufficient firmness to ascend. Paul, being the lightest, helped by his companions, had got up some way, when a gruff shout made them turn round, and old Charcoal, as they called the black, was seen

W. H. G. Kingston

shambling along on his crutches towards them. He beckoned Paul to come down from the tree in a way which showed that he would not be disobeyed. They saw that he had a basket on his back, and, pointing to the fountain to intimate that he wanted water, he set about turning its contents, which were of a very heterogeneous character, into the large stew-pot from which he had supplied their breakfast. The midshipmen, as before, saw enough to convince them that it would be wise not too minutely to examine the contents of the pot. The black produced some rum at dinner, which, though they partook of it sparingly, helped down the strange mess.

Two or three days passed by, and the black continued to treat them as at first, though O'Grady suggested that he was possibly like the ogre in the fairy tale—only fattening them up that he might eat them in the end. Still, it was agreed that he was a very good fellow, and the majority were of opinion that he would help them to reach the nearest British island if he had the power. However, hitherto not a word had been exchanged between him and them. He made no objection to their exploring the island, but their discoveries only convinced them that it was very barren, and that no means existed of their getting away from it. They came, to be sure, on a canoe, in which they concluded that the black occasionally went out fishing; but it was only just large enough to hold him, and the paddles were nowhere to be found. Soon after this, O'Grady, who was in advance, saw a large boat hauled up under some bushes. "Hurrah, boys! here's a craft which will carry us to Jamaica, if need be," he shouted, and ran on, followed by Paul and Alphonse.

The tone of his voice changed as he got nearer. "She has a mighty antique look about her, but she may still serve our purpose," he said. "But I'm not quite certain," he added, as he struck his fist against a plank, which crumbled away before the blow. A kick sent another plank into fragments. The whole boat was mere touchwood.

There was a smile on the countenance of old Charcoal, who came in sight directly afterwards and had evidently been watching them at a distance. They were in a certain sense his prisoners, and yet he could not mean them ill, or he would not have treated them with so much hospitality. How he procured their food, was a question, and certainly it was his wish that they should not be able to provide it for themselves. Over and over again they discussed the means by which they might get away; but when they expressed their wish to him by signs, he shook his head, and tried to show that it would be impossible to do so.

At last they began to suspect that he had some motive for detaining them. Not a vessel had been seen since the morning when they were thrown on the island; but one day, on waking, just as it was light, Paul got up, and going out, saw a schooner gliding along through the lagoon or creek leading to the hut. He called up his companions, who were speedily on foot, and all rushed out to see the stranger. She was a long, low, dark schooner, with mischief in her very look—such as was not at that time to be found in European waters.

"That craft doesn't go about on any lawful errand," observed old Croxton to Reuben.

"I should think not, mate. If ever there was a pirate, that 'ere craft is one," was the answer.

The matter was pretty well set at rest by the appearance of a black flag, which had hitherto hung against the mast, but which, now blown out by the breeze suddenly freshening up, exhibited the skull and cross-bones which the rovers of those days delighted to carry, either in the presence of a weak enemy, or to exhibit in triumph to their friends.

The midshipmen felt that their uniforms would not be looked on with a favourable eye by the pirates, and yet they could not nor would have attempted to hide themselves. The vessel was soon securely moored, and several boats being lowered, and hampers, casks, and cases placed in them, the crew, with shouts, and songs, and wild gestures, came on shore. They appeared to be men of all nations and of every hue, from the jet-black African, to the fair Englishman or Dane. They soon made it evident that they intended to indulge in a thorough debauch, for the greater number began without loss of time to unpack cases of wine and provisions in a shady spot under the trees. Several, however, surrounded the Englishmen, and one of them, stepping forward, inquired in a rough tone what had brought them there.

Devereux replied calmly that they had been cast on the island, and hoped that he and his companions would be treated with courtesy.

"That depends on how you behave yourselves, my spark," answered the man, gruffly. "We want a few hands to supply the places of those who were killed in our last engagement. If you like to join us, well and good; if not, look out for squalls."

# CHAPTER SIX

The midshipmen and their companions were in an unpleasant predicament. The pirates, after abusing them in no measured terms, ordered them, on the peril of their lives, to remain where they were while they themselves joined their companions, who were just commencing their feast. Old Charcoal, the black, soon appeared from the hole, and beckoning to Croxton and Reuben, he bade them carry a huge stew-pot full of viands, and place it in the midst of the pirates. The outlaws, when they had done this, ordered them to be off, and to wait till they were again wanted, and then set to in earnest, digging their long knives and daggers into the pot, and ladling out its more liquid contents, some with silver, and others with wooden spoons. It seemed a matter of indifference to them which they used. Cases of champagne and claret were soon broken open, and each man seized two or three bottles, from which he drank, or poured the contents into silver flagons, which he drained in a couple of draughts. Seasoned as were probably their heads, the result of these copious libations was soon apparent by the fiercer oaths they uttered, their louder laughter, and the quarrels which began to arise between those who apparently were strong friends a few minutes previously.

The black had taken his seat on the ground near them; but though they every now and then handed him a jug of wine,

W. H. G. Kingston

Paul observed that he poured the chief part of its contents on the ground. No long time passed before the wine began to take effect on the greater part of the crew. Some rose to their feet with their eyes glaring, and their unsheathed knives in their hands, vociferating loudly. Blows were exchanged, and wounds given, though on each occasion the combatants sank down again, and applied themselves afresh to their wine-cups. Some sang, others shouted and fired off their pistols in the air, and others again got up and danced wildly round their companions, till, wearied with their exertions, they reeled back to their former places. Old Charcoal shouted, and applauded, and clapped his hands with the rest. The day wore on—the orgies of the outlaws continued till the larger number lay helpless and unconscious on the ground, surrounded by broken bottles, though a few retained sufficient sense to reel towards the hut, where more comfortable couches than the ground could afford were to be found. The black followed, making a sign to Paul and his companions to remain where they were.

"He is our friend, sir, I am certain of it," said Paul to Devereux, who had not observed the sign; "there is a chance for us of escaping."

"By what means?" asked Devereux. "We could not get their vessel out of the harbour."

"No, sir, but in one of their boats. Before they recover their senses we might be far away out of sight of the island."

"Very good, Gerrard; but without knowing in what direction to steer we might too probably float about till we were starved to death, or overtaken by another hurricane," answered Devereux, shaking his head mournfully.

"But perhaps we may find a chart on board the pirate vessel," suggested O'Grady. "If Charcoal is really our friend, as I think he is, he will help us to get a chart, a compass, and provisions also. Hurrah! I feel quite in spirits at the thought that we shall get away."

"Be not over sanguine, young gentleman," observed old Croxton; "there's many a slip between the cup and the lip, and it's well to be prepared for reverses."

In spite of this warning, the boys remained as sanguine as ever, and anxiously waited the appearance of old Charcoal, who, at length, was seen cautiously creeping out of the hut. He came along very fast on his knees and hands. They were surprised to see him without his legs and crutches, till he gave them to understand that the pirates had put them away out of his reach. Paul's hopes were not to be disappointed; the black had resolved to take the opportunity for which he had long been waiting, while his hard taskmasters were overcome by drunkenness, to escape from their power.

"They will make us all slaves, and keep us to work for them if we don't escape," observed O'Grady. "I vote that we set about it at once."

"But I will try to get old Charcoal's legs and crutches first," said Paul.

"And I will not go vidout my cher violin," cried Alphonse; "it has been my good friend very often. It may be again."

The poor black signified his wish to have his wooden supporters, and together the two boys set off running to the hut, while the rest of the party, not to lose time, proceeded towards the schooner.

The door of the hut was opened. Paul and Alphonse stepped

W. H. G. Kingston

in cautiously, for any noise might arouse the sleepers. They looked about for the crutches; they were placed across the rafters in the centre of the hut. A tall man standing on the table had put them there. Paul saw that even with the help of Alphonse he could not reach up so high; but he was not to be defeated—so going to the wall he put his feet on his companion's shoulders, and climbing up he reached the beam, along which he clambered, till he got hold of the crutches, and then he handed them down to Alphonse, and fortunately without making any noise. The latter was now anxious to find his fiddle, for it was nowhere to be seen. At length, with almost a groan of despair, the young Frenchman pointed to it. A pirate had appropriated the case for a pillow. Was he to leave it? No!—he would perish first! Fortunately the man was among the most drunken, and was sleeping heavily. They agreed by signs to withdraw it, and to substitute something else. A bundle of flags had been overlooked in a corner. It might serve their purpose yet. It was hazardous work. Alphonse drew his dirk, which he had retained; but Paul implored him by a look to put it up again.

"If he does awake, only say that you want your fiddle-case to play a tune; he won't mind that," he whispered.

Paul went on one side, and gently lifted the pirate's head with one hand while with the other he held the bundle of flags to shove under it as Alphonse gently pulled away the case. All depended on the movement being regular. A sudden jerk would have awakened the man, who was a fierce-looking ruffian. One of his hands lay over the hilt of his dagger, which he seemed capable of using with effect at a moment's notice. The manoeuvre required great nerve and courage, scarcely to be expected in such young lads. It was not found wanting in them. With intense satisfaction Paul let the outlaw's head sink on the soft pillow. The man uttered a few inarticulate sounds, but gave no other signs of awaking. The boys held their breath, and for a minute dared not move lest they should make any noise which might even at the last arouse the man, or disturb any of the other sleepers. At last they crept silently away, picking up Charcoal's crutches on the way, and made their escape out of the hut. Darkness was coming on. It would have been well to have had daylight to get clear of the island. As soon as they had got a little distance from the hut, they set off running to overtake their companions. Charcoal was as delighted to get back his wooden legs and crutches as Alphonse was to recover his fiddle. They had to proceed cautiously as they passed the sleepers, and still more so when they entered the boat, lest the sound of an oar in the rowlock, or its splash in the water, might alarm them. One of the boats in which the pirates had come on shore was selected for the voyage; but they had first to visit the vessel to obtain the various articles they required. They quickly scrambled on board, and even the black showed a wonderful agility in getting up the side. On going below, he lighted a lantern with which to search for the articles they required. There would have been no difficulty in deciding on the character of the the vessel by the gorgeous and yet rude and tasteless style in which the chief cabin was furnished. Pictures of saints and silver ornaments were nailed against the bulkheads, interspersed with arms of all sorts, and rich silks and flags, while the furniture showed that it had been taken from vessels of various sorts—for there were damask-covered sofas, and rosewood cabinets, with deal three-legged stools, and a rough oak table; and hanging to the beams above, or in the racks against the sides, were battered pewter mugs and plates, mixed with silver tankards and salvers, and other utensils of the same precious metal. The party, however, had no time to pay attention to any of these things, or to wish even to possess themselves of any of them. They were only anxious to find the articles which would facilitate their escape. In a receptacle for all sorts of stores a ship's compass was found; but that without a chart, and oil for the lamp, would be of little use. Nearly the whole ship had been searched through and no chart could be found.

"We must find one though, unless the black knows the direction in which we should steer," exclaimed Devereux.

"Let us ascertain if he does. Does he know what we are looking for, though?"

O'Grady got Charcoal to come to the table, and drawing with a piece of chalk a chart on it something like the West Indies, pointed to one spot where he supposed they were, and then to others, and demanded by signs how they should get there. The black clapped his hands, and began looking about the cabins as a terrier hunts for a rat.

In a cabin evidently used by the captain from the greater number of weapons hung up in it, and its richer furniture, Charcoal discovered a locker hitherto overlooked. It was locked; but without ceremony it was broken open.

"Robbing thieves is no robbery, I hope," observed O'Grady, as he lent a hand.

"Necessity has no law, I've heard say, at all events," said Devereux.

Everything that could be required was at length discovered, and placed in the boat alongside, except one thing. They had shoved off, and were gliding noiselessly down the lagoon, when Paul, feeling his throat somewhat parched with the excitement he had gone through, asked Reuben for a mug of water from a cask he saw at his feet. Reuben tapped it. It was empty. To go without water would be destruction. There was none on board the vessel. An expedition to the fountain must be undertaken. Reuben and Croxton volunteered to go, as did

O'Grady. They had, however, first to return to the schooner to get more casks. There was a fearful risk of waking up the sleeping men near whom they had to pass. Not a word was spoken by either party. While one proceeded on their expedition, the other sat still as death in the boat. Paul wished that he had gone also, for he was very anxious about his friends; he could not help fearing that should the pirates be awakened they would at once fire at strangers moving near them. It appeared to him a very long time since they had left the boat. He asked Devereux if he might go in search of them, as he feared that they might have lost their way.

"They will be here soon," was the answer; "they have no light weight to carry between them."

The time seemed longer perhaps than it really was. At length footsteps were heard.

"Here they come," said Devereux, and some figures emerged from the darkness. They must be their friends; the pirates would have approached with cries and threats of vengeance. O'Grady led the way, staggering under the weight of a cask; the men followed with still heavier burdens.

"We must be off; we heard the fellows talking in the hut," he whispered. Not another word was spoken; it was a moment for prompt action, if they would save their lives, for if captured by the pirates they would be treated with scant ceremony or mercy. The black took the helm; indeed, he alone knew anything of the shape of the lagoon, or of the passage which led from it to the sea. There were oars for each of the party. They pulled on in perfect silence, placing their handkerchiefs in the rowlocks to lessen the noise of the oars. There were numerous turns in the lagoon, which prevented them at first from feeling the wind. After pulling some way, however, they discovered that a strong gale was

　　　　　W. H. G. Kingston

blowing directly into the mouth of the lagoon. It must have sprung up after they had visited the schooner, or they would have felt it before. A loud roar of breakers was heard, and the white surf could be seen breaking wildly over the surrounding reefs.

"We are in a trap, I fear," remarked O'Grady.

They were the first words which had been spoken since they embarked. There was no danger now of their being heard.

"Let us ascertain what the black thinks," said Devereux.

This was no easy matter in the darkness. He seemed disposed, at all events, to proceed, for he continued steering towards the sea. The rocks on either side were tolerably high, with numerous indentations, miniature bays, and inlets on either side. The boat now began to feel the seas as they rolled in. It seemed high time to stop unless they were to attempt passing through the rollers which came roaring in with increasing rapidity towards them. Suddenly the black touched Devereux's arm, and made a sign to him to cease rowing. He waited for a few minutes. They were full of suspense. Then he shook his head, and again signed for the starboard oars to pull round, and running back a little way, he took the boat into a small inlet, where she lay quiet, sheltered by the high rocks. The disappointment was very great. It would clearly have been suicidal to have attempted passing through the surf. It would be better to face the anger of the pirates. Poor Charcoal was most to be pitied. They would hang or shoot him, or beat him to death to a certainty.

"Could we not land him, and perhaps the pirates would not find out that he assisted in our attempt to escape?" suggested O'Grady.

"You forget, Mr O'Grady, that he could not have got his crutches without our help," observed Paul.

"The wind may moderate, and we may yet be away before daylight," remarked Devereux. "We could not leave him behind."

The question had not, however, been put to the black; indeed it was difficult to ascertain his wishes. He kept his seat, and made no sign. This made them hope that he still expected to get out of the lagoon before daylight. It was possible that the pirates might take to drinking again as soon as they awoke; and if so, more time would be obtained for their escape. These and similar speculations served to occupy the thoughts of the party as the dark hours of night passed by. Still the wind blew, and the seas, as they dashed over the coral reefs and broke on the sandy beach, roared as loud as before. The black made no sign of moving; indeed they all knew it would be useless. At length, with sinking hearts, they saw the first pale streaks of dawn appear. There is but little twilight in those southern latitudes; but the first harbinger of day is speedily followed by the glorious luminary himself, and the whole world is bathed with light.

"I wonder if it's pleasant," soliloquised O'Grady. "I don't know whether I should prefer being hung or having my throat cut."

"Hush," said Devereux, "see the black is signing to you not to speak."

"Nor will I, blessings on his honest face," answered O'Grady, whose spirits nothing could daunt. "But I propose that before we put our necks into the noose we have our breakfast. We shall have ample time for that before those honest gentlemen we left drunk last night will be up and looking for us."

The proposition met with universal approval, and in another instant all hands were busily employed in discussing a substantial breakfast of biscuit, dried meat, and fish, washed down by claret in as quiet a manner as if they were out on a pleasant picnic party. When it was over, some of the party scrambled up the rocks to ascertain if any of the pirates were yet on foot; but no one was to be seen moving on shore. It was possible that the pirates might suppose that they had already made their escape, and thus not take the trouble of looking for them. It was clearly their best chance to remain quiet, and so they all returned on board and lay down in the bottom of the boat. The day, as the night had done, passed slowly on. Their hopes again rose; they might remain concealed till night, and then make their escape, should the gale abate.

"We have reason to be thankful that we are not outside now," observed old Croxton, who had said little all the time; "no boat could live in the sea there is running."

"If we are discovered we may still fight for it," observed Reuben Cole. "We are a match for a few score of such buccaneering scoundrels as they are, I hope."

"I will play them one tune on my cher violin; they will not hang us if they hear that going," said Alphonse, evidently perfectly in earnest.

"We'll fight, undoubtedly, my friends," said Devereux. "If we are taken, we will make the best of it, and may even then save our lives without dishonour."

It was past noon. They judged from the continued roar that the force of the gale had in no way decreased, and that nothing could be gained by leaving their rocky shelter. Not a sound from the hut had reached them, when suddenly a loud shout reached their ears. It startled most of the party, who, overcome by the heat, had fallen asleep. Again and again the shout was repeated in tones of anger. There could be no doubt that the pirates had discovered their flight, and were searching for them. They were still at some distance, and might not look into the creek where the boats lay hid. If, however, they were to follow in a boat, they would scarcely pass by the mouth of the creek without exploring it. Paul, as the most active of the party, was directed to climb up the rock to try and ascertain in what direction the pirates were roaming. He clambered up the rock, concealing himself as much as possible by the projecting portions. He saw in the far distance on the level ground figures moving rapidly about; but only a small part of the island was visible. It was evident that those whose voices had been heard must have come much nearer. He came down and made his report.

"Hurrah! it never occurred to us before that we took the only boat they had on shore, and that those thieves of the world can't get aboard their vessel again," cried O'Grady, in great glee. "There are some ugly-looking monsters in the lagoon, sharks or alligators, and it's just that they don't like swimming off lest they should make a breakfast for some of those pretty creatures."

"Should your idea be correct, there is another chance for us; but they will not be long before they build a raft and get on board," said Devereux.

"Oh, by the pipers, but I wish that we had remained on board, and fought the thieves from their own craft," cried O'Grady. "We might have picked them off as they appeared on the shore one by one, and carried her out of the harbour in triumph. Would it be too late to go back to try that same just at once?"

"Too late to go back, except we wish to be picked off ourselves, yes indeed," said Devereux. "And hark! there is the sound of oars coming down the lagoon; the villains have got on board, and are in search of us. If we are silent, we may still avoid them."

The whole party remained still as death. The boat came nearer and nearer. She passed the mouth of the creek, and went down to the entrance of the lagoon. Those in her were apparently satisfied that their prisoners had escaped, for the splash of their oars, and their voices as they talked loudly, were again heard as they pulled up the lagoon. Paul and his companions breathed more freely under the belief that they had escaped their enemies. Poor Charcoal sat perfectly still, though he moved his large eyes about with an uneasy glance upwards and around on every side. He ate and drank with the rest, but made no attempt to communicate to others what was passing in his mind. The day was drawing on, when Paul, who, with the rest of the party, had dropped off into a drowsy state of unconsciousness, was aroused by a shout of derisive laughter, and a voice exclaiming:

"Ah, ah! my masters, you thought to escape us, did you? and you're like mice in a trap, and you'll find that you've cats with precious sharp claws to deal with."

On hearing this unpleasant announcement, Paul looked up and saw a hideous hairy face, ten times more hideous than that of Charcoal, because, though that of a white man, so fierce and sneering, grinning down upon them. The man, for man he was, though more like a huge baboon than a human creature, levelled a blunderbuss at Devereux's head.

"If you allow your men to put out an oar, I will fire," he exclaimed. "You cannot make your escape out to sea if you were to attempt it, and we can give you employment enough on shore; so we don't intend to take your lives."

Devereux guessed pretty accurately the meaning of these last words.

"Death rather than slavery, lads," he cried; "out oars, and let us make an attempt for liberty."

Scarcely had he uttered the words, while all hands were getting out their oars, than the pirate pulled the trigger. The moments of the young midshipman's life would have been numbered, but the firearm flashed in the pan. With a curse at his failure, the man again primed his piece; but the delay, short as it was, enabled the Englishmen to get away out of the creek. The blunderbuss was fired, but its shot fell harmless. The report, however, served to call others of the pirates, who were searching for the fugitives, to the spot, and as the boat proceeded down again towards the mouth of the harbour, they were seen clambering along the rocks, shouting and gesticulating violently. It bodied ill for the way they would treat their prisoners if they caught them. The mouth of the lagoon was reached, but the surf broke as furiously as before. The pirates were approaching, having climbed along over the rocks. Already their shot could almost reach the boat. The small arms of those days carried no great distance. It would be madness to attempt running the boat through the surf.

"What say you, friends, shall we make the attempt, or yield?" asked Devereux.

"Push through it," cried O'Grady and Reuben.

The black shook his head, and made a sign to them to pull round.

"Then let us get on a rock and fight it out; we might keep the pirates at bay for many a day, as long as our provisions last," cried O'Grady.

"There is one that will serve us, and the fellows may have no little difficulty in dislodging us."

He pointed to a rock close to the mouth of the lagoon, some eighty or a hundred yards in circumference. The sea dashed against it on one side, breaking into masses of foam, and the sides were high, steep, and slippery, so that neither could a boat approach, nor could a landing be effected; but on the other was a deep narrow inlet, scarcely wide enough to allow a boat to enter. They pulled towards it, and, much to their satisfaction, discovered that they could just push in their boat. As soon as they had secured her, they began carrying their water and provisions to the top. The rock was full of deep crevices and hollows, amply large enough to shelter them thoroughly, while they could completely command the passage, and destroy the crew of any boat attempting to enter. Scarcely had they made this arrangement, than a pirate boat was seen coming down the harbour. The pirates on the rocks pointed out to their companions where the Englishmen had taken refuge. Those in the boat seemed aware of the strength of the position, for they ceased rowing and held a consultation. The delay was of use to Devereux and his followers. It gave him time to dispose of them to the best advantage, and allowed them to distribute their ammunition and to load all their arms. They had fortunately brought a good supply of weapons and ammunition from the pirate vessel, so that they were prepared to stand a siege, although the most sanguine had very little hope of ultimate success. The pirates, too, had loaded their arms, and once more they came on with loud shouts and threats of vengeance. It appeared that they had only to climb up the rocks to wreak it on the heads of the small band. The task, however, was not so easy as it seemed, for the ocean itself favoured the brave defenders of the rock. There was but one spot at which, under ordinary circumstances, a boat could land, and just at the moment that the pirates were about to approach, a succession of huge rollers came tumbling in, surging round the rock, and threatening to dash the boat to pieces, unless she could hit the mouth of the inlet into which the English had run.

"Be cool, my friends," said Devereux, "and do not throw a shot away; I will tell you when to fire."

A cheerful "Ay, ay, sir," was the reply from all, except from the black. He nodded his head, however, tapped the lock of his musket, and grinned broadly, intimating that he clearly understood what was said.

The pirate boat lay off the rock, but her crew dared not, it was evident, pull in; and from the way she rocked about, it was impossible to take anything like a steady aim from her. Devereux pointed out these circumstances to his companions, and ordered them to reserve their fire, and to shelter themselves as much as possible in the hollows of the rock. It was well they obeyed, for the pirates, losing patience, began firing away as fast as they could load. The shot came pattering on the face of the rock, while some whistled by above the heads of the defenders.

"Steady, steady, boys!" cried Devereux. "Those pellets can do us no harm. We will keep our fire till it is wanted."

"They'll think that we don't fire because we are afraid, or have no powder," said O'Grady.

"Let them think what they like; we'll show them presently that we've powder and shot, too, if they tempt us," answered Devereux.

Volley after volley was fired by the pirates with the same want of result. No one was hit, though several of the bullets came near enough to them to show the besieged that they must not depend upon escaping with impunity. Before, they had wished the gale to moderate, now they prayed that it might continue till nightfall, when they hoped the pirates would retire, and give them a chance of escaping. They were not disappointed. Long before dark the enemy ceased firing, as was supposed, because they had expended their ammunition, and away up the lagoon they went.

"Hurrah! Let us give three cheers for victory," cried O'Grady. "We've beaten them off, anyhow, without firing a shot."

To celebrate their bloodless victory, the party took a hearty meal, and then, when night came on, each crouched down, with his musket by his side, in his hole, to snatch a short sleep, to be prepared, should the gale cease, to escape. It was, of course, arranged that one at a time should keep watch. It appeared to Paul that the gale was abating, but he very soon became unconscious of all sublunary affairs. He must have slept some hours, for he felt greatly refreshed. The gale had ceased. He was surprised that, whosoever was on watch, had not summoned the rest of the party. He was about to call out, when he found his shoulder clutched with a strong gripe, and looking up, he saw by the dim light of a young moon, the same hideous face which had appeared on the top of the rocks on the previous day, and a peal of derisive laughter broke forth, followed by the cries of his companions, as they found themselves in the power of their enemies. Paul could scarcely help hoping and believing that he was in a dream, till the truth flashed on his mind that the pirates, accustomed to practise every kind of trick, must have approached the rock with muffled oars, and have climbed up it while he and his companions were asleep, and surprised them. Such, indeed, was the case. Whichever of the party ought to have been awake had undoubtedly dropped into forgetfulness, or the pirates must have approached in a wonderfully stealthy manner. English seamen, when they have fought bravely, as they always do, and have striven to the last, and are overpowered, do not struggle or bluster, but yield to their destiny with calmness and dignity.

"So you thought to escape us, did you?" exclaimed one of the pirates, as he secured Devereux's hands. "What do you think you deserve, now, for running away with other people's property? Hanging is too good for you; that's the way you would have treated us, if we had been caught doing the same thing to you—ha, ha!" And the man laughed at what he considered a very good joke. "But come along, mister officer, we'll try you by judge and jury all fair and shipshape to-morrow morning, and if you're found guilty, you'll have no cause to complain," added the pirate, as he in no ceremonious manner dragged the poor young midshipman down the rock.

Paul found himself held tight by the savage who had at first seized him, and the whole party were quickly transferred to the boats, which proceeded up the lagoon.

Paul found himself in the boat in which they had attempted to escape, seated next to Alphonse, who had managed to secure his fiddle-case.

"De music vil soften de savage breast, I have heard—I vill try," said the young Frenchman, stooping down to open the case, for their arms were at liberty.

The pirates were amusing themselves by taunting and deriding their prisoners, some in one language, some in another. Alphonse took no notice of what was said—

probably he understood but little. Paul felt that he should like to jump up and attack them, but he wisely kept his seat. Alphonse at length succeeded in getting out his bow and violin, and without saying a word, struck up a French tune.

"Hillo, you are a merry young chap," exclaimed one of the English pirates. "Scrape away, we don't hear much like that."

Alphonse played on without stopping.

"Ah, c'est de ma patrie—c'est de ma belle France," cried a Frenchman from the bow of the boat, and Alphonse felt a hope that there was one near who would befriend him. On landing, the prisoners, including poor old Charcoal, were marched up to the hut, into one end of which they were thrust, and told that their brains would be blown out if they moved or spoke. This made but little difference. They could expect but one fate, and by no plan they could devise were they likely to escape it.

When the morning came, some biscuit was given them, and the black was ordered to go and bring them water. This gave them hopes that they were not, at all events, to be murdered forthwith. The pirates all the morning were either asleep or very sulky, but at noon, having spread a supply of provisions in the shade and broached a cask of wine, they became merry, and one of them, the ugly hirsute fellow before described, proposed as an amusement, that they should try the prisoners and punish them afterwards according to their deserts. The proposal was received with great applause, and Devereux and his companions were ordered to appear before their captors. The pirate captain was the judge, and two of the officers undertook to be counsel for the defendants. The case, however, was made out very clearly against them, and except extenuating circumstances, they had nothing to plead in their favour. Poor Charcoal had still less chance of escape.

"He is guilty of ingratitude, of robbery, of rebellion and high treason, for either of which he deserves hanging, and hanged he shall be forthwith," cried the judge, draining off a jug of wine. "We couldn't before have done without him, but now one of you can take his place. You are a stout fellow," he added, addressing Reuben Cole. "Are you inclined to save your life and to work honestly for your bread?"

"To work for you, so as to let you hang that poor dumb fellow, Charcoal? No, that I'm not, yer scoundrels," he exclaimed vehemently. "If you touch a hair of his head, you'll not get a stroke of work out of me as long as you live unhung."

This reply excited the laughter rather than the anger of the crew. The same question was put to Devereux and Croxton, and answers to the same effect were given. Still the voice of the majority was for hanging the black. He, meantime, stood resting on his crutches, the most unconcerned of all the actors in the scene.

"Well, then, the young Frenchman shall hang him," cried the hairy savage, with a grin, seizing poor Alphonse by the arm. "Or stay—the other two youngsters shall perform the office, while mounseer shall fiddle him out of the world while we dance to the tune."

"No, you villains; I vill not play, if you hurt one hair of dat poor man's head," exclaimed Alphonse, starting up with unusual animation. "I vill play from morn to night, and you shall dance and sing as much as you vill, but if you hang him, I vill casser mon cher violin into pieces, and it vill never play more—dere!"

His address was received with much applause by many of the party, and, encouraged by it, he seized his violin and commenced playing, vigorously, one of his most animating tunes. The effect was instantaneous. Many of the pirates leaped to their feet and began dancing furiously one by one; even the more morose joined them, and old Charcoal took the opportunity of hobbling off to get out of their sight, hoping that if he could escape for a day or two, they might possibly forget their evil intentions with regard to him. Still, Devereux knew that, from their treacherous nature, as soon as the dance was over, they were very likely, for the sake of the amusement, to hang him and his elder companions, at all events, and to make slaves of O'Grady, Paul, and Alphonse. While the excitement was at its height, the pirates, with their frantic gestures and loud shrieks and cries, appearing more like a troop of demons than human beings, a large boat was seen coming up the harbour, pulled at a rapid rate. Her crew leaped on shore, and the pirates rushed to meet them. A few words overheard by Paul served to explain their errand.

"Our craft was sunk—we were pursued by a British man-of-war. Hardly escaped them. Some of our fellows taken prisoners. Are certain to betray us and to bring the enemy down here. Not a moment is to be lost. Our only chance is to escape to sea."

From what he heard, Paul guessed that the new comers were part of the crew of a consort of the pirate schooner, and he thought it probable that the pirates might carry him and his companions off as hostages. He therefore hastened to Devereux, who was at a little distance, and told him what he had heard. Devereux fully agreed with him, and before the pirates had time to recover from the excitement into which the news had thrown them, he and his companions, separating so as not to excite observation, walked quietly away till they were out of sight of the pirates. They then, once more meeting, set off running as hard as they could go towards the extreme end of the island. Before long, as they halted to take breath, they had the satisfaction of seeing sail made on the schooner, and presently she glided down with a fair wind towards the entrance of the lagoon. Before, however, she reached it, Paul, as he turned his eyes towards the west, caught sight of another sail approaching from that direction. He pointed it out to his companions.

"She is a square-rigged ship," cried Devereux; "a man-of-war, too, if I mistake not, come in search of the pirates. Unless their craft is a very fast one, their career will soon be brought to an end."

# CHAPTER SEVEN

The look-out from the mast-head of the pirate schooner must have discovered the stranger soon after Paul had seen her, and her appearance must have caused some uncertainty and irresolution on board. The wind dropping, they furled sails, as if about to remain where they were and fight it out.

"It will give the boats of the man-of-war some work to do," exclaimed Devereux, when he saw this. "I wish that we could get off to them first, though. I would give much to have a brush with those piratical scoundrels."

Before long, however, the pirates again altered their minds. The breeze returning, sail was once more made, and the schooner, with the boats towing ahead, stood through the entrance. The time lost was probably of the greatest conesquence to them, and by the time that the schooner was clear of the reefs, the man-of-war had drawn so near, that her character was no longer doubtful. Devereux had been anxiously watching her for some time, so had Reuben Cole.

"What do you think of her, Cole?" asked Devereux.

"What you knows her to be, sir—the *Cerberus* herself, and no other," cried Reuben, in a more animated tone than he had indulged in for many a long day.

"I made sure it was she, sir, five minutes ago, but I was just afraid to speak; but when you axed me, sir, then I knowed it was all right."

"The *Cerberus*!" cried the rest of the party in the same breath.

"Ay, she's the fine old girl, no doubt about it," exclaimed O'Grady. "Three cheers for the *Cerberus*! Hurrah! hurrah! hurrah!"

All the party joined heartily in the shout. It was echoed from a distance, and old Charcoal was seen scrambling along on his crutches towards them. They congratulated him by signs at having escaped the fate which his cruel taskmasters had intended for him, and he seemed no less pleased than they were at the appearance of the English frigate. Their attention was, however, soon fully engrossed by the chase. The frigate had caught sight of the schooner, and was now crowding on all sail to overtake her. The latter was keeping as close in with the shore as the reefs would allow, with the intention, probably, of rounding the island and putting it between herself and her enemy. She, however, by keeping so close in, lost the sea breeze, which the frigate, keeping from necessity further out, retained. The pirates thus lost the advantage which the knowledge of the shore would have given them. Their craft was a fast one, but there was no faster frigate on the station than the *Cerberus*. She seemed putting forth all her speed, and it was soon evident that she was gaining rapidly on the chase. The wind, it must be understood, was off the land, along the south coast of which the vessels were standing towards the east. It was necessary, therefore, for the schooner, in order to get on the north side, either to stand a long way to the east, or else to make short tacks, so as to weather the eastern end of the island. The temptation to watch her proceedings was very great, and though the way round was long, and over soft sand in places, the party set off in that direction as fast as they could run. By the time they had reached a slight elevation, whence they could watch the further progress of the chase, the frigate had gained so greatly on the schooner, that the latter would, in a few minutes, be within range of her guns. The pirates must have seen that they had now little chance of escaping, but they would not give in.

"Hurra! There goes her first shot," cried O'Grady, as a puff of smoke and a flash was seen to proceed from the frigate's side, followed by a report, as the iron missile went leaping over the water, but falling short of the object at which it was aimed. For some half-hour or more the frigate did not throw another shot away; the schooner, meantime, made several tacks in shore, but the wind veered as she went about, and she gained far less ground than if she had continued on one tack. Still she managed nearly to weather the eastern point. The *Cerberus*, however, was by this time standing directly towards her, a point off the wind, so as to make her escape almost impossible. Again the frigate fired—the water was smooth, and her gunnery was good. The shot struck the schooner's hull. Another and another followed. Still she stood on. She was in stays; another tack or two would carry her round the point, and there were reefs amid which she might possibly make her escape, when a shot, flying higher than the rest, struck the head of her main-mast. Over the side went the topmast and topsail, down came the mainsail, and the vessel's head paying off, in five minutes she was hard and fast on a reef. The frigate had, meantime, been shortening sail, and scarcely had the schooner struck, when she dropped her anchor in a position completely to command the wreck with her guns.

"The villains will get their due now. Hurrah!" cried O'Grady. "But see, they are lowering their boats to escape on shore. If they fall in with us, they will knock us on the head to a certainty. Won't discretion with us be the best part of valour? and hadn't we just best get out of their way?"

"They will scarcely attempt to come on shore here, I should think," observed Devereux. "They will more probably pull along close in with the shore, and, if they can, get away from the island altogether."

The attempt of the pirates to escape was immediately seen from the frigate, which, thereon, opened her fire to prevent them, while at the same time her boats were lowered to cut them off. The frigate's shot had knocked one of the schooner's boats to pieces. Most of her crew crowded into the other two, which shoved off, leaving some on board, who loudly entreated them to return. But, overloaded as they were, they could not have done so had they wished, and it was with difficulty they reached the shore, swearing vengeance on the heads of their victors.

"It's time for us, at all events, to be off, if we would save our throats from being cut, or our heads from being broken," cried O'Grady, as he saw them about to land.

The rest of the party agreed with him, and signed to Charcoal to accompany them. But the old black seemed bewildered, and shook his head, to signify that he could not move as fast as they could, and that they must hurry on without him. In vain they urged him and showed him that they would help him on.

"Come, old fellow, just you get up on my back, and I will carry you," exclaimed Reuben Cole, who was by far the strongest of the party.

Still the black refused—the whole party were in despair. It

was high time, indeed, to move away from the spot, not only to escape the pirates, but to avoid the shot from the *Cerberus*, some of which, passing over the schooner, had struck the ground very close to them. One of the shot at length settled the dispute by flying along and striking the poor old man on the shoulder, and very nearly taking off Reuben's head at the same time. His moments were evidently numbered, and to move him while seemingly in the agonies of death, would have been cruelty. Devereux, therefore, reluctantly ordered his followers to run for their lives, before they were discovered and pursued by the pirates. It was doubtful, indeed, whether they had not already been seen. Paul, as they came along, had observed a patch of rocky ground to the south near the shore, with low shrubs growing about it. He pointed it out to Devereux.

"Right, Gerrard, the very place for us; we'll steer towards it," he answered.

By running on at full speed, they had just time to conceal themselves among the rocks as the pirates reached the shore. Devereux had ordered them all to lie down, so that they were unable to observe the direction the outlaws took. O'Grady and Paul were crouching down close to each other. Both felt a strong inclination to look out from their hiding-place.

"I say, Gerrard, don't you think that you could manage, just with half an eye above the rock, to see what the spalpeens of pirates are about there?" whispered the former.

"Beg pardon, sir, but our orders were not to look out at all," answered Paul, in a very low voice.

"Right, Gerrard, right; but by the powers, our fellows are a long time getting on shore from the frigate," said O'Grady.

"Silence, lads!" whispered Devereux, who overheard them talking. "I hear footsteps."

Sure enough, the tramp of men running fast was heard, and, it seemed, coming in the direction of the rock. Probably the pirates were hastening there for shelter. Paul was sure, as most likely were the rest of the party, that they would wreak their vengeance on their heads if they discovered them. He felt very uncomfortable; his satisfaction was not increased, when he heard a voice shout out, "Here they are, the scoundrels! don't let one of them escape."

As there was no object in remaining to be cut down, he was about to follow the ordinary instinct of nature, and to try and escape by flight, when another voice added, "Come on, men, here they are, a dozen or two skulking scoundrels, too."

There was a shrill squeak in the sound, which Paul was certain he had heard many times before. He was not mistaken. There, on the top of a rock, stood honest Bruff, and by his side, Tilly Blake.

"There are two of the villains—young ones, though," cried Tilly, pointing to O'Grady and Gerrard.

Then he stopped, with a look of astonishment which made them almost burst into a fit of laughter, as they sprang forward to meet him, while the rest of the party at the same time rose up from their lair.

"Why, Devereux, old fellow, I thought that you were safe in England with our prize by this time," cried Bruff, as he shook his messmate's hand.

Devereux could with difficulty reply, his feelings had so completely mastered him; so Bruff continued: "Ah, I see how it was; the scoundrels surprised and captured you, and brought you prisoners here. Well, I'm thankful we've got you back safe, though I conclude poor old Noakes has lost the number of his mess."

In a few words, Devereux, who soon found his tongue, explained what had occurred, and the whole party, with the rest of the frigate's crew who had landed, set forward in pursuit of the pirates. It was important to come up with them before they could have time to fortify themselves. In high glee, the whole party hurried on, led by Bruff, and guided by Devereux and O'Grady. It was likely that the pirates would make a stand either at the hut or on the top of a rocky mound on which some thick brushwood, with a few trees, grew. It was a strong post naturally, and might be made much stronger if the pirates had time to cut down the trees and form barricades. Bruff, therefore, with his small party, without waiting for reinforcements from the ship, pushed on. They had already passed round the head of the lagoon without finding the enemy.

"They must have got into the hut, and we must be cautious how we approach it, or they may pick us off without our being able to return a shot," observed Devereux, as they came in sight of it.

Bruff, in consequence of this, at once divided his men, sending one party to the right, another to the left, while he advanced directly towards the hut, keeping, however, under such shelter as the cocoa-nut trees and bushes afforded. Whether the generalship was good might be doubted, for should the pirates break out, they might overwhelm one of the smaller parties, and make good their retreat to another part of the island, where they might hold out till the frigate was compelled to leave the coast. This was Reuben's opinion, which he imparted to Paul. Still the enemy did not appear. The parties closed in—not a shot was fired. "Charge!" shouted Bruff. The door was burst open—the hut was empty. There were treasures of all sorts scattered about, which the pirates had not time to pack up when they hurriedly left the island.

The crew of the *Cerberus* very naturally wished to take possession of the plunder, but Bruff called them together, and ordered them to proceed at once to the mound where Devereux and O'Grady thought that the pirates must have gone. It was hot work. They stopped for a few seconds at the fountain to wash the sand out of their throats, and pushed on. The hill was soon in sight. The place looked naturally strong.

"The fellows are there, for they are cutting down the trees already," cried O'Grady. "If we could but wait for an hour or so, they'd be pretty well ready for us, and we should get heaps of honour and glory in taking them."

"Thank you, Paddy, but we'll not give them time to get ready," answered Bruff. "On, lads, on!"

So busily engaged were the pirates, that the English were close up to the mound, for hill it was not, before they perceived that their enemies were on them. Led on by Bruff and the other midshipmen, the seamen clambered up the hill in spite of all obstacles. The pirates stood to their arms and fought desperately. They were a fierce set of ruffians. The hairy baboon, as O'Grady called the man who had seized Paul on the rock, led them on. Their captain, probably, had been killed, for he seemed to be the principal officer among them. Among gentry of that class, when the day is going against them, no one is anxious to be looked upon as a leader. Whether he wished it or not, however, the hairy baboon was a conspicuous object. With three brace of pistols stuck in his belt, his arms bare, and a huge sword in his hand,

W. H. G. Kingston

he stood like a wild beast at bay. The pirates, when overpowered at other points, rallied round him. Again and again Bruff attempted to pick him out, in the hopes of cutting him down, but each time calling his men around him, the pirate avoided the combat.

The pirates were, however, getting the worst of it. Several of them had fallen, killed, or desperately wounded. Some of the English also had been hurt, and two killed. Bruff, determining to put an end to the conflict, once more dashed up the slope, and with his brave fellows, leaping over all obstacles, pushed up to where the savage stood behind the trunk of a fallen tree. Devereux was at his side, and Paul followed close behind, armed with a pistol which had been given him by one of the seamen. His great wish was, should opportunity occur, of being of use to Devereux, just as he had been, on a former occasion, to poor old Noakes. This was fiercer work, for quarter was neither asked nor taken. The English among the pirates were the most desperate, for they knew that they were fighting with halters round their throats. The pirate plied his weapon with right good will, and kept Bruff fully occupied, bestowing, indeed, more than one wound on him. Devereux was, meantime, engaged with another fellow, evidently an officer by his gay dress and ornaments. He also was a good swordsman; and while the English seamen were engaged on either side, he managed to strike down Devereux's cutlass, and would the next moment have cut him from the head to the neck, when Paul, seeing that the moment for action had arrived, springing forward, fired his pistol with so good an aim, that the pirate, shot through the heart, sprang into the air and fell forward over the tree, while Devereux, recovering his guard, saved his head from the blow of the falling sword, which he sent flying away among the pirates. At liberty for a moment, he turned on Bruff's antagonist, who, unable to parry his rapid blows, was at length brought to the ground. As he lay writhing in the agonies of death, he attempted to fire a pistol, which he drew from his belt, at his victor's head; but his eye was dim—the shot flew into the air, and his hand fell powerless by his side. The pirates, though they still fought on, were evidently disheartened at the fall of their leaders; but the English were proportionately encouraged, and dashing on once more, they cut down every pirate opposing them. Some attempted to fly, prompted by the instinct of self-preservation; but they were met by a party under O'Grady, sent round to attack them in the rear, and at last, in the hopes of prolonging their lives, they threw down their arms and begged for quarter. However fierce men may be, very few will fight on with the certainty of being killed if they do, and the possibility of escaping if they yield. The pirates were completely disarmed, and were then surrounded by seamen, with pistols at their heads, marched towards the spot where the boats of the *Cerberus* lay waiting for them. The hut and its contents were not forgotten, and one party of men was ordered to collect and bring along all the more valuable articles which could be found. As they marched along, Devereux called Paul up to him. "Gerrard, I am anxious to tell you that I feel how heavy a debt of gratitude I owe you," he said. "You have tended me with a brother's care since I was wounded, and I saw the way in which you saved my life just now. Fortunately, Mr Bruff saw it also, and as you thus certainly contributed to the success of the undertaking, I am certain that he will place your conduct in its most favourable light before the captain, and, for my part, I think that there is one reward which you ought to obtain, and which you will obtain, too."

"What can that be, sir?" asked Paul, innocently. "All I know is, that I wished to be of use to you, and I am very glad that you think I have been of use."

"Indeed you have, Gerrard," answered Devereux. "I should

W. H. G. Kingston

have been food for the land crabs if it hadn't been for you; but we'll not say anything more about the reward just now."

They were approaching the beach where the boats were waiting.

"Hillo, what is that?" cried O'Grady. "Oh, you vile scoundrels—you did that, I know you did."

He shook his fist at the prisoners as he spoke, and pointed to the body of the poor black, which lay in their course, with the head smashed to pieces. The pirates had evidently found him wounded on the ground when they landed, and had thus wreaked their vengeance on him.

The seamen stopped a few short minutes to bury him in the sand, and the midshipmen, as they passed on, muttered, "Poor old Charcoal, good bye."

The pirates would have had very little chance just then of escaping with their lives had the seamen been their judges, and in consequence of the cruel murder of the black, they got many a punch in the ribs and a lift with the knee as they were bundled into the boats. Hitherto, of course, those on board the *Cerberus* were ignorant that Devereux and his companions were on the island. As the boats approached the ship, all glasses were turned towards them; but it took some time after they had climbed up the sides to explain who they were and where they had come from, so haggard in countenance were they, and so tattered in dress, and blood and smoke-begrimed. Devereux lost not a moment in speaking to Captain Walford in warm terms of Paul's conduct throughout all the events which had occurred, adding, "To-day, sir, he saved my life by shooting a man who was on the point of cutting me down, and I must entreat you to give him the only reward he would value, or indeed, I believe, accept."

"What is that?" asked Captain Walford, smiling at the idea of a ship-boy being punctilious as to the style of reward he would receive.

"Why, sir, that you would place him on the quarter-deck," answered Devereux, boldly. "There is no one who will do it more credit, or is better fitted to become an officer than Paul Gerrard, sir."

"I will keep him in mind, and perhaps he may have an opportunity of distinguishing himself while under my eye," answered the captain; but he made no promise to promote Paul, and Devereux left him, fearing very much that he was displeased at his having mentioned the subject.

All the party were, however, warmly welcomed on board, and Alphonse, who had now learned a good deal of English, became a great favourite both with officers and men. As there happened to be no fiddler among the crew, his violin was in great requisition. He had no pride, and as he took delight in giving pleasure, he constantly went forward to play to the men while they danced. There was nothing they would not have done for the "little mounseer," as they called him.

Before the *Cerberus* left the island, one of the pirates declared that a large amount of treasure was hidden near the hut, and volunteered to show it, provided that his life was spared. Captain Walford would make no promise, but let the man understand that if the treasure was found, and he chose to turn king's evidence, the circumstance might possibly tell in his favour. The pirate held out for the promise of a pardon and refused to afford any further information unless it was given. The captain, however, sent a party on shore, under Mr Bruff with O'Grady, to search for the supposed treasure.

Reuben and Paul were of the party. There were two boats. They pulled up the lagoon.

"I feel very different now from what I did t'other day when the pirates were after us. Don't you, Paul?" said Reuben Cole, in a moralising tone. "Many are the ups and downs in the world. The pirates was then thirsting after our blood, and now we're thirsting after the pirates' gold. It's not much good our blood would have done them, and I'm afeared the gold won't do us much good either, if it's spent as most of us spends it when we gets ashore. Paul, don't you go and throw away your hard-earned gains as seamen generally do—you'll be sorry for it some day, if you do."

Paul promised to follow his friend's advice. He was very eager, however, to find the pirate treasure, as he hoped to be able to send his share home to his mother and sisters. He was not aware of the efforts Devereux had been making to get him placed on the quarter-deck, in which case the share would be considerably more than that of a cabin-boy. The search was commenced, but except a bag of dollars and a few gold doubloons, nothing of value could be found. The men dug about in every direction. There was no sign of the earth having been turned up.

"I say, Reuben, I wonder where all the gold we are looking for can be," exclaimed Paul, after they had searched in vain again and again.

"Just possible, nowhere," answered Reuben. "Them chaps is much more likely to spend their money ashore than to bury it in the ground."

It seemed very probable that Reuben's opinion was the right one. The seamen dug and dug more frantically and eagerly as the prospect of finding the gold became less and less. Reuben's spade at length struck something hard.

"Hurrah! Here it is," cried several voices, and half a dozen spades were plunged into the hole at the same time. A human skull was soon brought to view.

"All right," cried O'Grady. "The pirates always bury a man above their treasure, that his spirit may keep guard over it."

Thus encouraged, the seamen dug on, the bones were thrown up with very little ceremony, and all expected every instant to come upon an iron case, or an oak chest, or something of that sort, full of gold, and pearls, and diamonds. While thus employed, a gun from the ship was heard. They dug more desperately than ever. The gun was the signal for their return: it must not be disobeyed. Still, within the very grasp of their treasure, it seemed hard to lose it. They dug, and they dug, but there was no sign of treasure. Another gun was heard.

"We must be away!" cried the leader. "Shoulder spades, and march!"

O'Grady, stopping behind, leaped into the hole and ran his sword up to the hilt into the sand, but it met with no impediment. Again and again he plunged his sword in all directions. He saw that it was of no avail. "I must be out of this and run after the rest," he said to himself. But to propose was easier than to execute. In vain he tried to get up the sandy sides of the pit—he made desperate efforts. He ought not to have stopped behind, and did not like to cry out. "Oh! I shall have to take the place of the disinterred body, and that would not be at all pleasant," he muttered—"One more spring!" But no—down he came on his back, and the sand rushed down and half covered him up. He now thought that it was high time to sing out, and so he did at the very top of

W. H. G. Kingston

his voice. He shouted over and over again—no one came. His companions were getting further and further off. He scrambled to his feet and made another spring, shrieking out at the same time, "Help! help!"

Fortunately, Paul and Reuben were bringing up the rear, and Paul happening to speak of Mr O'Grady, observed that he was not in front. At that moment the cry of "Help, help!" reached his ears.

"It's Mr O'Grady," he exclaimed, and he ran forward to Mr Bruff and obtained leave to go and look. Reuben and several other men had, however, to go to his assistance to get poor Paddy out of the hole, and pretty hot they all became by running towards the boats, so as not to delay them. Nothing was said of O'Grady's adventure, and the captain did not seem much surprised at no treasure having been found. A course was steered for Jamaica, where the pirates were to be tried. The *Cerberus* arrived at her destined port without falling in with an enemy. Numerous witnesses came forward to prove various acts of piracy committed by the prisoners, the greater number of whom were condemned to death, and were accordingly hung in chains, as the custom of those days was, to be a terror and warning to like evil-doers, as dead crows and other birds are stuck up in a field to scare away the live ones wishing to pilfer the farmer's newly-sown seed.

The frigate having refitted in Port Royal harbour, was again to sail—like a knight-errant—in search of adventures. It was not likely that she would be long in finding them.

As soon as the commander-in-chief heard of the capture of the frigate by the mutineers, he became very anxious to re-take her. A brig of war before long arrived with a Spanish prize lately out of Puerto Cabello on the Spanish Main. Her crew gave information that the frigate was there fitting for sea by the Spaniards, to whom the mutineers had delivered her; that she was strongly armed, and manned with a half more than her former complement. It soon became known on board the *Cerberus* that Captain Walford had volunteered to cut out the frigate, but that the admiral objected to the exploit as too hazardous.

"Just like our skipper," exclaimed O'Grady. "He would try it and do it too. We'd back him, and so would every man on board."

"No fear of that," cried several voices. "Let us but find her, and she will be ours."

"I wish that we could have the chance," observed Devereux to O'Grady. "It would be a fine opportunity for Gerrard, and the captain would, I think, be glad of a good excuse for placing him on the quarter-deck."

As there was no longer a reason for Alphonse Montauban remaining on board the *Cerberus*, he had to be left at Jamaica to wait till an opportunity should occur for sending him to France. His friends parted from him with many regrets.

"We shall meet some day again, old fellow," said O'Grady, as he wrung his hands. "But I say, I hope that it won't be with swords in our fists."

"Oh no, no!" cried Alphonse; "I will never more fight against you English. I was told that you were little better than barbarians—a nation of fierce lords, money-making shop-keepers, and wretched slaves; but I find you very different. I love you now, and I love you for ever."

Alphonse parted in a most affectionate manner from Paul,

W. H. G. Kingston

telling him how glad he should be, when the war was over, if he would come and see him at his father's chateau, where he said he should go and remain quietly, and escape, if possible, being sent again to sea.

The *Cerberus* sailed with sealed orders. This was known. It was hoped that they would give permission to the captain to attack the Spanish frigate. The captain opened his orders off the east end of the island, when he found that he was to proceed off Cape Delavela, on the Spanish Main, a point of land about seventy leagues to leeward of Puerto Cabello, and that he was to remain as long as his provisions, wood, and water would allow, to endeavour to intercept the frigate supposed to be bound to the Havana. Thither the *Cerberus* accordingly proceeded. To wait in expectation of meeting a friend is a matter of no little interest; but when an enemy is looked-for, and there is the prospect of a battle, and a pretty tough one to boot, the excitement is immense. In this instance it was tenfold: the enemy was no ordinary one; the object was to win back a ship foully taken and disgracefully retained.

"There is no necessity to tell you to keep a sharp look-out," said the captain to the officers of the watch, as he went below the first night of their arrival on their cruising-ground.

"She'll be clever if she escapes us," was the answer. However, the captain was on deck that night several times, as he was on many subsequent nights, and sharp eyes were looking out all night and all day, and still no enemy's frigate hove in sight. Paul was very ambitious to be the first to see her. Whenever his duty would allow, he was at the mast-head till the hot sun drove him down, or darkness made his stay there, useless. He often dreamed, when in his hammock at night, that he heard the drum beat to quarters, and jumping up, slipped into his clothes, and hurried on deck, when finding all quiet, with no small disappointment he had again to turn in. "The opportunity will come, however, in some way or other," said Paul to himself as he tried to go to sleep, and succeeded, as ship-boys generally do. "I must have patience. Even if I were to be killed the next day, I should like to have been a midshipman." Week after week passed away; no enemy appeared. Now and then a prize was taken; but it was always the same story—the frigate was still in Puerto Cabello. At length it became known that the water and wood were running short, while it was a fact no one would dispute, that the provisions were very bad. The *Cerberus* must return to Jamaica. The disappointment was general.

"Och, the blackguards of Dons, to keep us waiting all this time, and not to give us the satisfaction of thrashing them after all!" cried Paddy O'Grady, as the matter was discussed in the midshipmen's berth.

"The fellow has probably slipped by us in the dark; but we'll catch him some day; that's a comfort," observed Devereux.

"Our skipper is not a man to take that for granted without ascertaining the fact," remarked Bruff.

He was right. Before a course was shaped for Jamaica, the *Cerberus* stood for Puerto Cabello. All hands were eagerly on the look out as they approached the port, to ascertain whether the frigate was still there. A shout of satisfaction broke from the throats of the crew as she was discovered with her sails bent ready for sea, though moored head and stern between two strong batteries, one on either side, at the entrance of the harbour. By herself, she looked no insignificant opponent; while the batteries, it was supposed, mounted not less than two hundred guns. The *Cerberus* stood in till she was within gun-shot of the enemy, and then continued her course, as if fearing a contest. Not a word was said by the captain as to what he intended doing. Hope returned when the ship was tacked. For two or three days the *Cerberus* continued cruising up and down before the port. Another day was drawing to a close, when, as it seemed, she had given a farewell to the port. Some of the officers had been dining with the captain. They came out of the cabin with an expression of satisfaction on their countenances.

"Something is in the wind," said Reuben to Paul. "They wouldn't look so pleased otherwise."

Not long after this, all hands were sent aft to the quarter-deck, where the captain stood, surrounded by his officers, ready to receive them.

"I told you so," whispered Reuben to Paul. "He's got some good news, depend on that; I see it in his eye."

"My lads, we have been waiting a long time to get hold of that villainous frigate in there," the captain began. "If we don't take her, somebody else will, and we shall lose the honour and glory of the deed. She will not come out to fight us fairly, and so we must go in and bring her out. It's to be done, I know, if you'll try to do it. What do you say to that?"

"That we'll try and do it," cried a voice from among the seamen.

"Hurrah! hurrah! hurrah!" Three hearty cheers broke from the crew. Again and again was given forth from the seamen's throats that soul-thrilling shout which none but Englishmen can utter.

"Thank you, my lads," cried the captain. "I knew that you would be ready to do it; and, what is more, I know that you will do it. It will not be your fault if that frigate is not ours before many hours are over. There will be six boats with their regular crews, and I have arranged already of whom the boarding-parties are to consist. I will myself lead."

Saying this, he handed a list to the first-lieutenant. All were eager to ascertain its contents. Bruff and Devereux had command of boats; the second-lieutenant had charge of another—the launch; the surgeon of a fourth. Paul, with no small delight, heard his name called out for the captain's boat—the pinnace. Reuben Cole was also to go in her. The expedition was to consist of two divisions; the first formed by the pinnace, launch, and jolly-boat, to board on the starboard-bow, gangway, and quarter; and the gig, black and red cutters, to board on the opposite side. Some of her crew were to remain in the launch to cut the lower cable, for which they were provided with sharp axes; the jolly-boat was to cut the stern cable and to send two men aloft to loose the mizen-topsail. Four men from the gig were to loose the fore-topsail, and in the event of the boats reaching the ship undiscovered, as soon as the boarders had climbed up the sides, the crews were to cut the cables and take the ship in tow. No arrangements could be more perfect, and all about to engage in the undertaking felt confident of success, eagerly waiting for the moment of action. The ship stood towards the harbour, and in silence the crews and the boarding-parties entered the boats and shoved off. Paul felt as he had never felt before. He had gone through a good many adventures; but the work he was now engaged in would probably be of a far more desperate character. Still his heart beat high with hope. If the undertaking should be successful—and he felt sure that it would be—he believed that he should secure that position he had of late taught himself so ardently to covet. The boats made rapid progress. The pinnace led; the captain with his night-glass keeping his eye constantly on the enemy. No light was seen, either on board her or in the batteries, or

W. H. G. Kingston

other sign to show that the Spaniards were aware that a foe was approaching. The night was dark; the water was smooth. There was a sound of oars. Two large gun-boats were seen at the entrance of the harbour. At the same instant the Spaniards, discovering the English, began firing. The alarm was given; lights burst forth in all directions, and round-shot and bullets came whizzing through the air. Some officers might have turned back; not so Captain Walford. Ordering the boats to follow, and not to mind the Spaniards, he gave three hearty cheers, and, dashing on, was quickly up to the frigate.

# CHAPTER EIGHT

The Spanish frigate lay moored head and stern, with her ports open, and the light from her fighting-lanterns streaming through them. The crew, awakened by the firing, had hurried to their quarters, and were now rapidly discharging their guns, sending their shot right and left, though happily, it seemed, without any definite aim. A shot passed close over the captain's head; so close that Paul expected for a moment to see him fall, but he did not even notice the circumstance, and only urged his men to pull up alongside the enemy. The pinnace was crossing the frigate's bows. Suddenly her way was checked.

"She's aground, sir," cried the coxswain. "A rope has caught our rudder—unship it, man," answered the captain, who was as cool as if about to go on board his own ship.

In another instant the pinnace had hooked on to the Spaniard's bows; and her crew, led by their brave captain, were climbing up to gain a footing on their forecastle. Paul's heart beat quick—not with fear, but with the belief that the moment for distinguishing himself had arrived. He resolved to follow the captain closely. Captain Walford had hold of the anchor which hung at the bows, when his foot slipped, and he would have fallen back, had he not caught at the lanyard and hauled himself up. The delay, though brief,

W. H. G. Kingston

enabled some of the men to be up before him. Paul was among the number; and, finding a rope, he hove it to the captain, which enabled him to gain the deck. Not an enemy was found; but, looking down on the main-deck, the English discovered the Spaniards at their quarters, not dreaming, it seemed, that the foe already stood on the deck of their ship. There they stood, some loading, others firing; fierce-looking fellows enough as the light of the lanterns fell on their countenances. The foresail had been left laid across the deck ready for bending, and the thick folds of the canvass served as a screen to the first of the gallant hoarders while the rest were climbing up. Not a moment was to be lost, and before the Spaniards had discovered that the English were on board, a party of the latter, led by their brave captain, were literally in the midst of them, fighting their way towards the quarter-deck, where it had been arranged that all the parties should rendezvous.

The Spaniards, taken by surprise, were cut down or leaped to the right hand or to the left to escape the cutlasses of the boarders. At length, however, some of the Spaniards rallied; and, led by one of their officers, made so furious an attack on the captain's party that he and most of his men were separated from each other. Paul had stuck by his captain from the first. His arm was not very strong, but he was active; and, while he managed to avoid the blows of his enemies, he bestowed several as he leaped nimbly on. He, with the captain and Reuben Cole, had nearly gained the quarter-deck when a Spaniard rushed at the latter, and knocked him over with the butt-end of a musket. At the same moment the captain's foot slipped, and another Spaniard striking him a furious blow on the head, he fell senseless on the coaming of the hatchway, very nearly going over below. Paul fully believed that his brave captain was killed, and that his last moment was come. The Spaniard was about to repeat the blow when Paul, springing in, regardless of consequences to himself, cut him so severely under the arm with his sword that the man missed his aim, and he himself fell headlong down the hatchway.

Paul then, while he laid about him with his weapon, did the best thing he could by shouting at the top of his voice, "Help! help!—the captain is down—help! help!" at the same time laying about him in so energetic a way that none of the Spaniards seemed disposed to come within reach of his weapon. His shouts quickly brought several of the crew of the *Cerberus* to the rescue; and, while some kept the Spaniards at bay, the others assisted the captain, who was recovering from the effects of the blow, to rise. Paul, as soon as he saw the captain on his feet, hurried with two of his companions to the assistance of Reuben Cole, just in time to prevent some Spaniards from giving him his quietus. Reuben's head was a tolerably thick one; and, notwithstanding the severity of the blow, he quickly came to himself; and, seizing his cutlass with right good will, joined the party under the captain, who were employed in preventing the Spaniards from regaining possession of the quarter-deck. Meantime, several separate combats were going on in different parts of the ship. The Spaniards, as they recovered from their first surprise, rallied in considerable numbers; and, attacking the boatswain's party, which had been separated from that of the captain's, fought their way forward and re-took the forecastle. Paul could only discern what was going forward by the flashes of the pistols of the combatants on deck, and of the great guns which those below still continued to fire. As yet, however, the English mustered but few hands, considering the magnitude of the enterprise. Paul anxiously looked for the arrival of the other boats. Now some dark forms were seen rising above the hammock nettings. The Spaniards rushed to repel them, but at the same moment the cry was raised that others were appearing on the opposite side. Others came swarming over the bows, another party climbed up on the quarter. The shouts and cries of the combatants increased. On every side was heard the clashing of steel and the sharp crack of pistols. The British marines now formed on deck, and, led by their officers, charged the Spaniards. The bravest of the latter, who had been attacking the captain, threw down their arms and cried for mercy or leaped below. They were quickly followed by Bruff and Devereux, who drove them into the after-cabin, where some sixty of them lay down their weapons and begged for quarter. Others, however, still held out. The game was not won; reinforcements might come from the shore, and the gun-boats might pull up and prove awkward customers. The deck was, however, literally strewed with the bodies of the Spaniards, while as yet not an Englishman was killed, though many were badly wounded. Many of the Spaniards still held out bravely under the forecastle, and others on the main-deck; but the gunner and two men, though severely wounded, had got possession of the wheel. The seamen who had gone aloft loosed the foretop sail, the carpenters cut the stern cable, the best bower was cut at the same moment, just in time to prevent the ship from canting the wrong way.

The boats took the frigate in tow, and though as yet those on deck were scarcely in possession of the ship, directly she was seen to be moving, the batteries on either side opened a hot fire on her, but, undaunted, the brave crews rowed on in spite of the shot whizzing over their heads, and the efforts of the yet unsubdued portion of the Spaniards to regain the ship. Those of the latter who attempted to defend the forecastle suffered most, and were nearly all killed or driven overboard. Still the victory was not assured; a cry was raised that the Spaniards retreating below were forcing open the magazine for the purpose of blowing up the ship.

Devereux was the first to hear the report, and calling on Paul, who was near him, and a few others to follow, he leaped down the hatchway, and sword in hand dashed in among the astonished Spaniards, who with crowbars had just succeeded in breaking open the door of the magazine. One man grasped a pistol ready to fire into it. Paul, who felt his spirits raised to the highest pitch, and ready to dare and do any deed, however desperate, sprang into the midst of the group and struck up the Spaniard's arm, the pistol going off and the bullet lodging in the deck above. Several of the others were cut down by Devereux and his men, and the rest, strange as it may seem, fell on their knees and begged for quarter; though an instant before they were preparing to send themselves and their foes suddenly into eternity.

"Quarter! Pretty sort of quarter you deserve, ye blackguards, for wishing to blow up the ship after all the trouble we've had to take her," cried Reuben, giving one of the Spaniards, who still stood at the door of the magazine, a kick which lifted him half-way up the ladder leading to the deck above.

All opposition after this ceased below, but there was work enough to secure the prisoners and prevent them from making any similar attempt to that which had just been so happily frustrated. The hands on deck were meantime employed in making sail with all speed; and good reason had they for so doing, for the shot from a hundred guns were flying above and around them, some crashing on board and others going through the sails and cutting the running and standing rigging; but in spite of the iron shower not a man aloft shrank from his duty. As soon as a brace was cut, or a shroud severed, eager hands were ready to repair the damage. The gallant captain, though bleeding from more than one wound, stood by the mizen shrouds conning the ship, and not till she was clear of the harbour and no shot came near her did he relinquish his post.

The triumphant moment was, however, when the two

frigates neared each other, and the victors shouted out, "We have got her—we have got her, without the loss of a man, though we have some pretty severe scratches among us. Hurrah! hurrah! hurrah!"

Loud and hearty were the cheers; but there was too little time for making speeches. Most of the prisoners were removed to the *Cerberus*. A prize-crew, under the command of the second lieutenant, was put on board the re-captured frigate, and a course was immediately shaped for Jamaica. When Paul at length was able to turn into his hammock he felt very low-spirited. Not a word had been said of anything that had been done. He felt that he had certainly saved the captain's life, and had in all probability prevented the ship from being blown up. Yet he would not be his own trumpeter, and he thought that very likely no one had observed what he had done, and that it would be entirely overlooked. "Well, I should not care so much for myself," he thought, "but dear mother—how she would rejoice to hear that I had made my own way up to the quarter-deck. It can't be helped, I must wait for another opportunity."

The fate Paul dreaded has been that of many who have struggled on year after year in the hopes of winning fame, and have after all missed the object at which they aimed.

It was reported that the captain was suffering severely from his wounds, and for some days he did not appear on deck. Devereux, however, had not forgotten Paul, and took the first occasion to tell him that he would mention him to the captain as having preserved the ship and all their lives from destruction. Paul, on this, felt very much inclined to say that he had been the means also of preserving the captain's life. "No, I won't, though," he thought; "the captain will make inquiries as to what happened when he was struck down, and the men who saw me defending him will surely tell him the truth."

He therefore simply thanked Devereux for his kind intentions.

"You know, sir, that what I did was to save my own life as well as that of others," he added.

"Very true, but still I think that the captain will consider your conduct worthy of reward," answered Devereux.

To Reuben, Paul was more communicative.

"But do you know which were the men who came when you called for help?" asked the former.

Paul could not be positive as to one of them, on account of the darkness and confusion.

"Then I must find out, my lad, and make all things square," muttered Reuben, as he walked away.

The victors had plenty of hard work in putting the prize to rights, in manning her and their own ship, and in looking after the prisoners. However, not long after they had lost sight of land, a sail hove in sight. Chase was made, and the stranger proved to be a Spanish schooner. She quickly hauled down her colours, and a boat was sent to bring her captain on board. The Don stood, hat in hand, trembling in every joint, at the gangway, his long sallow face drawn down to twice its usual length, expecting to be carried off a prisoner, and to have his vessel destroyed. As Captain Walford was unable to come on deck, Mr Order received him. If it had been possible for a Don to throw up his hat and to shout for joy, the Spanish skipper would have done it when the first-lieutenant told him, that if he would undertake to carry the prisoners back to Puerto Cabello in his schooner, he might go free. He did not skip, or throw up his hat, or sing, but advancing with a deep bow, one hand holding his hat, and the other pressed on his heart, he gave the lieutenant an embrace and then retired to the gangway. Mr Order did not exhibit any sign of satisfaction at this proceeding, but it was too ridiculous to make him angry; so he told him to get on board and prepare for the reception of his countrymen. The Spanish prisoners were soon tumbled into the boats, and heartily glad were the English seamen to be rid of them.

"Their habits are filthy, and as to manners, they have none," was the opinion generally formed of them on board.

"Now, if we'd have had as many mounseers, they'd have been fiddling and singing away as merry as crickets, and been good sport to us—long afore this," observed Reuben to Paul, as the schooner made sail to the southward.

Although the captain's hurts were severe, he was, after some days, able to come on deck. He looked pale and weak, but there was fire in his eye and a smile on his lip as he glanced at the captured frigate sailing at a few cables' length abeam.

"Let the people come aft, Mr Order," he said in a cheerful voice.

The crew were soon assembled, hat in hand, looking up to their captain with eager countenances as he opened his lips.

"My lads," he said, "I have been unable before to thank you, as I do from my heart, for the gallant way in which you carried out my wishes the other night when you re-took yonder frigate, so disgracefully held by the Spaniards. Where all did well, it is difficult to select those most deserving of praise, yet to the second-lieutenant and the boatswain and gunner my thanks are especially due, as they are to the surgeon for the able support he gave me. They will, I trust, receive the reward they merit in due time; but there is another person to whom I am most grateful, and whom I have it in my power to reward, as he fully deserves, immediately. To his presence of mind I find the preservation of the lives of all on board the prize is due, and I fully believe, that had it not been for his courage, I should not have been conscious of the glorious achievement we have accomplished. Paul Gerrard, come up here. Accept this dirk from me as a slight token of gratitude, and from henceforth consider yourself a quarter-deck officer—a midshipman."

Paul, his eyes sparkling, his countenance beaming, and his heart beating, sprang forward, helped on by the arms of the crew, all sympathising with his feelings. The captain shook him warmly by the hand before giving him his dirk—an example followed by all the officers and midshipmen, and by none more cordially than by Devereux and O'Grady. They then took him by the arm and hurried him below, where he found a suit of uniform, in which they speedily clothed him and returned with him in triumph on deck. Their appearance was the signal for the crew to give three as hearty cheers as ever burst from the throats of a man-of-war's crew. Paul's heart was too full to speak, and he could with difficulty stammer out his thanks to his captain. He felt indeed as if he had already reached the summit of his ambition. The captain reminded him, however, that he had a long way yet to climb, by observing that he had only just got his foot on the lower ratline, but that, if he went on as he had begun, he would certainly, if he lived, get to the top. The advice was indeed, from beginning to end, very good, but need not be repeated. Paul was so cordially received in the midshipmen's berth, that he soon felt himself perfectly at home, though he did not forget that he had a short time before served at the table at which he now sat.

The frigates arrived without accident at Jamaica, where the

W. H. G. Kingston

officers and crew received all the honours and marks of respect they so justly merited. The *Cerberus* required no repairs, and the prize was quickly got ready for sea. Captain Walford, however, suffered so severely from his wounds, that he was ordered home to recruit his strength. Devereux and O'Grady had never entirely recovered from their illness, and they also obtained leave to go home. Paul was very sorry to lose them, not being aware how much he was himself knocked up by the hardships he had gone through. Three or four days before the ship was to sail, the doctor came into the berth, and looking hard at him, desired to feel his pulse.

"I thought so," he remarked. "You feel rather queer, my boy, don't you?"

"Yes, sir, very ill," said Paul; "I don't know what is the matter with me."

"But I do," answered the doctor. "A fever is coming on, and the sooner you are out of this the better. I'll speak to the captain about you."

The fever did come on. Paul was sent to the hospital on shore, where he was tenderly nursed by Devereux, aided by O'Grady; the *Cerberus*, meantime, having sailed on a cruise under the command of Mr Order. As no ship of war was going home, Captain Walford took his passage in a sugar-laden merchantman, having Devereux and O'Grady with him, and he got Paul also invalided home. Paul's chief source of delight was the thought that he should present himself to his mother and sisters as a real veritable midshipman, in the uniform he so often in his dreams had worn, and of the happiness he should afford them. Their ship was not a very fast one, though she could carry a vast number of hogsheads of sugar, and was remarkably comfortable. The captain was more like a kind father and a good-natured tutor than most skippers, and they all had a very pleasant time of it. Paul had had no time for study while he was a ship-boy, and so the captain advised him to apply himself to navigation and to general reading; and he did so with so much good will, that, during the voyage, he made considerable progress. They were nearing the mouth of the Channel.

"In another week we shall be at home," said Paul.

"Yes, it will be jolly," answered Devereux. "You must come and see me, you know, at the Hall, and I'll introduce you to my family, and they'll make you amends somehow or other, if they can; they must, I am determined."

"Thank you heartily, Devereux," answered Paul; "but the short time I am likely to be at home I must spend with my mother, and though I know your kind wishes, people generally will not look with much respect on a person who was till lately a mere ship-boy."

"No fear of that, Gerrard; but we'll see, we'll see," answered Devereux.

"A sail on the weather bow," shouted the look-out from aloft, "standing across our course."

The West Indiaman, the *Guava* was her name, went floundering on as before; the master, however, who had gone aloft, kept his glass on the stranger. After some time he came down, his countenance rather paler than usual.

"She has tacked and is standing towards us," he said, addressing Captain Walford.

"Sorry to hear it, Mr Turtle. Is she big or little?"

"Why, sir, she has very square yards, and has much the look of a foreign man-of-war," answered the master.

"Umph! If she is Spanish we may beat her off, but if she proves French, she may be a somewhat tough customer; however, you will try, of course, Mr Turtle."

"If you advise resistance, we'll make it, sir, and do our best," said Captain Turtle, who, though fat, had no lack of spirit.

"By all means. Turn the hands up, load the guns, and open the arm-chest," was the answer.

The crew of the *Guava*, which was rather of a mixed character—blacks, mulattoes, Malays, Portuguese, and other foreigners,—were not very eager for the fight, but when they saw the spirit of the naval officers, especially of the young midshipmen, they loaded the guns, stuck the pistols in their belts, and girded on their cutlasses to prepare for the fight.

The *Guava*, of course, could not hope to escape by flight, so the safest course was to put a bold face on the matter, and to stand on. The stranger rapidly approached. There could no longer be any doubt as to her nationality, though no colours flew from her peak. She was pronounced to be French, though whether a national ship or a privateer was doubtful.

"If she is a privateer and we are taken, our chances of fair treatment are very small," observed Captain Walford.

"It will be hard lines for the skipper, after performing so gallant an action, to fall into the hands of the enemy," observed O'Grady. "For my part, I'd sooner blow up the ship."

"Not much to be gained by that," answered Devereux. "Let

us fight like men and yield with dignity, if we are overmatched."

"The right sentiment," said Captain Walford. "There is no disgrace in being conquered by a superior force."

"As I fear that we shall be," muttered the master of the *Guava*. "Now, if I'd been left alone, I'd have knocked under at once. We've not the shadow of a chance."

"Then it's not like Captain Turtle's own shadow," whispered O'Grady, who could even at that moment indulge in a joke.

Matters were indeed becoming serious. The stranger was, it was soon seen, a powerful vessel, cither a large corvette or a small frigate, against which the heavily-rigged, ill-manned and slightly-armed merchant ship, had scarcely a chance. Still, such chance as there was, the English resolved to try. The order was given to fire high at the enemy's rigging, and the rest of the crew stood prepared to make all possible sail directly any of the Frenchman's spars were knocked away. Paul had been so accustomed to believe that whatever his captain undertook he would succeed in doing, that he had no fears on the subject. The *Guava* rolled on, the stranger approached, close-hauled. Captain Turtle, with a sigh, pronounced her to be a privateer, and a large frigate-built ship. She would have to pass, however, some little way astern of the *Guava*, if she continued steering as she was then doing. Suddenly she kept away, and fired a broadside from long guns, the shot flying among the *Guava's* rigging and doing much damage. The merchantman's guns could not reply with any effect, her shot falling short. The Frenchman saw his advantage. His shot came rattling on board the *Guava*, her spars and blocks falling thickly from aloft. At length the former was seen drawing near, evidently to range up alongside; and many of the crew, fancying that resistance was hopeless, ran below to secure their best clothes and valuables, while the officers, with heavy hearts, throwing their swords overboard, saw Captain Turtle haul down the colours. The Frenchmen were soon on board. They proved to be, not regular combatants, but rascally privateers; fellows who go forth to plunder their fellow-men, not for the sake of overcoming the enemies of their country and obtaining peace, but for the greed of gain, careless of the loss and suffering they inflict. These were of the worst sort. Their delight was unbounded, when they found that they had not only taken a rich prize, for sugar at that time fetched a high price in France, but had taken at one haul a post-captain and several officers, for besides the three midshipmen, there were two lieutenants, a surgeon, and master, going home for their health. The privateer's-men began by plundering the vessel and stripping the crew of every article they possessed about them, except the clothes they stood in. They took the property of the officers, but did not, at first, take anything from their persons. Captain Walford retained his coolness and self-possession, notwithstanding the annoyances he suffered, and the insults he received. The other officers imitated him. They were all transferred to the privateer.

"To what French port are we to be carried?" he asked of his captain.

"To Brest—and it will be a long time before you see salt-water after that," was the answer.

"Probably never—if we are not to be liberated till France conquers England," said Captain Walford, quietly.

"Sa-a-a, you may be free, then, sooner than you expect," cried the Frenchman.

In about five days, the privateer, with her rich prize, entered

Brest harbour. The prisoners were treated on landing with very scant ceremony, and were thrust into the common prison—the officers in one small room and the men in another. In those days the amenities of warfare were little attended to. It was all rough, bloody, desperate, cruel work. In truth, it is seldom otherwise. The prisoners were not kept long at Brest, but one fine morning in spring, after a not over luxurious breakfast of black bread, salt fish, and thin coffee, were mustered outside the prison to begin their march into the interior. The midshipmen kept together and amused themselves by singing, joking, and telling stories, keeping up their spirits as well as they could. Their guards were rough, unfeeling fellows, who paid no attention to their comforts, but made them trudge on in rain or sunshine, sometimes bespattered with mud, and at others covered with dust, parched with thirst, and ready to drop from the heat. The country people, however, looked on them with compassion, and many a glass of wine, a cup of coffee, and a handful of fruits and cakes, were offered to them as they passed through the villages on their road.

"Och, if some of those pretty little villagers who are so kind with their cakes would just increase their compassion and help us to get out of the claws of these ugly blackguards, I'd be grateful to them from the bottom of my soul to the end of my days," said O'Grady to Paul, as they approached a hamlet in a hilly, thickly-wooded part of the country.

It was in the afternoon, and, although they generally marched on much later, to their surprise, the captain of their guard, for some reason best known to himself, called a halt. Instead of being placed in prison, as there was none in the village, they were billeted about in different houses, with one or two guards over each. Paul and O'Grady found themselves, together with Reuben Cole and two other men, in a neat house on the borders of the village. They were the first disposed of, so that where their companions were lodged they could not tell. The people of the house did not appear to regard their guards with friendly eyes, so that they concluded that they were not attached to the present order of things.

"See that you render them up safe to us to-morrow morning," said the captain to an old gentleman, who appeared to be the master of the house.

"I am not a gaoler, and can be answerable for no one," was the reply, at which the captain shook his fist and rode off, exclaiming, "Take care, take care!"

Though very unwilling to receive the prisoners, the old gentleman treated them with a courtesy which seemed to arise rather from respect to himself than from any regard he entertained for them. The two midshipmen were shown into one small room, and the seamen, with their guards, into another. In the room occupied by O'Grady and Paul, there was a table and chairs and a sofa, while the view from the window consisted of a well-kept garden and vineyard, a green meadow and wooded hills beyond. As far as accommodation was concerned, they had little of which to complain; but they were very hungry, and O'Grady began to complain that the old Frenchman intended to starve them.

"I'll go and shout and try to get something," he cried out, but he found that the door was locked outside.

The window was too high from the ground to allow them to jump out, and as they would probably be caught, and punished for attempting to run away, they agreed to stay where they were. At length the door opened, and a bright-eyed, nicely-dressed girl came in with a tray covered with edibles, and a bottle of wine in her hands. They stood up as she entered, and bowed. She smiled, and expressed her sympathy for their misfortunes. Paul had, hitherto, not let the Frenchmen know that he understood French.

"I think that I may venture to speak to her," he said to O'Grady. "She would not have said that if she didn't wish to assist us."

O'Grady agreed that it would be perfectly safe, and so Paul addressed her in the choicest French he could command, and told her how they had been coming home in a merchantman, and had been captured, and robbed of all they possessed, instead of being, as they had hoped, in a few days in the bosom of their families, with their mothers and brothers and sisters.

"And you both have brothers and sisters, and they long to see you, doubtless," said the little girl.

"Oh yes, and we long to see them," exclaimed Paul, believing that he had moved her heart.

She sighed. "Ah, I once had many, but they are all now in the world of spirits; they cannot come to me, but for their sakes I will try to serve you," answered the girl.

"Oh, thank you, thank you!" said Paul. "If you could help us to get out of this house, and to hide away till the pursuit is over, we should be eternally grateful."

She smiled as she answered—

"You are too precipitate. If you were to escape from this house, my father would be punished. Means may be found, however. We have no love for these regicides, and owe them no allegiance; but you must have patience."

"It is a hard thing to exercise; however, we are very much obliged to you," said Paul.

"Just ask her her name," put in O'Grady. "Tell her we should wish to know what to call one who for ever after this must dwell like a bright star in our memories, especially one who is so lovely and amiable."

"That's rather a long speech to translate, and perhaps she won't like all those compliments," remarked Paul.

"Won't she, though?" said O'Grady, who had seen rather more of the world than his companion; "try her, at all events."

Paul translated as well as he could what Paddy had said, and as the latter stood with his hand on his heart, and bowed at the same time, the young lady was not left in doubt as to who was the originator of the address. Paddy was remarkably good-looking and tall for his age, and the young lady was in no way displeased, and replied that her name was Rosalie, and that she was her father's only daughter. She had had two brothers, both of whom had been carried away by the conscription. One had been killed in a battle with the Austrians, and the other was still serving in the ranks, though he ought long ago to have been promoted.

"Ah! the cruel fighting," she added; "our rulers take away those we love best, and care not what becomes of them, or of the hearts they break, and bring with sorrow to the grave."

Rosalie soon recovered herself, and, wiping her eyes, told the midshipmen that she would come back again when they had eaten their supper, and would in the meantime try and devise some means to enable them to make their escape while they were travelling.

"She's a sweet, pretty little girl," observed O'Grady, after Rosalie had gone. "She'll help us if she can, and do you know I think that she is a Protestant, for I don't see any pictures of saints and such-like figures stuck about the walls as we do in most other French houses?"

"It is possible; but what difference can that make to you?" asked Paul.

"Why, you see, Gerrard, I have fallen in love with her, and I'm thinking that if she helps us to make our escape, when the war is over, I'll come back and ask her to marry me."

Paul laughed at his friend's resolve. It was not at all an uncommon one for midshipmen in those days to entertain, whatever may be the case at present. They enjoyed their meal, and agreed that they had not eaten anything half so good as the dishes they were discussing for many a long day. Rosalie came back in about an hour. She said that she had been thinking over the matter ever since, and talking it over with an old aunt—a very wise woman, fertile in resources of all sorts. She advised that the young Englishmen should pretend to be sick, and that if the captain consented to leave them behind, so much the better; but if not, and, as was most probable, he insisted on their walking on as before, they should lag behind, and limp on till they came to a certain spot which she described. They would rise for some time, till the road led along the side of a wooded height, with cliffs on one side, and a steep, sloping, brushwood—covered bank on the other, with a stream far down in the valley below. There was a peculiar white stone at the side of the road, on which they were to sit to pretend to rest themselves. If they could manage to slip behind the stone for an instant, they might roll and scramble down the bank to a considerable distance before they were discovered. They were then to make their way through the brushwood and to cross the stream, which was fordable, when they would find another road, invisible from the one above. They were to run along it to the right, till they came to an old hollow tree, in which they were to hide themselves, unless they were overtaken by a covered cart, driven by a man in white. He would slacken his speed, and they were to jump in immediately without a word, and be covered up, while the cart would drive on. They would be conveyed to the house of some friends to the English, with whom they would remain till the search for them had ceased, when they would be able to make their escape to the coast in disguise. After that, they must manage as best they could to get across the Channel.

"The first part is easy enough, if Miss Rosalie would give us the loan of a little white paint or chalk," observed O'Grady; "but, faith, the rest of the business is rather ticklish, though there's nothing like trying, and we shall have some fun for our money at all events."

"I wish that Reuben Cole could manage to run with us. He'd go fast enough if Miss Rosalie's friends would take care of him," remarked Paul.

"You can but ask her," said O'Grady. "Tell her that he's been with you ever since you came to sea, and that you can't be separated from him."

Rosalie heard all Paul had to say, and promised that she would try to arrange matters as he wished. Paul then described Reuben, and gave Rosalie a slip of paper, on which he wrote: "Follow the bearer, and come to us." Though Reuben was no great scholar, he hoped that he might be able to read this.

"Tell her she's an angel," exclaimed O'Grady, as Rosalie took the paper. "I wish that I could speak French, to say it myself;

but I'll set to work and learn at once. Ask her if she'll teach me."

Rosalie laughed, and replied that she thought the young Irishman would prove an apt scholar, though she could not understand how, under the circumstances, she could manage to do as he proposed.

"Och! but I've a mighty great mind to tell her at once all I intend to do, and just clinch the matter," cried Paddy; but Paul wouldn't undertake to translate for him, and advised him to restrain his feelings for the present.

It was getting near midnight, when a gentle rap was heard at the door, and Reuben poked in his head. The arrangements which had been made were soon explained to him, and he undertook to feign lameness and to drop behind and roll down the bank as they were to do.

"You sees, young gentlemen, if they goes in chase of me, that'll give you a better chance of getting off. If they catches me, there'll be no great harm done; they won't get me to fight for them, that I'll tell them, and if I get off scot free, why there's little doubt but that I'll be able to lend you a hand in getting to the coast, and crossing the water afterwards."

The arrangements being made, Reuben stole down to rejoin the other seamen, and the midshipmen then coiling themselves up in their blankets in different corners of the room, resolved to remain there till summoned in the morning, were soon asleep.

When their guards appeared, they made signs that they could not move, O'Grady singing out, "Medecin, medecin," by which he wished to intimate that he wanted physic, and they thought that he asked for a doctor. In spite, however, of all their remonstrances, they were compelled to get up and dress by sundry applications of a scabbard.

They found a breakfast prepared for them in the hall, though they had but a few minutes allowed them to consume it before they were driven on through the town to join the rest of the prisoners, no time being allowed them to bid farewell to Rosalie and her father. She, indeed, had wisely kept out of their way to prevent any suspicion. They limped along, looking as woe-begone as they could, though their hearts were in no way sad. Their only regret was, that they must part from Devereux and their captain, but they consoled themselves by believing that they could report where they were, and thus manage to get them exchanged.

"We are nearing the spot," said Paul. "This is the scenery Rosalie described, and this must be the hill. I hope Reuben understands what he is to do. Ah! there is the stone. Come, let us sit down."

They made signs to the last guard that they would follow. Believing that they were ill he allowed them to remain. They saw that Reuben was watching them.

"We mustn't stay long, though," said O'Grady.

"No; now's the time. Over we go," cried Paul; and suiting the action to the word, over he rolled, followed by O'Grady, and both were speedily hid from sight in the brushwood.

# CHAPTER NINE

The two midshipmen rolled away down the hill at a very rapid rate, and then, getting on their feet, rushed on through the brushwood, not minding how much they tore their clothes, and running no little risk of scratching out their eyes. As yet no shouts had reached their ears, which they knew would have been the case had their flight been discovered. They had got so far that they did not mind speaking, and were congratulating each other on escaping so well, when they heard several voices cry out, and some shots fired in rapid succession.

"That must be Reuben," cried Paul. "Oh, I hope that they haven't hit him."

"The first shot did not, or they wouldn't have fired others, and they wouldn't have fired at all had he not got to some distance before they shouted, on discovering that he had escaped," observed O'Grady. "However, as we cannot help him, we must push on, or we shall be retaken ourselves."

Paul saw that his friend was right, though he did not like the idea, as he thought it, of deserting Reuben.

"If he does not join us, we must send or come and look for him. He is not likely to leave the shelter of the wood,"

W. H. G. Kingston

he observed.

They spoke as they ran on, verging always to the right. They forded the shallow though rapid stream, found the road, and continued their flight, till they came to the remarkable old tree which had been described to them. There was an entrance on one side into the interior.

"Up, up, Gerrard!" said O'Grady. "If we are pursued, they are certain to look in here, but I see a cavity, some way up, into which we may get, and the soldiers might look in and still not find us."

They climbed up. There was not room for both in one hole. Fortunately Paul found another, and there they sat, as O'Grady said, like owls in their nests, waiting for the cart. They heard voices—men shouting to each other. They must be the soldiers still searching for them. They came nearer and nearer. There was a laugh and an oath. Paul heard a man say, "Ah! they must be in there—just the place for them to hide in."

He gave up all for lost. He drew in his legs, shut his eyes, and coiled himself up in as small a space as possible, hoping that O'Grady would do the same. He heard a man stop and lean against the tree, as if looking in. Fortunately a cloud at that moment passed across the sun, and prevented the man from seeing the holes.

"No, they are not here—they must have gone the other way," shouted the soldier.

"Then the sailor must have gone with them. It is strange— they must have known the country. Such a thing could not have happened at any other spot on the road."

"Very glad that we did not miss the opportunity," thought Paul. "Reuben, too, has not yet been taken—that's a comfort."

They waited and waited. They were afraid to get out of their holes, lest their enemies should still be looking for them. At length, the wheels of a cart were heard in the distance. Paul, by climbing a little higher, could look out. It was a covered cart, driven by a man in white.

"All right," he said; "we must be prepared to jump in."

The cart came slower. They slid down, and a quick pair of eyes alone could have detected them as they ran across the road, and, without a word, leaped into the cart. The driver did not even look behind him, but, as soon as he heard Paul whisper *Nous sommes ici*, he lashed his horse and drove on faster than ever.

"Miss Rosalie is a brick," whispered O'Grady, as he and Paul crept under some sheepskins which the cart contained. "Hasn't she done the thing beautifully?"

They drove on rapidly for many miles. Of course they had not the slightest notion where they were going. Paul was chiefly anxious about Reuben, while O'Grady feared, as they were going so far away, that they might not meet Rosalie. Still, they were not very unhappy, though rather hot under the sheepskins. They would, however, have gone through greater inconvenience for the sake of gaining their liberty. At last, passing through a forest, the trees of which had lost most of their branches, lopped off for firewood, they reached an old grey chateau, with high pointed slate roof, and no end of towers and turrets, and gable ends, and excrescences of all sorts. The cart drove into a paved court-yard, on two sides of which were outhouses or offices. The entrance-gate was then shut, and the driver backed the cart against a small door on

W. H. G. Kingston

one side. Not a soul appeared, and he did not shout for any one to come and help him. Pulling out the skins, he whispered, *Descendez, mes amis—vite, vite*; and Paul, pulling O'Grady by the arm, they jumped out, still covered by the skins, and ran through the open door. Had any curious eyes been looking out of any of the windows of the chateau, they could scarcely have been seen. They were in a passage, leading on one side to a sort of store-room, but the man told them to turn to the left, and to go on till they came to a door, where they were to wait till some one came to let them through.

"What fun," whispered O'Grady. "I delight in an adventure, and this will prove one and no mistake. We shall have some old woman coming and shutting us up in an apple-loft or a ghost-haunted chamber, or some place of that sort. It may be weeks before we get to the coast, and something new turning up every day. I wouldn't have missed it for anything."

He was running on in this style when the door opened, and Miss Rosalie herself appeared, with a countenance which showed how pleased she felt at the success of her arrangements. O'Grady was, at first, quite taken aback at seeing her, and then very nearly bestowed a kiss and an embrace on her in the exuberance of his delight. Whether she would have found great fault with him it is impossible to say; she merely said, "I must not stop to listen here to what you have to tell me—but come along to where we shall not be interrupted, and then I will gladly hear all that has happened."

She forthwith led them up by a winding stair to the top of one of the towers, where there was a small room with very narrow windows.

"There you will be safe enough," she remarked, "for if you were to look out of the casement, no one could see you from below, and it will be pleasanter than being shut up in a cellar or a lumber-room, where, if anybody came to search the chateau, they would be sure to look for you. See, too," she added, "there are further means of hiding yourselves—for we cannot be too cautious in these sad times. Here is a panel. It slides on one side, and within you will find a ladder, which leads to a space between the ceiling and the roof. You might there manage to exist for some days—not very pleasantly, but securely at all events."

The ceiling was pointed the shape of the roof, and it was difficult to suppose that there could be space sufficient between the two to admit a person. Rosalie, however, pulled aside the panel and showed the ladder, that there might be no mistake. She charged them also not to leave anything about which might betray them. "If I were to tell you all we have gone through, you would not be surprised at my caution," she remarked.

She then inquired about the sailor they hoped would have accompanied them. Paul told her that he believed Reuben had escaped from the guards, and was probably still lurking about in the same neighbourhood.

"We will send and try to find him," she answered at once. "Our faithful old servant will undertake the work. Here, write on a slip of paper that he is to follow the bearer and do whatever he is told. It is important to find him before night, as he might otherwise, growing hungry, come out of his hiding-place in search of food, and be discovered. I will tell our worthy Jaques to sing out his name as he drives along, and perhaps that may draw him from his lair. What is it?"

Paul told her. "Oh, that is a very good name to pronounce,— Rubicole! Rubicole! Jaques can cry out that very well."

So away she went, leaving the midshipmen to their own reflections—O'Grady more in love than ever. As they had nothing to do, they looked through the window, and saw the cart which had brought them driving rapidly away. Rosalie came back soon afterwards with a very nice dinner on a tray. She said that she alone would attend on them, for though she could safely trust the people in the house, the fewer who knew that they were there the better. The chateau, she told them, belonged to her uncle, a Royalist, a fine old gentleman, who had nearly lost his life in the Revolution. She had come over that day, as had previously been arranged, to attend on her uncle, who was ill, and would, therefore, be unable to see them, but hoped to do so before their departure. She concluded that they were in no great hurry to be off.

"Not in the slightest, tell her," exclaimed O'Grady, when Paul explained what she had said: "we are as happy as bees in a sugar-bason."

Rosalie did not object to stay and talk with the midshipmen, but she had her uncle to attend on. She told them that she would close a door at the bottom of the turret steps; when opened, it would cause a small bell to ring in the room, and that the instant they should hear it, they were to retreat by the panel and take refuge in the roof. She again cautioned them not to leave anything in the room which might betray them; and having placed a jug of water, a bottle of wine, and some bread and cheese in the recess, she carefully brushed up the crumbs, and carried the tray with her down-stairs.

"Well, she is first-rate," cried O'Grady; "she's so sensible and pretty. I don't care who knows it—I say she'll make a capital wife."

"I dare say she will," said Paul. He did not think it prudent to make any further remark on the subject.

Having exhausted the subject of Miss Rosalie, and declared fully fifty times over that she was the most charming person alive, Paddy relapsed into silence. They waited hour after hour for the return of the cart, hoping that it might bring in Reuben. At last they rolled themselves up in their blankets and went to sleep. Rosalie had brought them in with pillows, and reminded them that they must drag the whole up with them into the roof, if they heard the bell ring. When Rosalie appeared the next morning, she said that Jaques had returned, but that he had seen nothing of the English sailor.

Several days passed by, and at last Rosalie said that her uncle would be well enough, she hoped, to visit them on the following day. They would have found their time pass somewhat heavily, had not she frequently visited them. She also brought them a French book, and, with it to assist him, Paul set to work to teach O'Grady French. Rosalie, when she came in, corrected his pronunciation, which was not always correct. O'Grady learnt very rapidly, and he declared that he thought it was a pity that they should not remain where they were till he was perfect.

"You see, Gerrard," he observed, "we are living here free of expense. It's very pleasant, and we are not idling our time."

Paul, however, who was not in love, though he thought Rosalie a very amiable young lady, insisted that it was their duty to get back to England as fast as they could. He also wished to see his mother and sisters, and to put them out of their anxiety about him. At last he told O'Grady that he wouldn't help him any longer to learn French if he did not put such foolish notions out of his head, and that he was very sure without him he would never get on. Paddy had sense enough to see that he must knock under, and that Paul was, in reality, the better man of the two. They were to see *Mon Oncle*, as Rosalie always called the owner of the chateau, on the following day. They were not allowed to have a light in the turret, lest it should betray them; so, as soon as it was dark, they went to sleep. The weather outside was unpleasant, for it was blowing and raining hard. They had not long coiled themselves up in their respective corners, when there was a loud knocking at the chief door of the chateau, the noise resounding through the passages up to their turret.

"Some benighted travellers seeking shelter from the storm," observed O'Grady. "I am glad that we are not out going across country in such a night as this."

There was a pause, and again a loud knocking.

"Old Jaques is in no hurry to let in the strangers," observed Paul. "He suspects that these are not friends; we must keep our eyes open. Remember what Rosalie told us."

"Ay, ay, mate, I am not likely to forget what she says," answered Paddy, who had not quite got over his feeling of annoyance with Paul.

They listened attentively. Those outside were at length admitted, they fancied; but, further than that, they could make out nothing. They waited all ready to jump up and run into their hiding-place, for they were persuaded that this evening visit had reference to them. They heard doors slamming and strange sounds produced by the blast rushing through the passages and windows.

"Yes, I am certain that there is a search going on in the house," whispered O'Grady. "I hope *Mon Oncle* won't get into a scrape on our account, or dear Rosalie," (he had got to call her "dear" by this time.) "Hark! how the wind roars and whistles."

There was a door banged not far from the foot of the stairs; it made the whole tower shake. They were silent for a minute, when a bell tinkled. Before it had ceased to vibrate, the midshipmen had started up, and, seizing their bed-clothes, had rushed to the panel. They started through and closed it behind them, but only just in time, for the door opened as the panel closed. What midshipmen were ever in a more delightful situation? They were not frightened a bit, and only wished that they could find some crevice through which they could get a look at the intruders, and O'Grady regretted that they had not a brace or two of pistols with which they could shoot them. They sprang up the ladder only as cats or midshipmen could do, and had placed themselves on the roof, when they heard the clank of sabres and spurs, and the tread of heavy men, and a gleam of light came through a crevice in the wooden ceiling. It was close to Paul's head, and looking down he saw three gendarmes peering round and round the room. They were evidently at fault, however. Behind them stood old Jaques with a lantern from which he sent the light into every corner of the room. There was a book on the table, and a chair near it.

"Who reads here?" asked one of the men.

"My young mistress, of course," answered Jaques, promptly.

"She said just now that she was here to attend on her uncle," remarked the gendarmes.

"So she is, and good care she takes of the old gentleman; but he sleeps sometimes, so I relieve her," returned Jaques. "She is fond of solitude."

"That is a pity; I should like to keep her company," said the gendarme, with a grin, which made O'Grady clench his fist, and Jaques look indignant. The man put the book under his arm, and having been unable to discover anything apparently, ordered his companions to fallow him down-stairs. O'Grady was for descending into the room at once from their uncomfortable position; but Paul held him back, observing that they had not heard the door at the foot of the stairs shut, and that they might easily be surprised. He advised that they should as noiselessly as possible take their bed-clothes up to the roof, and sleep there, however uncomfortable it might be to do so.

"Not for our own sakes alone, but for that of Rosalie and *Mon Oncle*, we are bound in honour to do so."

That settled the question—fortunately—for before long the door opened softly, and one of the gendarmes crept in on tip-toe. He crept round and round the room with a lantern in his hand, like a terrier hunting for a rat which he is sure has his hole thereabouts. O'Grady had gone to sleep, and had begun to snore. Happily he had ceased just as the man appeared.

Paul was afraid that he would begin again, and he dared not touch him lest he should cry out. He leaned over towards him till he could reach his ear, and then whispered, "Don't stir, for your life!"

O'Grady pressed his hand to show that he heard. He moved his head back to the chink. Had he made any noise, the storm would have prevented its being heard. The gendarme was not yet satisfied. He ran his sword into every hole and crevice he could find, and attacked several of the panels. For the first time Paul began to fear that they should be discovered. As yet he had passed over the moving panel. He began to grind his teeth in a rage, and to utter numerous "*sacres*" and other uncouth oaths, and at last made a furious dig close to the panel. His weapon, however, instead of going through the wood, encountered a mass of stone, and broke short off. The accident increased his rage, and produced numerous additional *sacres*, and, which was of more consequence, made him trudge down-stairs again, convinced that there was no hole in which even a rat could be concealed. He slammed the door after him; but Paul, suspecting that this might be a trick, persuaded O'Grady to remain where they were.

The night passed on, and both midshipmen fell asleep. When they awoke they saw that daylight was streaming full into the room below them, though it was dark up in the roof; still they wisely would not stir, for they felt sure that, as soon as the gendarmes were fairly away, Rosalie would come to them and bring them their breakfast.

"I hope she may," observed Paddy, "for I am very peckish."

Paul thought that he could not be so very desperately in love.

At last they heard the tramp of horses' hoofs, and about a quarter of an hour afterwards, though they thought it much longer, Rosalie appeared with a tray, with coffee, and eggs, and bread, and other substantial fare. They were down the ladder in a twinkling, and warmly expressing their thanks. They did not require much pressing to set to; indeed, O'Grady had begun to cast ravenous glances at the viands alternately, with affectionate ones towards her, while Paul was translating what he desired him to say. She looked very pale, and told them that she had been very anxious, though the gendarmes had come, not to look for them, but for a political criminal, a royalist of rank, who had been concealed in the chateau, but had fortunately escaped. About noon she came back with a very nice old gentleman, a perfect picture of a French man of rank of the old school—buckles, knee-breeches, flowered waistcoat, bag, wig, and all. She introduced him as *Mon Oncle*. He at once began to talk with Paul, and soon became communicative.

"I once had two brave boys," he said. "I have lost both of them. One perished at sea; the other has been desperately wounded fighting in a cause he detests; yet he was dragged away without the power of escaping. I scarcely expect to see him again; but if he recovers, my prayer is that he may be taken prisoner, for I am sure that he will be kindly treated by the brave English people. That is one of the reasons that I desire to help you. I have other reasons. One is, that I hope through the English the cause I espouse may triumph. I am sorry to say, however, that my chateau is no longer a safe abode for you. It will be subject to frequent visits from the police, and I myself may be dragged away with all my domestics, when you must either starve or be discovered."

The midshipmen agreed to the wisdom of this, and Paul, after thanking the old gentleman again and again for the refuge he had afforded them, said that they thought with him that it would be wise for them to start immediately on their journey to the north. They had consulted with Rosalie how they were to proceed, and they thought with her that they might make their way dressed as country lads from some place in the south of France where a patois was spoken scarcely known in the north; that he, Paul, was to act as spokesman, and that O'Grady was to pretend to be deaf and dumb. As a reason for their journey, Paul was to state that their father was a sailor, and that they had heard he was lying wounded at some place on the coast, and wanted to see them before he died.

This story, it must be understood, was concocted by Miss Rosalie, whose active fingers had been engaged night and day for nearly a week in making the costumes for the two midshipmen. They had reason to be thankful to her. The day was spent in preparing for the journey. The clothes fitted beautifully. Rosalie said that she did not know she was so good a tailor. The difficulty was to make them look sufficiently worn. Rosalie suggested, however, that they were to be the grandsons of a small farmer of a respectable class, by whom they had been brought up, and that therefore they would be well clothed, with some little money in their pockets. She had also fastened up in two belts some gold and silver coins, all the little money she possessed, and she told them that they must take it and repay her when they could. O'Grady, who fully intended to come back, had no hesitation about accepting the money, but Paul wished that they could manage without it; however, he yielded when the former observed, "You don't suppose that we can get on without money in France more than in any other country, and if we intend to starve we had better have remained prisoners."

In the afternoon Jaques drove the cart into the court-yard, and backed it up to the door by which they had entered. Rosalie came up to the midshipmen; her eyes were red with crying; still she looked very pretty.

"I have come to tell you that it is time for you to go; you will follow out the directions you have received as nearly as possible."

It had been arranged that they should go on in the cart till dark, and then walk as far as they could on foot during the night, concealing themselves in some secluded spot in the day-time. If they were discovered, they were to plead fatigue for resting; they were not to court observation, though they were not to dread it, if it could not be avoided. They were, however, on no account to enter a town, by night or by day, if they could help it. No one, indeed, could have arranged a more perfect plan than Miss Rosalie had done. There's nothing like the wits of an honest clear-sighted woman when people are in trouble, to get them out of it.

Rosalie had provided them with wallets well filled with food, so that they need not for some days stop at any village to procure food—not, indeed, till they were well to the north of the line of road the Brest prisoners passed.

Both the midshipmen were very, very sorry at having to part from Rosalie, and O'Grady felt more in love with her than ever; still they must be away. Her uncle gave them a kind embrace, and she accompanied them down-stairs, and kissing them both as if they were young brothers going to school, hurried them into the cart. It was loaded with sacks of corn going to the mill to be ground, with several span new sacks to fill with flour. There was a clear space formed by placing two sacks across two others, with the empty sacks thrown over the inner end. Into this they crept. They could look out from behind the loose sacks, and as the cart drove out of the court-yard they could see Rosalie watching them with her apron to her eyes. They drove rapidly on, though more than once Jaques stopped and talked to some one, and then on he went at the same pace as before. One man asked for a lift, but he laughed and said, that the cart was already laden heavily enough with so many sacks of wheat, and that it would break down if a burly fellow like the speaker were to get into it, or the horse would refuse to go. It was getting dark, but the sky was clear, and as they could see the stars by which to steer, they had little doubt that they should find their way. Jaques drew up in a solitary spot a little off the read.

"Farewell, young gentlemen, farewell!" he said, as he helped them to get from under the sacks: "may you reach your native land in safety. Go straight along that road; you will make good way before the morning. I wish that I could go further with you, but I dare not. Farewell, farewell!" Saying this, he shook them by the hand, and giving them a gentle shove on in the direction they were to take, as if his heart longed to go with them, he jumped into the cart and drove rapidly away.

They now felt for the first time how helpless they were, and the difficulty of their undertaking; but they were brave lads, and quickly again plucked up courage. They had been provided with sticks, and trudged on boldly. Mile after mile of dusty road, up and down hill, and along dead flats, were traversed.

"It will make us sleep all the sounder," observed O'Grady, who had a happy facility for making the best of everything. "If we were at sea now we should have to be pacing the deck with a cold breeze in our teeth, and maybe an occasional salt shower-bath."

Paul agreed, though they were not sorry when daylight came and warned them to look out for a resting-place. They saw a forest some way from the high road, and, going into it, before long discovered numerous piles of wood prepared for burning.

"They are not likely to be removed for some time," observed O'Grady; "if they do, they will begin on the outer ones, and we shall have time to decamp. Let's make ourselves some nests inside; see, there is plenty of dry grass, and we shall sleep as comfortable as on beds of down."

By removing some of the logs the work was easily accomplished, and no one outside would have observed what they had done. They crept in, and were very soon fast asleep. They awoke perfectly rested, and prepared to resume their journey; but on looking out they found that it was not much past noon, and that they had the greater part of the day to

W. H. G. Kingston

wait. This they did not at all like. O'Grady was for pushing on in spite of their first resolutions; Paul wished to remain patiently till the evening. No one had come to remove the wood, so that they were not likely to be disturbed. As they were hungry they ate some dinner, emptying their bottle of wine, and then tried to go to sleep again—not a difficult task for midshipmen.

Paul, after some time, was awoke by hearing some one singing. He touched O'Grady's arm. They listened. The words were English, and they both had an idea that they knew the voice. The singer appeared to be near, and employed in removing the logs of wood. Paul slowly lifted up his head. A shout and an expression indicative of astonishment escaped from the singer, who stood, like one transfixed, gazing at Paul. The shout made O'Grady lift up his head, and they had ample time to contemplate the strange figure before them. His dress was of the most extraordinary patchwork, though blue and white predominated. On his head, instead of a hat, he wore a wisp of straw, secured by a handkerchief; his feet were also protected by wisps of straw, and round his waist he wore a belt with an axe stuck in it. Altogether, he did not look like a man possessed with much of this world's wealth. The midshipmen looked at him, and he looked at the midshipmen, for a minute or more without speaking.

"It is—no it isn't—yes it is!" exclaimed the man at length. "Why, young gentlemen, is it really you? you looks so transmogrified, I for one shouldn't have known you!"

"What, Reuben Cole, is it really you? I may ask," cried Paul, springing out of his lair, and shaking him by the hand, followed by O'Grady. "This is a fortunate meeting."

"Why, that's as it may turn out; but how did you come to

look like that?"

Paul told him, and then put the same question to him.

"Why, do ye see, when I got away from our Jennydams, I found a hole in the hillside close under where I jumped off the road. Thinks I to myself, if I tumbles in here, they'll all go pelting away down the hill through the wood, leaving me snug; and so they did. I heard them halloing, and cursing, and swearing at one another, and I all the time felt just like an old fox in his cover till they'd gone away on their road wondering where I'd gone. I then started up and ran down the hill just in time to see a cart driven by a man in white. I shouted, but he didn't hear me, and so I hoped it would be all right for you, at all events. Then I went back to my hole, and thinks I to myself, if I goes wandering about in this guise I'll sure to be taken: so I remembers that I'd got in my pocket the housewife my old mother gave me, and which the rascally privateer's-men hadn't stolen; so out I takes it and sets to work to make up my clothes in a new fashion. I couldn't make myself into a mounseer—little or big—by no manner of means, so I just transmogrified my clothes as you see them, that I mightn't be like a runaway prisoner. It took me two days before I was fit to be seen—pretty smart work; and that's how the servant the old gentleman sent out missed me. At last I set out for the sea; but I was very hungry, and I can't say if I'd fallen in with a hen-roost what I'd have done. I got some nuts and fruit though, enough to keep body and soul together. Three days I wandered on, when I found myself in this very wood. I was getting wickedly hungry, and I was thinking I must go out and beg, when I sees a cart and a man coming along, so I up and axes him quite civilly if he'd a bit of a dinner left for a poor fellow. I was taken all aback with astonishment when he speaks to me in English, and tells me that he'd been some months in a prison across the Channel, and knows our lingo, and that he was treated so kindly that

W. H. G. Kingston

he'd sworn he'd never bear arms against us again, if he could help it. With that he gives me some bread and cheese and wine, and when his day's work was over he takes me to his house, at the borders of the forest, near a village. As I wouldn't eat the bread of idleness, I offered to help him, and as I can handle an axe with most men, I have been working away ever since as a wood-cutter. Now I know that if you'll come with me to his cottage, he'll gladly give you lodging and food as long as you like to stay, and then, of course, I must pack up and be off with you."

The midshipmen told Reuben how glad they were to find him, though they agreed that by his travelling on with them their difficulties would be somewhat increased, as they were puzzled to know what character he could assume. He was so thoroughly the English sailor that even his very walk would betray him.

He acknowledged this; but after scratching his head for five minutes, and giving sundry tugs at his rather curious-looking breeches, he exclaimed: "I've hit it. I'll go on crutches and follow in your wake; when no one is looking I'll make play, and I'll keep up with you, I'll warrant. If I'm axed who I am, I'll pretend that I'm a 'Talian, or some other furriner, who can't speak the French lingo, and just make all sorts of gabblifications. Just you leave it to me, young gentlemen, if you'll let me come with you."

Though there was considerable risk in the plan, the midshipmen could think of no other. They agreed to go to the wood-cutter's hut, and if, after talking the matter over, they could not improve on Reuben's plan, to start the following evening. Having assisted him to load his cart, they set forward at once. The path led them for most of the way through the forest. It was still broad daylight when they approached the cottage. It stood at the edge of a green, on which a number of villagers were seen collected. They were themselves perceived before they had time to retreat, which it would have been wise for them, they felt, to do.

"Let us put a bold face on the matter and go forward!" exclaimed O'Grady. "Reuben, go on with the cart; we had better have nothing to say to you at present."

They at once walked on towards the villagers without exhibiting any marks of hesitation. Reuben looked after them with as indifferent an air as he could assume, as he drove his cart up to the woodman's cottage.

"I see a high road; let us turn towards it, and walk along it as if we were not going to stop at the village," observed Paul; "we may thus avoid questions, and we may come back to the wood-cutter's when it is dark; Reuben will prepare him for our appearance."

O'Grady agreed to this plan, and they were walking along pretty briskly, hoping to pass an auberge, or inn, at the side of the road, when the aubergiste, or inn-keeper, who happened to be in very good humour after his evening potations, caught sight of them, and shouted out, "Come in, come in, mes garcons! there is no other auberge in the place, and you would not pass by the house of Francois le Gros!" And he patted his well-stuffed-out ribs, for there are fat Frenchmen as well as fat Englishmen.

Thus appealed to, the midshipmen thought it wiser to go up to the man, and Paul told him that as they had very little money, they preferred stopping out at night when the weather was fine.

"That will never do," cried honest Francois. "Tell me all about yourselves, and you shall have board and lodging free.

Numerous great people stop here, and so does the diligence, and as I am patronised by all around, I can afford at times to help young wayfarers like yourselves."

Paul, anxious especially to avoid so public a place as an inn, made more excuses. While he was speaking the landlord looked very hard at him. Several other villagers did the same.

"Why, you do not look very like what you say you are!" he exclaimed. "Come nearer, and let me have a better look at you."

"Thank you," said Paul; "if you don't believe me, I won't ask you to do so; but let us go on, and we will not trouble you."

This speech did not satisfy the landlord, and several disagreeable remarks were made by the bystanders. Altogether, matters were looking very bad, when the attention of the villagers was called off by the sound of the loud cracks of whips, the tramping of horses, the rumbling of wheels, and the appearance of a cloud of dust, out of which emerged a huge lumbering vehicle with a vast hood in front, a long big body covered with boxes and baskets, and drawn by six horses, governed by two postillions dressed in huge jack boots, cocked hats, and gold-laced coats. They dashed up to the inn with as much clatter and noise as they could make. More of the villagers collected; and while the horses were being brought out, and the landlord was engaged in attending to his customers, O'Grady whispered to Paul that he thought they might possibly slip out of the crowd unobserved; and while some of the villagers had to move out of the way of the released horses, they moved round on the other side of the diligence and walked rapidly along the road.

At that moment Francois had come out with a jug of wine for

an old gentleman in the inside, and as he was returning, his eye fell on the fugitives. His suspicions now increased; he shouted to some of his cronies to make chase and bring them back. As the villagers were making holiday and had nothing to do, a dozen or more set off in chase.

"I wish that we hadn't tried to get away," said Paul. "Let's go back boldly, and say that we hoped to get on to the next village; but as they are determined to keep us, we will stay with them."

They, however, had barely time to turn before their pursuers were upon them; and in no very happy state of mind they were dragged back to the village. They came in sight of the inn just as the diligence had driven off. One passenger had remained behind, who stood watching them with a look of considerable interest while the landlord was describing to him how they had made their appearance, and expressing his opinion that they were no better than they should be.

# CHAPTER TEN

Paul and O'Grady, as they were dragged back by the villagers to the inn, felt certain that their true character would be discovered, and that they would be sent to prison. Paul was especially unhappy under the belief that his bad French had betrayed him. He wished that he could give Reuben warning to keep out of the way of the meddling villagers, lest he also should be captured. Still, he was not a lad to give in, and he determined to play the part he had assumed as long as he could. When the villagers saw Francois, they shouted out to him that they had got the young rogues fast enough. Paul at once began to expostulate with the inn-keeper, and, with a volubility which did him credit, gave the whole story which had been arranged by Rosalie. The traveller, who had retired on one side, but had remained near enough to hear what Paul said, now stepped forward, exclaiming, "Of course—all they say is true. I know all about them. Their grandfather is a most estimable man—a tenant of my maternal uncle, the Sieur Caudbec. I saw him when last I was in the south of France, and these lads, I think I saw them—yes, surely I know both of them. You know me, the son of the Baron de Montauban—one who was always kind to the poor, and a friend of true liberty."

Paul glanced at the speaker; he was very young. He looked again. There could be no doubt about it. Though somewhat disguised by his travelling costume and civilian's dress, there stood before him Alphonse Montauban. He ran forward and took Alphonse's hand, not to shake it, however, but, remembering their supposed relative ranks, to put it to his lips. O'Grady, though not understanding what had been said, and wondering why he did so, followed his example.

"Come, worthy Francois," said Alphonse; "though I had intended to proceed across the country, I will rest here to-night; and as I take an interest in the family of these lads, they shall spend the evening with me, and live at my cost. Let a good supper be prepared for us all, and, mark you, a bottle of your best wine."

Saying this, Alphonse led the way into the inn. He stopped at the door, however, and taking some money out of his purse, handed it to the landlord, saying, "Let some of these honest people here, after their quick run, have wherewithal to drink my health."

Alphonse, with considerable dignity, walked into a private room in the inn, and taking a chair, beckoned to the seeming peasant lads to sit near him, while the landlord received his orders for supper. As soon as Francois had retired, he burst into a fit of laughter, and, jumping up, shook the midshipmen warmly by the hand, and begged them to tell him how they came to be there. They gave him, as rapidly as they could, an account of their adventures.

"And do you not know the name of the old gentleman, 'mon oncle,' as you call him, and that of the chateau? But I do. He is my dear father, and that pretty little Rosalie is my very sweet cousin. The story is just such as I could have supposed she would have invented. And they think me dead. That is very natural, for when the *Alerte* escaped from the *Cerberus*, of course her people would have reported all on board their consort drowned. You will be surprised that I should not have reached home before this, but I had a long voyage, and as I had no wish to go to sea again, when I found on landing that it was not known I had escaped, I made the best of my way to the house of a relative near the coast, who provided me with clothing and funds, and I have only lately been able to commence my journey homeward. Now, however, I have a great inclination to turn back and to see you safely embarked to cross the Channel."

The English midshipmen would not, however, hear of his carrying out such a proposal. If caught, he would be more severely dealt with than they would, and they felt sure that, if they were cautious, they should be able to reach the coast by themselves. At length, Alphonse, seeing the wisdom of their arguments, and remembering his duty to his father, consented. He, however, said that he must first communicate with Reuben Cole, and let him know the road they had taken, that he might follow them. Alphonse had become quite an Englishman in his habits, and the three old friends spent a very pleasant evening. They were up before daylight, when Alphonse, slipping out, hurried off to the woodman's hut. The woodman and his new mate were on foot, and Reuben, having ascertained that the young strangers were at the auberge, was very doubtful how to proceed. He rubbed his eyes, and hitched away convulsively at his belt, when he saw Alphonse, for some minutes, before he dared believe his own eyes.

"Well, sir, things do come about curious," he exclaimed at last. "First I falls in with the young gentlemen, and then they falls in with you, just in time for you to save them from being packed off to prison."

As Alphonse knew that part of the country well, he was able to fix on a spot about three miles from the village, where he suggested that they and Reuben should lie concealed during the remainder of the day, and travel on, as they had proposed, at night. Having made these arrangements with Reuben, he returned to the auberge. Once more, after an early breakfast, the friends parted; Alphonse starting in a wonderfully old-fashioned *caleche* on two wheels, which gave promise of breaking down on its way to his father's chateau, and the midshipmen proceeding northward on their own sturdy legs. They fell in with Reuben Cole at the spot arranged on, and then all three, plunging into the forest, made themselves comfortable for the rest of the day. Night after night they travelled on. Sometimes they met people during the day, and either little notice was taken of them, or Paul easily answered the questions put to him. Reuben always had his crutches ready, and in a wonderfully quick time he was on his wooden leg, and hobbling along at a rate of a mile or so an hour, so that no one would have suspected that he had a long journey before him. The whole party were in very good spirits, for as they had found friends when they least expected it, and got out of difficulties when they thought that they were irretrievably lost, so they hoped that they might be equally fortunate another time. O'Grady declared that this life was that of a perpetual picnic. They generally took shelter during the day in a wood, or among hills, or in some deserted hut, or, like gipsies, under a hedge in some unfrequented district; or, if it rained, which was not very often, they got into some barn or shed in the outskirts of a hamlet; and twice they found caves into which they could creep, and several times some old ruins of castles or chateaux afforded them shelter. Their plan was to walk on till daybreak, and then O'Grady or Paul climbed a height or a tree, and surveyed the country ahead. If no habitations were to be seen, they pushed on further, and then took another survey of the country, to find a place of shelter for the day. When they required food, they generally first passed through a village, and then Paul went back, towards the evening to purchase it. As soon as he had bought it, they proceeded

W. H. G. Kingston

onward, so that, should the villagers have any suspicions, they were not likely to overtake them. They were now approaching the coast, and greater caution than ever was, of course, necessary. Their greatest difficulty, however, would be finding a fit boat, and getting away unperceived.

"I suppose that it will not be wrong to steal a boat," said Paul. "I don't quite like the thoughts of that."

O'Grady laughed, and remarked, "Why, you see, Gerrard, that necessity has no law. The owner of the boat will not be pleased to lose it, but then he is one of a nation with whom England is at war, and we have as much right to run away with his boat, as his countrymen have to keep us prisoners."

At length, after a long walk, at break of day the sea appeared in sight in the far distance, somewhere between Cherbourg and Barfleur. With beating hearts they went on. They could not resist the temptation of trying to ascertain whereabouts they were, and if there was a boat near which might serve their purpose. It might have been wiser had they, as usual, lain by during daylight. They walked on till they reached the top of a cliff overlooking the Channel. Across those waters was the land they so earnestly desired to reach. To the west a blue line of land stretched out into the sea. It was the promontory on which Cherbourg is situated. If they were able to get to the end, they would have much less distance to go by sea, and might, in the course of little more than a day, reach the Isle of Wight. The great point was to find a boat. Not one was in sight. It was a question whether they should go east or west in search of some fishing village, where they might find one. They carefully examined the coast, and as the sun rose in the sky, his beams lighting up the shore on the west, they fancied that they could make out some buildings in the distance. They at once turned in that direction. As they advanced, they found that they were not mistaken. Before concealing themselves, as they proposed doing, till night, they carefully reconnoitred the place from the cliff above it. There was a tower, and a small harbour with several small craft and boats at anchor in it, and two or three better sort of houses, besides numerous cottages and huts, and, at a little distance, a chateau of some pretension to architecture. They would have preferred a place where there were no gentlemen, who would naturally be less likely to believe their story. In other respects, they could not have desired to reach a more satisfactory locality. The cliffs appeared to be full of caves, in one of which they could lie hidden till night. They calculated that their food would last them for a couple of days, so that by husbanding it, even if their voyage were prolonged, they would have enough to support life. After hunting about for some time, they selected a cave half-way up the cliff, which sailors alone, and that not without some difficulty, could reach. The entrance was small, but there was ample room for them to lie down, and, what was of importance, they were not at all likely to be disturbed. As they had walked all night, and had been scrambling about all the morning, they were very tired, and directly they had taken some breakfast, they fell fast asleep. Paul was awoke after some time by the roaring sound of the waves dashing against the shore. He could see through the narrow opening dark clouds scouring across the sky, the rain descending in torrents, while ever and anon there came vivid flashes of lightning, followed by loud, rattling peals of thunder, which seemed to shake the very rock above their heads. The wind, too, blew fiercely, and the whole ocean before them was covered with white-topped billows. Reuben awoke and looked out. He came back and seated himself.

"Well, young gentlemen," he said quietly, "one thing is certain—we may make up our minds to have to remain here for some days to come. That sea won't go down in a hurry, and till it does, it will be hard to come at a French boat which

W. H. G. Kingston

will carry us safe across."

It was very evident that Reuben's observation was correct, yet it was very provoking to be thus, delayed when their expedition was so nearly, as they thought, brought to a happy conclusion. Two days passed, and the gale did not abate. It now, therefore, became necessary for Paul to go in search of provisions. His companions wished to accompany him, but he preferred going alone, and, if possible, to some inland village where there was less risk of their object being suspected. He set off early in the morning, and after walking for nearly three hours, he entered a village where he hoped to find both bread and meat. He could not get it, however, without being asked some rather searching questions. He replied promptly, that he had a brother with him, and that as they had still some way to go, and did not wish to delay on the road, he wished to lay in a stock of provisions at once. Fortunately there were three or four small shops in the place, at each of which he made some purchases, filling up his wallet at a farm-house, where he got a supply of eggs and a ham. Highly satisfied with the success of his undertaking, he took his way back to the cave. He had got within a couple of miles of the end of his journey, rather tired with the weight of the provisions he carried, when, on sitting down on a bank to rest, he saw that somebody was following him. He was puzzled what to do. Should he go on, his retreat would be discovered; if he stopped, he would be overtaken, and disagreeable questions might, perhaps, be asked of him. So he got up and went on again as fast as his legs could carry him. More than once, however, he looked back. The man he had seen was still behind. "He may, perhaps, only be going the same way that I am," thought Paul. "I will take the first turning I can find to the right or left, and he may then, perhaps, pass on and miss me."

The opportunity occurred sooner than he expected. The road

made several sharp turns. A narrow path, between high banks, led off to the right. He turned sharp into it, and by running rapidly along, was soon out of sight of the high road. He sat down and waited. No one came. He hoped that he had escaped his pursuer. At last he came cautiously out and looked about. No one was in sight. He walked on swiftly towards the cliff. He had to descend and then to mount again to reach the cave. His companions welcomed him on their own account as well as on his, for they were nearly starved. There was a stream, however, of good water close at hand, which had prevented them from suffering from thirst. They had now provisions to last them, they hoped, till they reached England. Paul had bought a tin saucepan, in which they could boil their eggs and make some soup, and as O'Grady had collected a supply of drift wood, they were able to cook their dinner and to enjoy the warmth of a fire. Altogether, they had not much reason to complain of their detention. Three more days passed, and the wind abating, the sea went down, and once more the calm ocean shone in the beams of the rising sun.

"Hurrah!" cried O'Grady; "we may sail to-night, and, if we're in luck and the wind holds, we may sight the shore of old England before the world is two days older."

The day passed very slowly away, as they had nothing with which to employ themselves. Fortunately, midshipmen, as O'Grady boasted, have a powerful knack of sleeping; and so they passed most of the time, in the intervals of their meals, lost in oblivion of all sublunary matters. As the shades of evening drew on, they roused up and were all animation. They had reconnoitred the path to the village, and found that it would be necessary to get down to the beach while there was still daylight to enable them to see their way. They hoped to find shelter in some boat-shed or out-house till the inhabitants had gone to bed. They went on cautiously, Paul

W. H. G. Kingston

in advance, lest they should meet any one; Reuben hobbling forward on his wooden leg and sticks. The lights in the village were being put out as they approached. "They are early people—so much the better for us," thought Paul. "We can easily seize a boat and get off."

The thought had scarcely passed through his mind, when a voice exclaimed, "Hallo! who goes there?"

"A friend," answered Paul.

"How many friends?" asked the man. "Let me see: two young lads and a lame man—answers the description. Come along with me, my friends, for I have more to say to you."

The two midshipmen and Reuben followed, much crest-fallen. They were in the hands of the police; of that there could be no doubt. Should they keep up their assumed characters, or acknowledge their true ones and brave the worst. They could not venture to speak to consult with each other. Paul thought that the best plan would be to keep silent till compelled to speak. He therefore got as near O'Grady as he could, and, pretending to stumble, put his finger against his friend's lips. O'Grady passed on the signal soon afterwards to Reuben. This matter arranged, they quietly followed their captor—O'Grady doing his best to hum a tune which he had heard Rosalie sing, and forgetting that he pretended to be deaf as well as dumb. There was still sufficient light for them to see that their captor was a gendarme, a discovery far from pleasant, as it led them to suppose that some person in authority was at the place, who might dispose of them in a somewhat summary manner. The man turned round once or twice, and told them, in no pleasant voice, to walk quicker, while he led the way to the chateau they had observed from the cliff. They found themselves standing before the chateau. It looked vast and gloomy in the dark. In another minute they were in a large hall in the presence of several persons, one of whom, a fierce-looking bearded official, inquired who they were, where they had come from, whither they were going.

Paul, with a fluency which surprised himself, narrated the story which had been arranged by Rosalie, O'Grady going through his part, pointing to his lips, and making inarticulate sounds, while Reuben imitated him in a way which seemed to try the gravity of those before whom he stood. Paul thought that all was going on smoothly, when he was considerably taken aback by seeing the officer laugh, and hearing him say in fair English:—

"You speak well, certainly, for one who has been so short a time in the country, but I should have understood you better had you spoken in English; and now I should like to know what your young friend here, and your lame companion, have to say for themselves. There's a salt-water look about them which makes me suspect that they know more about a ship than a vineyard."

The midshipmen saw that all further disguise was useless.

"Well, sir," exclaimed O'Grady, "if you know that we are English officers, you will understand that we were captured in a merchantman returning home invalided, and that as we were not on our parole, we had a full right to endeavour to make our escape."

"Granted, young sir," said the officer, blandly; "and not only had you a right to endeavour to escape, but you shall be allowed to proceed if you will answer me a few simple questions."

"What are they?" asked Paul and O'Grady, in a breath.

"Oh, a mere trifle," said the officer. "Who concealed you when you first made your escape? who assisted you to obtain your disguise? who invented your well-arranged story? and who forwarded you on your way?"

The midshipmen looked at each other.

"Shall I answer, Paddy?" asked Paul, eagerly.

"No, no, it's myself that will spake to the gentleman," exclaimed O'Grady, in that rich brogue in which an Irishman indulges when he is about to express a sentiment which comes up from the depth of his heart. "If your honour is under the belief that British officers are made up of such dirty ingredients that they would be capable of doing the vile, treacherous, ungrateful act you have insulted us by proposing, you never were more mistaken in your life. We are prisoners, and you have the power of doing whatever you like with us; but at least treat us with that respect which one gentleman has a right to demand from another."

The French officer started back with astonishment, not unmixed with anger. "How have I insulted you? How dare you address me in that style?" he asked.

"When one man asks another to do a dirty action, he insults him, and that's what you've asked us to do, Mounseer," exclaimed O'Grady, indignantly. "And just let me observe, that it is possible we may have had wits enough in our own heads to concoct the story we told you without being indebted to any man, woman, or child for it, especially when we were stimulated with the desire of getting out of this outlandish country, and being at you again; and as to the clothes, small blame to the people who sold them when they got honest gold coins in exchange."

"That story will not go down with me, young gentleman," observed the officer with a sneer. "However, enough of this trifling; we shall see in a few days whether you will alter your mind. Monsieur," he continued, turning to an elderly gentleman standing at the side of the hall, "we must have these persons locked up in one of your rooms. I beg that you will send your steward to point out a chamber from whence they cannot escape, and give us the trouble of again catching them."

"Monsieur," said the old gentleman, drawing himself up with an indignant air, "all the rooms are occupied; my chateau is not a prison, and I have no intention of allowing it to become one."

"Ho! ho!" cried the officer, pulling his moustache, and stamping with rage, "is that the line you have taken up? I was ordered to respect your chateau, and so I must; but take care, citoyen... However, sergeant, take them to the old tower; there is a room at the top of that where they will be safe enough. The wind and rain beat in a little, to be sure, but for any inconvenience they may suffer, they will be indebted to my friend here. Off with them!"

With scant ceremony the sergeant dragged them through the hall, Reuben stumping along after them on his wooden leg. They soon reached the tower, which was close to the little harbour. It was a very old building of three low stories, surrounded by sand, and the stones outside were so rough and so frequently displaced, that even by the light of the now risen moon it seemed as if there could not be much difficulty in climbing up to the top from the outside, or descend by the same means.

The sergeant shoved them on before him up a winding stair, which creaked and groaned at every step.

W. H. G. Kingston

"En avant, en avant!" cried the sergeant when O'Grady attempted to enter one of the lower chambers; and at length they found themselves in a room at the very top. The sergeant, grumblingly observing that they would not require food till the next morning, gave Reuben a push which nearly sent him sprawling into the middle of the chamber, closed the door with a slam, and locked and bolted it securely.

Reuben whipped off his wooden leg, and began flourishing it about and making passes at the door whence the sergeant had disappeared, exclaiming with a laugh, "Well, the beggars haven't found me out, and they'll be surprised at what a man with a timber toe can do!"

He tied it on again, however, very soon, for a heavy step was heard on the stairs, and they saw by the light of the moon that their own wallets and a jug of water were placed on the floor just inside the door.

"We have a friend somewhere, probably the old gentleman at the chateau, or we should not have got back those things," observed Paul; "so let's cheer up: we might have been much worse off."

All agreed to the truth of this remark, and, as they were hungry, took some supper, and then Paddy proposed that they should reconnoitre the premises.

The windows were very narrow, with an iron bar down the centre, so that it was impossible to get through them. There was not a particle of furniture in the room, nor anything which would serve for their beds.

"It isn't cold yet, and we must make ourselves as comfortable as we can in the least windy corner of the place," observed Paul.

"What do you think of trying to get away instead?" asked O'Grady.

"With all my heart!" answered Paul; "but what do you say to the moon? Should we not be seen?"

"It might help us, and it might betray us," said O'Grady. "Let us ask Cole."

Reuben said that he must have a look round from the windows, before he pronounced an opinion. The midshipmen helped him up to each of them in succession. He considered that in so bright a light they were nearly certain to be seen; but as the moon rose later every day they would have a fair chance of making good their escape. That they could not go at once was very evident, so they dusted a corner, and coiled themselves up to sleep. Daylight revealed the dirty condition of the room, and also the rotten state of the roof. Reuben pointed it out and remarked, "There, if we can't get through the windows, it will be hard if we do not make our way out by the roof. If they keep us here many days, we'll do it."

In the course of the morning a man appeared with a fresh jug of water, and some bread and cheese, and dried figs. It was better than ordinary prison fare, and as the man did not look very savage, Paul thought that he would try and move him to procure them something on which to sleep. He explained, in the most pathetic language he could command, the misery they had suffered, and begged for bedding of some sort. The man nodded, and returned in the evening with some bundles of straw.

"But there is nothing to cover us, and barely sufficient to keep us from the floor," observed Paul.

The man smiled, and replied, "To-morrow, perhaps, I may

find something of more use to you."

The following day he came again, loaded with a bundle of old sails. "Seamen have no reason to complain who can obtain such coverlids as these," he remarked, as he threw them down, and again left the room.

Each time that he went, they heard the sound of the door being locked and bolted. On undoing the sails they found that ropes were attached to them, and on examining these they were found to be sound and strong.

"That man is our friend, and depend on it these ropes were not sent in here by chance," observed O'Grady positively. "Very likely the old gentleman at the chateau sent him."

They were confirmed in the opinion that the rope was intended for use, by the appearance of the man, in the evening, to bring them a fresh supply of provisions.

"I've heard it said that it's no easy matter to keep English seamen in a cage when they have the will to get out," he remarked, as he turned round towards the door.

"Are we likely to be kept here long?" Paul asked.

"Until directions have been received from head-quarters, and as they are some way off, and yours is not a matter of importance, it may be a month or more," was the answer.

"He means to say that we may select our time for escaping," said Paul when the man had gone; "unless the rope was sent as a trap to tempt us to try and escape."

"Oh, they would not take that trouble," observed O'Grady. "If they had wished to treat us ill, they would have done so."

Three more days passed. The moon did not now rise till nearly midnight. This would give them ample time to get away out of sight of land before daylight. That evening their friend brought, with other provisions, a small keg of water, and a bottle of brandy, which he placed under the sails, and nodding, took his departure.

"No time to be lost," said O'Grady; "as soon as our guard has paid us his last visit, we must commence operations."

Just before dark a gendarme as usual put his head in at the door, looked round the room, and then stamped down-stairs again to a guard-room, in which it seemed that three or four men were stationed.

"There is no time to be lost, if it is to be done, gentlemen," exclaimed Reuben, stumping about the room as soon as the man was gone. "If we can't get through a window, I have marked two or three spots where we can through the roof, and we've rope enough to help us out either way. We have first to make up some packs to carry our stores."

It was important to do all this while daylight remained, now fast fading away. The packs were soon made, and the various lengths of rope fastened together. Reuben then, with the aid of his younger companions, climbed up to the roof, and, without difficulty, pulled down first the wooden lining, and then the slates, which he handed to them to avoid making a noise, and soon had a hole large enough for them to get through. The slates and ropes and their packs were then hid under the straw, in case any one should visit them before the hour of starting, not that such an event was likely to occur. They then threw themselves on their beds to be ready to pretend to be asleep at a moment's notice. The hours passed slowly. The night was calm; that was fortunate, or any little wind there was came from the south, which was better. They

W. H. G. Kingston

could hear a clock strike, that probably on the tower of the little church attached to the chateau. It was already nine o'clock, and they thought that all chance of interruption was over, when they heard steps on the stairs. The sergeant and a guard entered. He held a lantern in his hand. They lay trembling lest the light should be thrown upwards, and the hole in the roof be discovered.

"They seem to be asleep," observed the sergeant; "it is wonderful what power of sleeping these Englishmen possess. However, I must awake them. Rouse up, my boys, and understand that you are to march to-morrow for Paris at an early hour; but the worthy citizen Montauban has directed me to say that he will supply you with funds for your necessary maintenance, and to enable you to make your defence should you be accused, as he fears you may be, of being spies."

Paul started up on hearing this address, with as much terror as he could assume, considering that he had hoped in a few hours to be out of the reach of all French myrmidons of the law, and in a few words thanked the citizen Montauban for his kind purpose, adding that a French midshipman of the same name had long been his companion.

"Undoubtedly a nephew of citizen Montauban's, and his heir. The young man was long supposed to be lost; but he was here a short time back, and it is owing to the kind way he was treated by the English, that the old gentleman takes so warm an interest in you. However, lie down; I will tell him what you say, and he will communicate with you to-morrow, unless something should occur to prevent him. Good night."

"I hope that something will occur," cried Paul, jumping up as soon as the officer was gone. "Very kind of the old gentleman, and just like Alphonse to interest his uncle in our favour."

"Yes, indeed," said O'Grady; "curious, though, that we should have fallen in with so many of his relations."

Just then, however, they were too much engrossed with the work in hand to talk on the subject. They considered it safer to wait another hour or more before moving, lest they should encounter any straggler on their way to the harbour, or be seen descending the tower.

"Time to start," cried O'Grady, who, as the senior officer, was to take the command.

Their knapsacks were soon secured to their backs. Reuben used his wooden leg to assist in securing the rope by driving it into the wall. They all soon climbed up to the roof, and let down the rope, which reached nearly to the bottom, as far as they could judge. Should it not prove long enough, and stones be underneath, broken limbs would be the consequence. Paul was certain that there was sand (as they had gone nearly round the tower when looking for the door), and, as the youngest and lightest, volunteered to go first. He without hesitation flung himself off; but at the moment he began to descend, it occurred to him that he might possibly have to pass before one of the windows of the guard-room, and he half expected to find himself seized and dragged in by a gendarme. It was too late, however, to go back. All must be risked. So down he cautiously slid, doing his best to make no noise. He kept his feet tightly pressed against the rope, that he might ascertain when he had reached the end. Suddenly he felt that there was no more rope. At all events all the windows had been avoided. He lowered himself more cautiously than ever, till his hand grasped the very end in which Reuben had made a knot. He hung down by it by one hand, and looked down. He could see the ground; but it seemed still some way below him. Should he risk a fall? He recollected the uneven character of the wall, and hauling

W. H. G. Kingston

himself up a little, he was able to stretch out his feet sufficiently to reach it. He put out one hand in the same direction, and caught hold of an iron staple. He could now clutch the wall, and feeling his way, he descended about eight feet to the ground. It was fortunate that he had not jumped, for, instead of sand, there was a slab of hard rock on which he would have fallen. Scarcely had he time to get under the rope, than he saw another figure descending.

"Try to get to the wall," he whispered, "and I will help you down."

It was Reuben. After several efforts he reached the staple, and scrambled down. Paddy quickly followed at a much greater speed. There was no time to warn him that the rope was too short, and had not Reuben and Paul stretched out their arms and broken his fall, he would very likely have broken his legs.

"I thought that I heard some one coming upstairs," he whispered. "Not quite certain, but could not stop to learn. Away for the harbour!"

They stepped lightly till they were on the soft sands, and then they ran on as fast as their legs could move. They examined the harbour; but not a boat could they find of any size on the shore. They had all probably been removed by the order of the police, to prevent either prisoners of war or refugees from escaping. A small one, however, lay moored off a little distance from the shore.

"I will bring her in," whispered Paul; and without another word he stripped off his clothes, and, with knife in his mouth, slipped noiselessly into the water, and struck boldly out towards the boat. O'Grady and Reuben anxiously watched him, or rather the phosphorescent wake he left in the water. Even that after a time disappeared. Could the brave boy have sunk? The hearts of both his friends trembled. Every instant they expected to be pounced upon by gendarmes; but though they listened earnestly as may be supposed, no sounds came from the tower. At length the boat began to move. Paul must have got on board all right, and cut the cable. Yes, there he was standing up on a thwart, and working her on with a single paddle.

"Jump in," he whispered, as soon as he reached the shore; "there are lights in the old tower, and our flight will quickly be discovered. It may be some time, however, before they find a boat to pursue us."

O'Grady and Reuben required no second bidding. The former, however, very nearly forgot Paul's clothes. He sprang back for them, and narrowly escaped a tumble into the water.

"You dress while we pull out to look for a fit craft," said Paddy, seizing a paddle. But Paul kept hold of his own, in his eagerness declaring that he did not feel the cold.

To select a craft was easy; but it was possible that there might be people on board who might dispute their possession. However, that must be risked. O'Grady pointed out a small sloop of some eight or ten tons. She was not likely to have many people on board. They must be surprised and silenced immediately. While the boat drifted alongside, Paul put on his clothes. It would not have been pleasant to fight as he was; and besides, he might not have had time to dress afterwards. Taking care that their boat should not strike against the side of the little vessel, the three adventurers leaped on board as noiselessly as possible. The after hatch was closed. No one could be in the cabin. But as they crept forward they discovered that the fore hatch was open.

Reuben signed that he would go down first. The midshipmen waited an instant, when they heard a noise, and leaping down they found their companion struggling with a powerful man, whom a boy, who had just leaped out of his berth, was about to assist.

"You are our prisoners," cried Paul, throwing himself on the boy; while O'Grady assisted Reuben, and so completely turned the tables, that the Frenchman was quickly secured. The boy who had struggled bravely with Paul, for the purpose, it seemed, of getting his head up the hatchway to sing out, then gave in.

"You will be well treated, my friends, if you remain quiet; but if you make the slightest noise, I cannot answer for your lives," said Paul.

To prevent any risk of the sort the hatch was clapped on after they had examined the vessel.

"We will get ready to make sail, while you, Gerrard, cut the cable, and then go to the helm," said O'Grady. "Cut!" he cried, in a few seconds.

A light breeze came off the land. Paul cut, and then hurried to the helm. He started as he turned his glance towards the shore; for there, in the direction of the old tower, a bright light was burning. It quickly increased in magnitude—bright flames burst forth. "It must be the old tower itself," he thought, for there was no time to say anything. The flames increased, and it now became evident that it was the tower itself; for the whole building was soon wrapped in flames, the glare reaching far down the harbour, and lighting up the sails of their vessel.

"We shall be seen and pursued, I'm afraid," cried Paul.

"Seen, or not, we must stand on; and at all events we shall have the start of them," answered O'Grady. "It's not impossible that they may think we have perished in the flames. I am sorry, though, for Reuben Cole's timber toe. Ha! ha! ha! it would have enraged the monsieurs to find that they had been so completely duped."

All this time the little vessel was gliding out from among a number of others, and the curious eyes of many persons were glaring at her, who wondered whither she was going. The probabilities that the midshipmen and Reuben would be retaken seemed very great.

W. H. G. Kingston

# CHAPTER ELEVEN

The bold often succeed where the timid fail. The young midshipmen and their companion, nothing daunted by the dangers which surrounded them, kept on their course. The flames quickly ascending to the top of the old tower, sent their ruddy glare far across the ocean; and as their light fell on the adventurers and their little craft, it occurred to Paul that their strange, unseamanlike costume would at once betray them.

"The chances are that the Frenchmen have left some jackets in the after-cabin," he observed; and as he spoke, jumping below, he soon returned with several garments and hats, with which they quickly dressed themselves.

"Now we look pretty decent mounseers," observed Reuben, as he eased off the main-sheet a little. "If we're hailed, you'll have to tell 'em, Paul—I mean Mr Gerrard—beg pardon—that we're bound for Cherbourg, and don't like to lose the breeze. It's coming pretty strongish, and if I could but find a squaresail, for I sees there's a squaresail boom, we'd make the little craft walk along."

Reuben was in high spirits, and indeed so were the midshipmen, at their hazardous enterprise having thus far succeeded. Still they were not out of danger. If it was believed that they had been burnt in the tower, they would not be pursued, unless the owners of the sloop or the remainder of her crew on shore should catch sight of her sailing away. There were still several vessels to pass; but they intended to give them as wide a berth as possible. O'Grady was at the helm. Paul and Reuben were removing the main-hatch in hopes of finding the squaresail, when a cry from O'Grady made them jump up, and they saw the head of the Frenchman, with his mouth open, as if about to shout out, rising above the covering of the forehatch. An Englishman generally carries a weapon ready for immediate use, which at the end of a stout arm is of a somewhat formidable character—his fist. Reuben with his dealt the Frenchman a blow which stopped his shout, knocked three of his teeth down his throat, and sent him toppling over into the fore-peak, from which he had emerged; he, Reuben, and Paul following so rapidly, that the boy, who had been capsized by his companion, had not time to pick himself up. They this time took good care so to secure both their prisoners, that there was very little fear of their escaping, as the man had done before by expanding the muscles of his legs and arms while Reuben was securing him.

"Please tell them, Mr Gerrard, that if they cry out or attempt to play any more tricks, we must shoot them," said Reuben. "And now we'll go and look for the squaresail."

The sail was found and bent on, and, Paul going to the helm, O'Grady and Reuben managed to set it. The vessel felt the effects of the additional canvas, as she drew out more from the land, and rapidly glided past the different vessels in the roadstead. There were only two more. One of these, however, they were compelled to pass uncomfortably near.

"When we are clear of her, we shall be all right," said O'Grady, looking back, and seeing nothing following. "She

W. H. G. Kingston

looks like an armed vessel—a man-of-war perhaps; but it won't do to go out of our course; we must chance it."

They stood on. Although they were now some distance from the land, the old tower continued blazing up so fiercely, that a strong light was still thrown on their canvas. Being between the suspicious vessel and the light, they were abreast of her before they were seen. Just then a hail came from her, demanding who they were, and where they were bound.

"Answer, Gerrard, answer!" cried O'Grady.

But he did not tell him what to say; so Paul put up his hands and shouted, "Oui, oui; toute vite!" with all his might.

"Heave-to," shouted the voice, "and we will send a boat aboard you."

"Very likely," said Paul; and so he only cried out as before, "Oui, oui, to-morrow morning, or the day after, if you please!"

As a vessel running before the wind cannot heave-to at a moment's notice, the sloop got on some little distance before any attempt was made to impede her progress. Another hail was heard, and after the delay of nearly another minute, there was a flash from one of the stranger's ports, and a shot came whizzing by a few feet astern.

"If any of us are killed, let the others hold on to the last," cried O'Grady. "We are suspected, at all events, and may have a near squeak for it."

Reuben, the moment the first shot was fired, jumped down into the hold—not to avoid another; no fear of that. Directly afterwards he shouted out, "I have found the square-topsail.

Lend a hand, Paul, and we'll get it up."

The square-top-sail was got up, rapidly bent on to the yard, and in another minute or two hoisted and set. The man-of-war meantime kept firing away; her shots falling on either side of the little vessel; but as she was riding head to wind, it was evident that only her stern chasers could be brought to bear.

"I wonder that she does not follow us," observed Paul, as the shots began to fall wider and wider of their mark.

"Perhaps most of her crew are on shore, or we are thought too small game to make it worth while to get under weigh for," answered O'Grady. "However, don't let us be too sure; perhaps she will come, after all. We've got a good start of her though."

"The mounseers are generally a long time getting under weigh, and to my mind they don't know what to make of us," observed Reuben, as he eyed the Frenchman with no loving glance.

The breeze continued freshening, and the little craft, evidently a remarkably fast one, flew bravely over the water, increasing her distance from the French shore, and from the light of the burning tower. As the night was very dark, there was yet a chance of her escaping in the obscurity. The adventurers were already congratulating themselves on having got free, when Reuben exclaimed, "The Frenchman thinks more of us than we hoped. He's making sail."

A sailor's eyes alone, and these of the sharpest, could have discovered this disagreeable fact; and even Paul could distinguish nothing but the dark outline of the coast. Reuben kept his eye on the enemy.

"I doubt if she can see us," he observed. "And if she doesn't, we may still give her the go-by. I'd haul up a little to the eastward, Mr O'Grady, sir. The tide will be making down soon, and we shall just check it across. She'll walk along all the faster, too, with the wind on the starboard-quarter, and no risk of jibing. We'll take a pull at the main-sheet, Mr Gerrard. Now we'll ease off the squaresail sheet. That'll do, sir. Now the sail stands beautifully."

O'Grady wisely followed Reuben's advice, and took no notice of his doing things which were so clearly right without orders.

The sloop was now steering about north-east by north, and should the Frenchman stand a little to the westward of north, the two vessels would soon be out of sight of each other. Reuben declared that he could still see the enemy now making all sail in chase, but could not tell exactly how she was standing. It was anxious work. O'Grady made her out, as well as Reuben, and all hoped devoutly that she was a slow sailer. They kept the little vessel on a steady course, and for an hour or more scarcely a word was uttered. Sometimes Reuben lost sight of the enemy; but before long she was again seen. It proved that she did not sail very fast, and that the course they had taken was suspected. Thus hour after hour they stood on, till dawn began to break.

"It's all up with us if she sees us now," cried O'Grady. "But I vote we die game any how, and not give in while there's one of us alive to steer the craft."

The increasing daylight soon revealed them to the Frenchman, who at once began blazing away in a manner which showed that the long chase they had given him had made him not a little angry. The shot, however, fell short; but he on this made more sail, and soon gained on them. He ceased firing for half an hour or more, and then again began, the shot flying by on either side, or over the mast-head. They came, indeed, much too near to be pleasant. Reuben took the helm, and the two midshipmen stood facing their enemy, knowing that any moment might be their last; still, however, as resolved as at first not to yield. In another twenty minutes or half an hour they must be killed or prisoners; escape seemed out of the question.

"I wish that I could let my father, and mother, and brothers, and sisters at Ballyshannon know what has become of me," said Paddy, with a sigh.

"And I wish that I could have again seen my dear mamma," said Paul, "and my sweet sister Mary, and jolly old Fred, and Sarah, and John, and pretty little Ann. They know that I am a midshipman, and I suppose that that will be some consolation to them if they ever hear that I've been killed."

"Don't talk like that, young gentlemen. Look there. What do you say to that?" exclaimed Reuben, pointing to the north-west, where standing towards them, close-hauled, and evidently attracted by the firing, was a large, ship, the beams of the rising sun shining brightly on her wide-spread canvas.

"The enemy must see her, but fancy that she is French," observed Reuben. "But they are greatly mistaken, let me tell them."

"Hurrah! they've found out that they're wrong, then," cried O'Grady.

As he spoke, down came the Frenchman's studden sails, and with a few parting shots, which narrowly missed their mark, he hauled his wind, and stood close-hauled towards the coast of France. He sailed badly before the wind; he sailed worse

W. H. G. Kingston

close-hauled. The stranger, which soon proved to be an English frigate, her ensign blowing out at her peak, came rapidly up. The adventurers cheered as she passed, and received a cheer in return. Those on board evidently understood the true state of the case.

"Why, I do believe that is Devereux himself!" cried Paul, in a tone of delight.

"Well, it is difficult to be certain of a person at such a distance; but it is very like him," said O'Grady. "But, again, how could he be there? He could not have made his escape from prison."

The sloop hove to in order to watch the chase, which was soon terminated, for the frigate came up hand over hand with the slow-sailing brig, which found to her cost that instead of catching a prize she had caught a Tartar. The midshipmen consulted together whether it would be wiser to continue their course for the Isle of Wight, or to get on board the frigate. But as the Channel swarmed with the cruisers of the enemy, they decided to do the latter; and accordingly, when they saw the frigate returning with her prize, they stood towards her. They were soon up to her, and, a boat being sent to them, as they stepped up her side the first person they encountered was Devereux.

"Why, old fellows, where have you come from in that curious guise?" he exclaimed, as he warmly wrung their hands.

"Oh, we ran away, and have been running ever since, barring some few weeks we spent shut up in an old castle and a tumble-down tower," answered O'Grady.

"And the captain, and I, and a few others, were exchanged

two weeks ago for a lot of French midshipmen without any trouble whatever."

"As to that, now we are free, I don't care a rope-yarn for all the trouble we have had, nor if we had had ten times as much. But we ought to report ourselves to the captain; and we think—that is, Gerrard does—that we ought to let our prisoners take back the sloop which we ran away with."

"I agree with Gerrard, and so I am sure will the captain," said Devereux.

The frigate on board which the three adventurers so unexpectedly and happily found themselves was the *Proserpine*, Captain Percy, of forty-two guns. As she was on her trial cruise, having only just been fitted out, she was short of midshipmen, and Captain Percy offered to give both O'Grady and Paul a rating on board if Reuben would enter. This he willingly did, and they thus found themselves belonging to the ship. The occupants of the berth received them both very cordially, and paid especial attention to Paul, of whom Devereux had spoken to them in the warmest terms of praise. The surprise of the Frenchman and boy on board the sloop was very great, when Paul and Reuben, accompanied by some prisoners from the prize, appeared and released them; and when Paul told them that they might return home, and that some countrymen had come to help them navigate the ship, to express his joy and gratitude, he would have kissed them both had they allowed him; and he seemed at a loss how otherwise to show it, except by skipping and jumping about, on his deck. When he shortly afterwards passed the *Proserpine*, he and his companions waved their hats, and attempted to raise a cheer; but it sounded very weak and empty, or, as Reuben observed to one of his new shipmates, "It was no more like a British cheer than the squeak of a young porker is to a boatswain's whistle."

The prize thus easily gained was sent into Portsmouth, and the *Proserpine* continued her cruise. O'Grady and Paul would have liked to have gone in her; but they thought it better to wait till the frigate herself returned to port, when they might get leave to go home and visit their friends, and perhaps take a little prize-money with them to make up for what they had lost. They easily got a temporary rig-out on board, so that there was no absolute necessity for their going. Paul had hitherto, young as he was, held up manfully in spite of all the fatigue and anxiety he had gone through; but no sooner had the prize disappeared, than his strength and spirits seemed to give way. He kept in the berth for a day or two; but could scarcely crawl on deck, when Devereux reporting his condition to the surgeon, he was placed in the sick list. Both his old shipmates, Devereux and O'Grady, attended him with the fondest care, and he would have discovered, had he possessed sufficient consciousness, how completely he had wound himself round their hearts. He had done so, not by being proud, or boastful, or self-opinionated, or by paying them court, by any readiness to take offence, or by flattery, or by any other mean device, but by his bravery and honesty, by his gentleness and liveliness, by his readiness to oblige, and general good-nature and uprightness, and by being true to himself and true to others—doing to them as he would be done by. They became at last very sad—that is to say, as sad as midshipmen in a dashing frigate, with a good captain, can become during war time; for they thought that Paul was going to die, and the surgeon gave them no hopes. No one, however, was more sad than Reuben, who for many a watch below, when he ought to have been in his own hammock, sat by the side of his cot, administering the medicines left by the doctor, and tending him with all a woman's care and tenderness. The thoughts of his friends were for a time, however, called off from Paul by an event which brought all hands on deck—the appearance of a strange sail, pronounced to be a French frigate equal in size to the *Proserpine*. All sail was made in chase. The ship was cleared for action, and Paul with other sick was carried into the cockpit to be out of the way of shot. The gunner went to the magazine to send up powder; the carpenter and his mates to the wings, with plugs, to stop any shot-holes between wind and water; and the various other officers, commissioned and warrant, repaired to their respective posts. Paul had sufficiently recovered to know what was about to take place, and to wish to be on deck.

"Couldn't you let me go, doctor—only just while the action is going on?" he murmured out. "I'll come back, and go to bed, and do all you tell me—indeed I will."

"I am sorry to say that you could be of no use, my brave boy, and would certainly injure yourself very much; so you must stay where you are," answered the surgeon, who was busy in getting out the implements of his calling. "You will have many opportunities of fighting and taking other prizes besides the one which will, I hope, soon be ours."

The remarks of the surgeon were soon cut short by the loud roar of the guns overhead, as the frigate opened her fire on the enemy. Then speedily came the crashing sound of the return shot, as they tore through the stout planks, and split asunder even the oaken timbers. It was evident that the two ships were very close together by the loud sound of the enemy's guns and the effects of his shot. Not many minutes had passed since the firing commenced, when steps were heard descending the ladder, and first one wounded man, and then another, and another, was brought below and placed before the surgeon. He had scarcely begun to examine their wounds, when more poor fellows were brought below badly wounded.

"Ah! sir," said one of the seamen who bore them, as he was

W. H. G. Kingston

hurrying again on deck, in answer to a question from the surgeon, "there are many more than these down for whom you could do nothing."

"What, is the day going against us?" asked the surgeon.

"No, sir; I hope not. But the enemy is a big one, and will require a mighty deal of hammering before she gives in."

Paul looked out; but he soon closed his eyes, and he would gladly have closed his ears to the shrieks and groans of anguish which assailed them, while the poor fellows were under the hands of the surgeons, or waiting their turn to have their wounds dressed, or their limbs amputated. Paul was more particularly anxious about his old friends; and whenever anybody was brought near him, he inquired after them. The report was, from those who had seen them, that they were at their posts as yet unhurt. Again he waited. Now there was a cessation of firing. Once more it was renewed, and the wounded were brought down in even still greater numbers than at first. Paul's spirits fell very low. He had never felt so miserable, and so full of dread. What, if after all the *Proserpine* should be overmatched, and he and his companions again fall into the hands of the French, or should perhaps Devereux, or O'Grady, or his firm friend Reuben Cole, be killed! Suddenly he remembered what his mother often had told him, that in all troubles and difficulties he should pray; and so he hid his face in the pillow, and prayed that his countrymen might come off victorious, and that the lives of his friends might be preserved. By the time he had ceased his fears had vanished; his spirits rose. He had done all he could do, and the result he knew was in the hands of Him who rules the world. Still the battle raged. He heard remarks made by the wounded, by which he guessed that the enemy was indeed vastly superior, and that many a man, if not possessed of an indomitable spirit, would have yielded long ago; but that their captain would fight on till the ship sunk beneath his feet, or till not a man remained to work the guns. Several officers were among the badly wounded, and many were reported to be killed. At length there was a cry of grief, and their brave captain himself was brought below. Still the first-lieutenant remained to fight the ship, and his captain's last order to him was never to yield while the remotest hope of victory remained.

"Am I likely to survive?" asked the captain of the surgeon, after his wound had been examined.

"It is possible, sir; but I will not disguise from you that your wound is dangerous," was the answer.

"I should be resigned," said the captain, "could I know that the victory would be ours."

At that instant the sound of cheering came down into the cockpit. The captain heard it, and lifted up his head with a look of intense eagerness. Directly afterwards an officer appeared. His head was bound up, and his coat at the shoulder was torn and bloody. It was Devereux.

"The enemy has sheered off, sir, and is making all sail to the southward," he exclaimed, in a hurried tone. "We are unable to follow, for our fore-top-mast and main-mast are gone, and the fore-mast and mizen-mast, until they are fished, cannot carry sail."

"Thank heaven! thank heaven!" whispered the captain, falling back. The surgeon, whom he had sent to attend to others worse wounded than himself, as he thought, hurried back to him with a restorative cordial; but he shook his head as he vainly put it to his mouth: it was too late. In the moment of victory the gallant spirit of the captain had

W. H. G. Kingston

departed. The enemy with which the *Proserpine* had for so long thus nobly sustained this fierce engagement, was a 74-gun ship, more than half as large again as she was, and having on board nearly twice as many men. The sea was fortunately calm, and the masts being fished, sail was made, and in two days the frigate reached Portsmouth. As she had suffered much in the action, she required extensive repairs; and the sick and wounded were sent on shore to the hospital. In the list of the former was Paul; in the latter, Devereux. Paul still continued very weak and ill. Devereux was not dangerously hurt; but the surgeons would not allow him to travel to go to his friends, and they showed no disposition to come to him. Paul was too weak to write home himself, but he had got Devereux to do so for him, making, however, as light as he could of his illness.

Two days had scarcely elapsed, when they were told that a young lady was below, waiting to see Mr Gerrard.

"It must be my dear sister Mary," whispered Paul. "Oh, do go and see her before she comes here, Devereux, and tell her how ill I am, and prepare her for the sort of place she is to come to."

Hospitals in those days, especially in the war time, were very differently arranged to what they are now, when every attention is paid to the comfort and convenience of the patients. At that time, even in the best regulated, were sights, smells, and sounds, trying to the sensibilities even of ordinary persons, but especially so to those of a young lady brought up in the quiet and retirement of a rural village; but Mary Gerrard, who now entered the Portsmouth hospital, escorted by Devereux, had at that moment but one feeling, one thought—an earnest desire to reach the bedside of her brave young brother, who she thought was dying. After the first greetings were over, Paul, seeing her look very sad, entreated her not to grieve, as he was sure that he should get well and go home and see them all.

She prayed he might, and so did Devereux, though from what the doctor said, there could be little doubt that he was very ill. Mary did not tell him that his dear mother was very ill also, being sure that the knowledge of this would agitate him, and retard, if it did not prevent, his recovery. She entreated that she might remain night and day with her brother; but this was not allowed, and so she was obliged to take lodgings near at hand, where she remained at night when turned out of the hospital. Devereux, however, comforted her by promising that he would sit up as long as he was allowed with his friend, while O'Grady and Reuben Cole came on shore and assisted in nursing him; so that Paul was not so badly off after all. The consequence was, that in spite of the doctor's prognostications, Paul rapidly improved. As soon as he was in a fit condition to be moved, he was conveyed to some nice airy lodgings Mary had engaged; and here Devereux, who was also recovering from his wounds, and allowed to go out, was a constant visitor, that is to say, he came early in the morning, and stayed all day. He came at first for Paul's sake; but it might have been suspected that he now came for the sake of somebody else. He was no longer a midshipman, for he had received his commission as lieutenant soon after landing, provisionally on his passing the usual examination, in consequence of the action in which he had taken part, when he had acted as second in command, all the other officers being killed or wounded. Mary could not fail to like him, and although she knew the whole history of the disastrous lawsuit between her father and the Devereux family, she had never supposed that he belonged to them in any way.

It did not occur to Paul that his friend and his sister were becoming sincerely and deeply attached to each other. He

W. H. G. Kingston

asked Devereux one day why, now that he was strong enough, he did not go home to see his friends.

"Do you wish me gone?" asked Devereux.

"No, indeed, I do not," answered Paul; "but it surprised me that you should not be anxious to go and see them."

"Did they show any anxiety to come and see me, when they supposed I was wounded and ill, and perhaps dying?" he asked, in an animated tone. "No, Paul; but there is one who did come to see my best friend, who saved my life, and watched over me with more than the tenderness of a brother when I was sick, and for that person I have conceived an affection which I believe will only end with my life."

"Who can you mean, Devereux?" asked Paul, in a tone of surprise.

"Why, who but your sister Mary!" exclaimed Devereux. "Do you think that I could have spent so many days with her, and seen her tending on you like an angel of light, as she is, and not love her with all my heart?"

"Oh, my dear Devereux, I cannot tell you how I feel about it," said Paul, warmly taking his hand; "though I am sure Mary does not know that you belong to that family we all fancy have treated us so ill; yet, when she does come to know it, as she ought to know, still I do not think that it will bias her in her sentiments towards you. When she knows that you love her, I am sure that she must love you."

"Thank you, Paul; thank you, my dear fellow, for saying that. Then I will tell her at once," said Devereux.

And so he did; and Mary confessed that Paul was not far

wrong in his conjectures.

It had, curiously enough, never occurred to her to what family Devereux belonged, and when she heard, she naturally hesitated about allying herself to people who, if they could not despise, would assuredly dislike her. Devereux, however, overcame all her scruples, which is not surprising, considering that he was scarcely twenty-one, and she was only nineteen.

When Paddy O'Grady heard of the arrangement he was delighted.

"All right, my dear fellow," he exclaimed. "When you marry Mary Gerrard, I'll run over to France and pop the question to little Rosalie Montauban, and bring her back to live in some snug box of a cottage I'll take near you. Won't it be charming?"

Midshipmen, when they think of marrying, always think of living in a snug little box of a cottage, just big enough for themselves, forgetting that they may wish for servants, and may some day expand somewhat in various ways.

Devereux ventured to suggest that Miss Rosalie might not be as willing to come away as O'Grady supposed, at which Paddy became very irate, the more so, that some such idea might possibly have been lurking within his own bosom. However, as the war was not over, and might not be for some time, he could not go just: then.

Paul was now sufficiently recovered to be moved, and Devereux got leave to help Mary in taking him home. They were also accompanied by Reuben Cole. Mrs Gerrard had begun to recover from the day that she heard Paul was out of all danger. She joyfully and proudly received them at her neat and pretty, though small cottage; and from the day of his arrival Devereux found himself treated as a son. Devereux had admired Mary watching over her sick brother. He admired her still more when affectionately tending on her mother, and surrounded by her younger brothers and sisters. Paul was made so much of that he ran a great chance of being spoilt. He had to put on his uniform, and exhibit himself to all the neighbourhood as the lad who had gone away as a poor ship-boy, and come back home as a full-blown midshipman. At last, one day Devereux received a letter from his home, suggesting that as he was in England he might possibly be disposed to pay them a visit. He went, though very reluctantly. He was greatly missed, not only by Paul and Mary, but by all the younger Gerrards. Not ten days had elapsed when he again made his appearance.

"They have had enough of me," he said, as he entered laughing. "But, Mary, dear," he added, after he had gone the round of handshaking, and, it may be, with a kiss or two from the lady part of the family, "the best news I have to tell you is that they will not oppose our marriage, if we will wait till I am made a commander, and then my father promises me three hundred a year, which, with my pay, will be a great deal more than we shall want. To be sure, I had to undertake to give up some thousands which might some day come to me; but it would not be for a long time, at all events, and, in my opinion, perhaps never; and I was determined not to risk the danger of losing you for money, or any other cause."

"Oh, my dear Gilbert! and have you sacrificed your fortune and your future prospects for my sake?" said Mary, her eye's filling with tears; and yet not looking, after all, as if she was very sorry.

"No, no! not in the slightest degree. I have laid them out, as a merchant would say, to the very best advantage, by securing what I know will tend to my very great and continued happiness," answered Gilbert Devereux, adding—

But never mind what he said or did after that. Certain it is, Mary made no further objections, and Mary and he were regularly betrothed, which is a very pleasant state of existence, provided people may hope to marry before very long, and expect, when they do marry, to have something to live on.

Soon after this Gilbert Devereux went to Portsmouth to pass his examination, and came back a full-blown lieutenant, with an epaulette on his left shoulder, which, when he put on his uniform, was very much admired.

Paul awoke very early the morning after Devereux had returned, in the same little room in which he slept before he went to sea, and which he had so often pictured to his mind's eye as he lay in his hammock tossed by the stormy sea. A stout sea-chest stood open in the room, and over it was hung a new uniform with brass buttons; a bright quadrant, and spy-glass, and dirk, and gold-laced hat, lay on the table, and the chest seemed filled to overflowing with the articles of a wardrobe, and a variety of little comforts which his fond mother and sisters, he was sure, had prepared for him. He turned round in his bed and gazed at the scene.

"I have dreamed this dream before," he said to himself. "It was vivid then—it is vivid now; but I will not be deceived as I was then!—oh, how bitterly—No, no, it is a dream. I fear that it is all a dream!"

But when the bright sunbeams came in and glittered on the quadrant and buttons, and the brass of the telescope, and on the gold lace, and the handle of the dirk, and the birds sang cheerily to greet the glorious sun, and the lowing of cows and the bleating of sheep was heard, and the crack of a carter's whip, and his "gee up" sounded not far away from under the window, Paul rubbed his eyes again and again, and, with a shout of joy and thankfulness, exclaimed—

"It is true! it is true! I really am a midshipman!"

And when he knelt down to say his prayers, as all true honest Christian boys do, he thanked God fervently for having preserved him from so many dangers and granted him fully the utmost desire of his young heart. When Paul appeared at breakfast, did not his mother and brothers and sisters admire him, even more than they did Gilbert Devereux, except, perhaps, Mary; and she certainly did not say that she admired Paul less. They were a very happy party, and only wished that to-morrow would not come. But such happiness to the brave men who fight Old England's battles, whether by sea or land, must, in war time at all events, be of brief duration. A long official-looking letter arrived for Devereux, and another of a less imposing character, from the first-lieutenant of the *Proserpine*, ordering Paul, if recovered, to join forthwith, as the ship was ready for sea. The letter for Devereux contained his appointment to the same ship, which was a great satisfaction to all concerned.

We will not describe what poor Mary felt or said. She well knew that the event was inevitable, and, like a true sensible girl, she nerved herself to endure it, though we dare say she did not fail to let Gilbert understand, to his satisfaction, how sorry she was to lose him. It is, indeed, cruel kindness to friends to let them suppose when parting from them that you do not care about them.

Reuben Cole, who had spent his holiday in the village with his old mother, and left her this time cash enough to make her comfortable, according to her notions, for many a day, came to the cottage to say that his time was up. The three old shipmates therefore set off together for Portsmouth. On their arrival they found that Mr Order, who had been made a commander in the West Indies, and had lately received his post rank, was appointed to command the *Proserpine*. The *Cerberus* had arrived some time before, and several of her officers and men had, in consequence of their regard for Captain Order, joined the *Proserpine*. Among them were Peter Bruff, still a mate, Tilly Blake, and old Croxton. The midshipmen's berth contained a merry party, some youngsters who had come to sea for the first time, full of life and hope, and some oldsters who were well-nigh sick of it and of everything else in the world, and longed to have a leg or an arm shot away that they might obtain a berth at Greenwich, and have done with it. At that time, however, there were not many of the latter sort.

At first it was supposed that their destination was foreign; but whether they were to be sent to the North American station, to the Mediterranean, to the Pacific, or to India, they could not ascertain; so that it rather puzzled them to know what sort of stores they should lay in, or with what style of garments they should provide themselves. However, on the morning they were to sail Captain Order received a dispatch directing him to join the Channel fleet.

"Do you know what that means?" asked Peter Bruff of the assembled mess. "Why, I will tell you, boys, that we shall be attached to the blockading squadron off Brest, and that month after month, blow high or blow low, we shall have to kick our heels there till we have kicked holes in them."

Those present expressed great dissatisfaction at the prospect in view; but Devereux, when the subject was discussed in the gun-room, was secretly very glad, because he hoped thus to hear more frequently from Mary, and to be able to write to

W. H. G. Kingston

her. His brother officers took up the idea that he was an author, from the sheets upon sheets of paper which he covered; but, as may be supposed, nothing could induce him to exhibit the result of his labours. While others were weary; discontented, and grumbling, he was always happy in the belief that Mary was always thinking of him, as he was of her.

Blockading is always disagreeable work, as there must be an ever watchful look-out, night and day, and ships are often kept till all their provisions are expended, or the ships themselves can stand the wear and tear no longer. The *Proserpine* had, as was expected, plenty to do. Paul, though not finding it pleasant more than the rest, was satisfied that it was calculated to give him ample experience in seamanship, and to make him the good officer he aspired to become.

However, as disagreeable as well as agreeable times must come to an end some time, if we will but wait that time, the *Proserpine* was relieved at length, and returned to Portsmouth. She was not allowed to remain there long, for as soon as she could be refitted, and had taken in a fresh supply of provisions, wood, and water, she again put to sea to join a squadron in the North Seas. Winter came on, and as she lay in Yarmouth Roads, directions were sent to Captain Order to prepare for the reception of an ambassador, or some other great man, who was to be conveyed to the Elbe, and landed at Cuxhaven, or any other place where he could be put on shore and make his way to his destination.

It was early in February, but the weather was unusually fine, and off the compact little island of Heligoland a signal was made for a pilot, who came on board and assured the captain that there was not the slightest difficulty in getting up the Elbe to Cuxhaven, if he would but proceed at between half-flood and half-ebb, when he could see the sand on either hand. All the buoys in the river had, however, been carried away, he observed, to prevent the enemy from getting up. With a favourable breeze the frigate stood up the river, guided by the experienced pilot. While the weather continued fine, the task was one of no great difficulty, though with a wintry wind blowing and the thermometer far down below the freezing-point, it was anything but a pleasant one.

"Faith, I'd rather be back stewing away among the niggers in the West Indies, would not you, Gerrard?" exclaimed Paddy O'Grady, beating his hands against his sides to keep them warm.

"I should not mind it for a change, if it was not to last long; but I confess I don't wish it to be colder," said Paul.

"Why, lads, this is nothing to what I have had to go through in the North Seas," remarked Bruff. "I've known it so cold that every drop of spray which came on board froze, and I've seen the whole deck, and every spar and rope one mass of ice, so that there was no getting the ropes to run through the sheaves of the blocks, and as to furling sails, which were mere sheets of ice, that was next to an impossibility. I warn you, if you don't like what we have got now, you'll like still less what is coming. There are some heavy snow-clouds driving up, and we shall have a shift of wind soon."

The frigate had now got up to within four miles of Cuxhaven, when, at about four o'clock, as the winter's day was closing in, it, as Bruff had anticipated, came on to snow so thickly that the pilot could no longer see the marks, and it accordingly became necessary to anchor. Later in the evening, when darkness had already set in, the wind shifted to the southward of east, and the snow fell with a density scarcely ever surpassed, as if the whole cloud mass of snow were descending bodily to the earth. Added to this, the high wind drove the ice, which had hitherto remained fixed to the shore, high up, directly down on the ship, threatening every instant to cut her cables, when she must have been driven on shore and lost.

"All hands on deck!" turned many a sleeper out of his hammock, where, if not warm, he was not so cold as elsewhere. All night long the crew were on deck, fending off the ice, which in huge masses came drifting down on them.

"What do you think of this, Paddy?" asked Bruff.

"Why, by my faith, that when a thing is bad we have good reason to be thankful that it's no worse," answered O'Grady. "Can anything be worse than this?"

"Yes, indeed, a great deal worse," said Bruff.

The morning broke at length, and as it was evident that the ambassador could not be landed at Cuxhaven, it was necessary to get out of the Elbe without delay, that he might be put on shore on the coast of Holstein, if possible.

The wind blew as strong as ever—a severe gale; but, the snow ceasing partially, the pilot was enabled to see the land. The ship stood on under one sail only—the utmost she could carry—a fore-topmast stay-sail.

"Hurrah! we shall soon be out of this trap, and once more in the open sea," exclaimed O'Grady. "So the pilot says."

"Are we well clear of the outer bank?" asked the captain.

The answer was in the affirmative; but it was scarcely given when the ship struck heavily, and, her keel cutting the sand, she thus became, as it seemed, firmly fixed. Then arose the cry from many mouths—

"We are lost! we are lost!"

"Silence!" exclaimed Captain Order; "until every effort has been made to get her off, let no one under my command say that."

W. H. G. Kingston

# CHAPTER TWELVE

When a captain finds his ship on shore, even though he is in no way to blame, he feels as did Captain Order, that a great misfortune has happened to him. No sooner was the *Proserpine's* way stopped, than the ice drifting down the river began to collect round her. Still the captain did not despair of getting her off. The boats were hoisted out for the purpose of carrying out an anchor to heave her off; but the ice came down so thickly with the ebb, which had begun to make, that they were again hoisted in, and all hands were employed in shoring up the ship to prevent her falling over on her side. Scarcely was this done when huge masses of ice came drifting down with fearful force directly on the ship, carrying away the shores as if they were so many reeds, and tearing off large sheets of the copper from her counter.

"I told you that matters might be worse. What do you think of the state of things?" said Bruff to Paul.

"That they are very bad; but I heard the captain say just now that he still hopes to get off," answered Paul. "I suppose that he is right on the principle Mr Devereux always advocates, 'Never to give in while the tenth part of a chance remains.'"

"Oh, Devereux is a fortunate man. He is a lieutenant, and will be a commander before long, and so looks on the bright side of everything, while I am still a wretched old mate, and have a right to expect the worst," answered Bruff, with some little bitterness in his tone. "I ought to have been promoted for that cutting-out affair."

So he ought. Poor Bruff, once the most joyous and uncomplaining in the mess, was becoming slightly acidulated by disappointment. He had good reason on this occasion for taking a gloomy view of the state of affairs.

The ice drove down in increasingly larger masses every instant. One mass struck the rudder, and, though it was as strong as wood and iron could make it, cut it in two, the lower part being thrown up by the concussion on to the surface of the floe, where it lay under the stern, the floe itself remaining fixed in that position by the other masses which had collected round the ship.

The ambassador and members of his suite looked uncomfortable, and made inquiries as to the best means of leaving the ship; but she was Captain Order's first command, and he had no idea of giving her up without making a great effort for her preservation. At length came an order which showed that matters were considered bad in the extreme:

"Heave overboard the guns!"

Rapidly the guns were run out, and, aided by crowbars, were forced through the ports; but so strong was the ice that they failed to break it, and lay on its surface round the ship. Mr Trunnion, the gunner, hurried about, assisting in the operation; but as each gun went overboard he gave a groan, and made a face as if, one by one, his own teeth were being drawn.

"Never mind, mate, the good ship holds together, and we'll get her off, I hope," observed the carpenter.

"The ship! What's the value of her compared to the guns?" exclaimed the gunner, turning on his heel.

The stores (to the purser's infinite grief) and water followed. Anchors and cables were now carried out, and the ice astern with infinite labour was broken away; but the efforts of the crew were in vain, and the ship still remained firmly fixed in her icy prison when night drew on.

What a night was that! Down came the snow thicker than ever, the fierce wind howled and shrieked through the rigging, and when the ebb tide made, the ice in huge masses came down, crashing with fearful force against the sides of the frigate, mass rising above mass, till it seemed as if it were about to entomb her in a frozen mountain. The science and experience of the oldest officers were set at nought, all the exertions of the crew were unavailing; the wind increased, the snow fell thicker, and the ice accumulated more and more. The cold, too, was intense, and with difficulty the men could face the freezing blast.

Paul thought of how often he had heard people complaining of the heat of the West Indies, and now how glad would they have been to have obtained some of that caloric they were then so anxious to be rid of. Already the masses of ice reached up to the cabin windows. A loud crack was heard. It came from the after part of the ship. The carpenter and his mates descended to ascertain the mischief. He soon returned with a long face and a look of alarm on his countenance, and, touching his hat to the captain, reported that the stern port was broken in two, and parts of the stern stove in, so that there was small chance of the ship floating, even should she be got off.

"Well, well, Auger, keep up your spirits, man," observed Mr Grummit, the boatswain, to his brother warrant officer; "the masts are standing, and in spite of the gale the spars are uninjured, and you may manage, after all, to copper up the old barkie to get her out of this."

"Ah, that's just like the way of the world, Grummit," said Trunnion. "As long as your masts are standing, you don't care how much harm happens to the hull under Auger's charge; and while the hull was undamaged, Auger didn't care for my guns; but just let's see your masts going over the side, and we should have you singing out as loudly as any one— that we should, I know; and just you look out, they'll be going before long."

The indignant gunner turned away. It seemed very probable that his prognostications would prove true, for already in all directions the gallant ship cracked and groaned as the ice pressed in from every quarter on her stout timbers.

Paul met Devereux, and asked him what he thought was going to happen.

"One of two things, my dear Gerrard," answered the young lieutenant; "we must either try to get on shore, or we must be ready to go down with the ship, should the wind drift her out of her present position. I know that you will be prepared for whatever we are called to encounter; but whatever occurs, keep near me. I shall not be happy if we are separated."

As Paul was in Devereux's watch, this he could easily promise to do. Hour after hour wore on. The cold increased. The weather gave no signs of mending. Death, in a form, though not the most terrible, yet calculated to produce intense suffering, stared them in the face. The men looked at each other, and asked what was next to happen. The captain and most of his officers, and the ambassador, were in consultation in the cabin. Many of the men believed that the ship herself could not much longer resist the violent pressure to which she was exposed, and expected every instant that her sides would be crushed together.

The calmest, as usual, was old Croxton, who had been actively going about his duty without making any demonstration.

"Lads, just listen to me," he observed. "Some of you are proposing one thing, and some another; but let me advise you to go on steadily doing your duty, smartly obeying our officers, and leaving all the rest in the hands of Providence. It is the business of the officers to plan and command, and, depend on it, they'll order us to do what they believe to be best."

A few minutes afterwards the drum beat for divisions, and as soon as the men were mustered, the captain addressed them, and told them that, at the desire of the ambassador, it had been resolved to abandon the ship.

"At the same time, my lads, you will remember that while she holds together, you still belong to her," he added. "While, for your own sakes, you will maintain that strict discipline which has done you so much credit ever since I have had the satisfaction of commanding you."

A hearty cheer was the answer to this address.

The men were then directed to provide themselves each with a change of clothing, and a supply of provisions for two days. All knew that the undertaking was perilous in the extreme. The nearest inhabited part of the small island of Newark was upwards of six miles distant. No one knew exactly the direction. The snow continued to fall thickly, the cold was intense, and the wind blew fiercely, while it was possible that the ice might break away and carry them with it before they could gain the land.

They were to march in subdivisions, each under their respective officers. With heavy hearts the officers and crew went down the side of the ship, and formed on the ice under her lee. The sick—fortunately there were very few—were supported by their comrades. There were some women and children; for them it was truly fearful work. The captain, having ascertained that no man was left on board, was the last to quit the ship. He could not speak as he came down the side and took his place in the van. The order to advance was given. Slowly, with heads bent down against the freezing blast, the party worked their way. In some places the tide or the wind had forced the water over the ice, and pools of half-frozen slush had been formed, through which they were compelled to wade. In others they had to climb over the huge slabs of ice which had been thrown up in wild confusion. On they toiled, however, those who kept close together assisting each other; but some, alas! in the thick snow separated by the inequalities of the surface over which they travelled, sunk unseen, and not, in many cases, till their comrades had advanced too far to render assistance, was their absence discovered. A poor boy—who, though somewhat weak and sickly, was a favourite with the men—was one of the first missed. He had been complaining of the cold, but had been encouraged to proceed by those near him.

"Oh, let me just lie down and rest for a few moments, I am so weary, I will come on with the others," he murmured.

"You will get no rest to do you good," was the answer. "Cheer up, cheer up, lad!"

A friendly hand was stretched out to help him. For some way he struggled on. Then there arose a huge pile of ice slabs, and he escaped from the friendly hand which held him.

"Ah, now I will rest quietly," he thought, as he laid himself down on a crevice of the ice filled with snow.

From that sleep he never awoke.

Among the women, one toiled on with a child in her arms. Many of the seamen offered to carry it; but she would not part with her treasure. On and on she moved. Her words became wandering, then scarcely articulate. She ceased at length to speak. Still she advanced. The snow fell thicker. The road became more uneven. Each person had to exert himself to the utmost to preserve his own life. They thought not of the poor woman and her child till they discovered that she was not among them. But not only did the weak sink down. Strong men in the same way disappeared from among their comrades. No one at the time exactly knew how. No one saw them fall. They were by the side of those who still walked on alive one moment, and the next they were gone.

Paul kept near Devereux. They conversed together as much as they could, and often addressed words of encouragement to the men, who, though often sinking, it appeared, with fatigue and cold, were revived, it seemed, and proceeded with as much spirit as at first.

Paul himself at length began to grow very weary, and to long to lie down and rest.

"If I could stop back for three minutes, I could easily run on and catch them up," he thought to himself; yet he did not like to make the proposal to Devereux, who, he still had sense enough to believe, would not agree to it.

Poor Paul, was this to be the termination of all your aspirations for naval glory, to sink down and die on a frozen sand-bank, within a few miles of a spot where you may obtain food, shelter, and warmth?

"I can stand it no longer, I must rest," he said to himself. "There is a snug spot between two slabs of ice, quite an arm-chair. I must sit in it, if only for two minutes."

Devereux must have divined his thoughts, or probably observed the irregular and faltering steps he was making, for, seizing him by the arm, he exclaimed, with judicious roughness—

"Come, rouse up, Paul, my dear fellow! We must have none of this folly. I did not expect it from you."

The words had their due effect. By a powerful effort Paul threw off his lethargy, and once more sprang on with the rest, continuing to talk and encourage his companions.

Still no one could tell whether or not they should ever reach their destination. The snow fell thicker than ever, and not a windmill, a spire, or a willow, or any of the objects which adorn the shores of the Elbe, could be seen to indicate that they were approaching the haunts of men. It was too evident that many of their number had passed from among them since they began their march, and no one could say who might follow. Many were complaining bitterly of the cold, and others had ceased to complain, as if no longer conscious of the effect it was producing.

Suddenly there was a shout from those in advance. The rear ranks hurried on. A house was seen, then another, and another. They were in the middle of a village. Kind people came out of their houses to inquire what had occurred; and at once there was no lack of hearty invitations, and the whole

W. H. G. Kingston

party were soon enjoying warmth, hot drinks, and dry clothing, which soon revived the greater number, though some who had been frost-bitten required considerable attention before they were set to rights.

The next day the storm raged as furiously as before, and so it continued for nearly a week, and all had reason to be thankful that they had reached a place of safety. At length, the weather moderating, and provisions on the island growing very scarce, the ambassador and his suite, and half of the ship's company, proceeded on, though not without great difficulty and hazard, to Cuxhaven, while the rest remained on the island, in the hope of saving some of the ship's stores.

Among the latter were Devereux, Paul, and O'Grady, with Reuben Cole. The next day they, with a party of men, volunteered to visit the wreck, to report on her condition, and to bring back some bread, of which they stood greatly in need. They succeeded in getting on board, and found the ship in even a worse condition than they had expected. She was on her beam ends, with upwards of seven feet of water in her, apparently broken asunder, the quarter-deck separated six feet from the gangway, and only kept together by the ice frozen round her. Their task accomplished, with a few articles of value and a supply of bread, they returned to the shore.

Considering that the risk was very great, the captain decided that no further visits should be paid to the ship.

However, one morning, the weather becoming very fine, it being understood that the captain had not actually prohibited a visit to the ship, Devereux, Paul, and O'Grady, with Cole and another man, set off to pay, as they said, the old barkie a farewell visit. The captain, who was ill in bed, only heard of their departure too late to recall them. The frost was so severe that the ice was well frozen, and thus they must have got on board; but it was supposed that they had remained on board till the tide changing made their return impossible. They were looked-for anxiously during the evening, but no tidings came of them. At night the wind again got up, and their shipmates, as they sat by the fires of their hospitable host, trembled for their safety. As soon as daylight returned the greater number were on foot. Not a vestige of her could be seen. The tide and wind rising together must have carried down the masses of ice with terrific force, and completely swept her decks.

When Captain Order heard of this, his feelings gave way. "To have lost my ship was bad enough," he exclaimed; "but to lose so many fine young fellows on a useless expedition is more than I can bear. It will be the cause of my death."

The few officers who remained with the captain could offer no consolation. The pilots and other people belonging to the place were consulted. They declared that from the condition of the ship when last visited, it was impossible that she could withstand the numerous masses of ice which during the past night must have, with terrific violence, been driven against her, that she had probably been cut down by degrees to the water's edge, and that thus the ice must have swept over her. They said that if even those on board had been able to launch a boat, no boat could have lived amid the floating ice; and that even, had she escaped from the ice, she must have foundered in the chopping sea running at the mouth of the river. Probably, when the weather moderated in the spring, portions of the wreck would be found thrown up on the shore, and that was all that would ever be known of her fate. The captain, after waiting some days, and nothing being heard of the frigate or the lost officers and men, being sufficiently recovered, proceeded with the remainder of the

W. H. G. Kingston

crew to Cuxhaven.

Devereux, Paul and O'Grady were general favourites, and their loss caused great sorrow among their surviving shipmates; but sailors, especially in those busy, stirring days, had little time for mourning for those who had gone where they knew that they themselves might soon be called on to follow. Some honest tears were shed to their memory, and the captain with a heavy heart wrote his despatches, giving an account of the loss of his ship, and of the subsequent misfortune by which the service had been deprived of so many gallant and promising young officers. The ambassador and his suite had for some time before taken their departure, as the French were known to be advancing eastward, and might have, had they delayed, intercepted them. For the same reason Captain Order and his officers and crew anxiously looked forward to the arrival of a ship of war to take them away, as they did not fancy finishing off their adventures by being made prisoners and marched off to Verdun, or some other unpleasant place, where the French at that time shut up their captives. At length a sloop of war arrived, and they reached England in safety. Captain Order and his officers had to undergo a court-martial for the loss of the frigate, when they were not only honourably acquitted, but were complimented on the admirable discipline which had been maintained, and were at once turned over to another frigate, the *Dido*, lately launched, and fitting with all possible dispatch for sea.

But there were sad hearts and weeping eyes in one humble home, where the loss of two deeply loved ones was mourned; and even in the paternal hall of O'Grady, and in the pretentious mansion of Devereux, sorrow was expressed, and some tears were shed for those who had thus early been cut off in their career of glory. We will not attempt to pry into the grief which existed in Gerrard's home. It did not show itself by loud cries and lamentations, but it was very evident that from one heart there all joyousness had for ever flown. Still Mary bore up wonderfully. All her attention seemed to be occupied in attending to her mother, who, already delicate, felt Paul's loss dreadfully. Her young brothers and sisters, too, required her care. As usual, she taught them their lessons, made and mended their clothes, helped to cook their dinners, and attended them at their meals. None of these things did she for a day leave undone, and even Sarah and John, whispering together, agreed that Mary could not have cared so very much for Gilbert, and still less for poor Paul.

Some weeks passed on, when one day, when Mary was out marketing, Mrs Gerrard received a letter curiously marked over—not very clean, and with a high postage. Fortunately she had just enough to pay for it. She read it more than once. "Poor, dear, sweet, good Mary!" she exclaimed; "I almost fear to tell her; the revulsion may be too great. I know how much she has suffered, though others don't."

A writer has a great advantage in being able to shift the scene, and to go backwards or forwards in time as he may find necessary. We must go back to that fine, bright, but bitterly cold morning when Lieutenant Devereux and his companions set off to visit the frigate. They were strong and hardy, had thick coats, and, besides, the exercise kept them warm. The way was difficult, often through deep snow, into which they sank up to their middles. They looked in vain for trace of any of their lost shipmates. They were already entombed beneath the glittering snow, not to be again seen till the warm sun of the spring should expose them to the gaze of passers by. They at length reached the ship, and climbed up through a main-deck port. How silent and melancholy seemed the deserted ship, lately crowded with active busy human beings never more again destined to people its decks.

They looked into the cabins and selected a few articles they had before forgotten, taking some articles from the cabins of their messmates which they thought might be valued. On the main-deck the injuries which the ship had received were not so apparent.

"Would it be possible to save her?" exclaimed Devereux. "If she could be buoyed up with empty casks and got off into deep water, we might patch her up sufficiently to run her over to Yarmouth Roads. I would rather see her bones left there than here."

"Anything you like I am ready for," said O'Grady, and Paul repeated the sentiment.

"I do not mean to say that we can do it by ourselves; but if we can form a good plan to place before the captain, perhaps he will let us have the rest of the people to carry it out," said Devereux. "However, before we begin, let us have some food. I am very hungry after our walk, and I daresay you all are."

All hands agreed to this; there was no lack of provisions. Some time was occupied in the meal, and then they set to work to make their survey. As they wished to be exact, and to ascertain the number of casks on which they could depend for floating the ship, the business occupied a longer time than they had expected. They had nearly completed their plans when Paul, looking through one of the ports, saw the water rushing by with great rapidity, carrying with it large blocks of ice capable of overwhelming anybody they might have struck. The tide had turned, it was too evident, some time, and their retreat to the shore was cut off. Paul reported the circumstance to Devereux. There was no doubt about the matter. They stood at the gangway gazing at the roaring torrent, full of masses of ice leaping over and grinding against each other. No one but a madman would have ventured to cross it. It seemed doubtful if even a boat could live in such a turmoil of waters. If the flood ran up thus strong, what might be the effects of the ebb? It would not be low water again till past midnight, and it would then be very dangerous, if not altogether impracticable, to get on shore. They must, therefore, make up their minds to remain on board till the following day.

"The old ship is not going to tumble to pieces just yet," said Devereux. "We might have had worse quarters than she can still afford, so we shall have to turn into our berths and wait till the sun rises again."

Whether the young lieutenant felt as confident as he expressed himself might have been doubted; but he was one of those wise people who always make the best of everything, carrying out practically the proverb "What cannot be cured must be endured." As they had plenty to do, and were able to light a fire in the cabin stove and another in the galley to cook their supper, they passed their time not unpleasantly. Their habits of naval discipline would not allow them to dispense with a watch, so, while the rest turned in, one officer and one man at a time walked the deck, though, as O'Grady remarked, "We are not likely to run foul of anything, seeing that we are hard and fast aground, and nothing will purposely run foul of us; and if anything does, it may, for we can't get out of its way." Devereux took the dog watch, O'Grady was to take the first, and Paul the middle. Paul was not sorry to turn in, for he was very tired. He had not slept, as he thought, when he felt O'Grady's hand on his shoulder, telling him that it was time to turn out.

He was on deck in a minute, where he found O'Grady, who was waiting his coming. Just as O'Grady was going down, a loud, grating, crushing noise assailed their ears. It was blowing very strong, and freezing extremely hard. The night also was very dark, and occasionally heavy falls of snow came on, making the obscurity greater. The rushing noise increased. The tide they knew must have turned, and was now coming down with terrific force.

"I say, Gerrard, I doubt if Devereux's plan will succeed, if the ice continues to come down in this fashion; more likely to cut the old barkie to pieces," observed O'Grady.

"I am afraid so," said Paul; "I'll ask Cole what he thinks of the state of affairs."

Reuben was found, and confessed that he did not like them. The wind had increased to a fearful gale, which howled and whistled through the shrouds, and between the intervals of these gusts the roar of the distant ocean could be heard, as the seas met together, or dashed in heavy rollers on the coast.

While the midshipmen and Reuben were talking, they became conscious that the ship was moving; her deck rose and fell very slowly certainly, but they felt the sensation of which perhaps only seamen could have been aware that they were standing on a floating body. They instantly called Devereux, and he was convinced of the awful fact that the frigate was moving. In her present condition she could not float long, and though they might lower a boat, it was impossible that a boat could live among the masses of ice rushing by. Perhaps the frigate might ground again. They sounded the well; she had not made much water since they came on board, so she might float for some time longer. Perhaps she was still in shallow water, and just gliding over the bottom. A lead was found and hove for soundings; but instead of striking the water, it came upon hard ice. The mystery was explained. The whole floe in which the ship was embedded was floating away. There could be little doubt about that. But where was it driving to? That was the question. It might drive out to sea, and becoming broken by the force of the waves, allow the ship to sink between its fragments. Still even then they might possibly be able to escape in a boat. One was therefore cleared and got ready for landing, and a supply of provisions, a compass, and water, were placed in her, with some spare cloaks and blankets to afford them a slight shield and protection from the inclemency of the weather. After this they could do no more than pray that warning might be given them of the ship's sinking, and wait patiently for day.

The cold was so intense that they would have been almost frozen to death had they not been able to keep up a fire in the cabin stove, round which officers and men now clustered. It might possibly be their last meeting on this side a watery grave, and yet they had all, young and old, been so accustomed to face death, that they did not allow the anticipation of it altogether to quench their spirits. They talked of the past and even of the future, although fully aware that that future on earth might not be for them.

Day came at last, cold and grey. They looked out; they were, as they had conjectured, surrounded by a solid floe of ice—so thick that there seemed little danger of its immediately breaking up. Beyond it was the leaden sea foaming and hissing—but, in spite of the gale, not breaking heavily, owing to the floes of ice floating about and the direction of the wind; while in the distance to the south, and on either hand, was a low line of coast, with islands here and there scattered now and then.

The prospect was uninviting. The ship was driving out to sea, and could not then long hold together. O'Grady proposed making an attempt to gain the shore in the boat; but Devereux pointed out the difficulty there would be in making headway against the furious gale then blowing, in addition to the risk of having the boat stove in by the ice.

"No, no; let us stick to the ship as long as she keeps above water," he added.

Of course all agreed that his decision was right. They were not idle, however. Paul suggested that if a boat could not live, a strong raft might; and as soon as breakfast was over, they set to work to build one. As they had plenty of time and materials, they made it big enough and strong enough to carry fifty men, and in the centre built a store-house to hold provisions for several days. Fortunately the ice did not move very fast; and before they had drifted far off the coast, the wind shifted, and drove them along it at the same rate as before. Still it continued freezing hard. A rapid thaw they had most to fear, as it would melt away the supporting floe, and let the ship sink. But then they might take to their boat. Had it not been for the anxiety they felt as to what might happen, they had no great cause to complain, as they had shelter and firing, and were amply supplied with provisions, besides, as O'Grady observed, enjoying the advantage, when the raft was finished, of having nothing to do. The third night they had spent on board came to a close. They kept a very strict watch, that should any change occur, they might not be taken unawares. On looking out they found the land much nearer than before. This was accounted for, as the wind had shifted, and now blew almost directly on shore.

"Our voyage will come to an end sooner than we expected last night," observed O'Grady. "For my part I am almost sorry; it's very good fun."

"It will be no laughing matter, if the wind increases, and a heavy surf breaks on the shore," said Devereux, who overheard the remark.

The ship, still surrounded by its mass of ice, to which it acted as a sail, drifted slowly, but steadily, towards the shore. The rate of progress was increased, however, before long by the rising wind, and the deck of the ship, hitherto only gently undulating, began to be tossed about with a motion more rapid than pleasant. As they drove on, the land opened out, and appeared on either hand; so that they found that they were at the entrance of an estuary, or the mouth of a wide river. But the sea rolled in very heavily, and they feared, if it increased, that the ice round the ship would break up. Still there would be ample warning given, and they dreaded no immediate danger. The raft and boat were both got ready. Should the ship sink, the former would in all probability float, and afford them a refuge should the boat be unable to live.

"And now all our preparations are made, we'll pipe to dinner," said Devereux.

And the whole party sat down to a not unsubstantial meal round the cabin stove. Dinner was over. It had been somewhat prolonged, for there was nothing to do, and they had been talking of by-gone days, and fighting their battles over again. It was time, however, to look out to see what progress they had been of late making. It was O'Grady's watch, and when he opened the cabin door to go out, he saw a mass of smoke eddying round in the fore-part of the deck. His companions soon joined him to ascertain beyond a doubt that the ship was on fire. It might still be overcome. But the fresh water had been started; there was only ice alongside, and the pumps were choked. The party made a rush towards the fire, in the hopes of beating it out; but they were soon convinced that it had gained hold of the ship, and that no efforts they could make to extinguish it would avail. How it had originated there was no time to consider. Probably some coal jerked out of the galley-fire had found its way below, and had ignited some of the stores. The flames now burst forth, and spread rapidly—bursting through the hatchways and ports, and soon enveloping the whole of the fore-part of the ship. The party were now exposed to even a more terrible danger than any they had anticipated. Their raft would no longer avail them. Their entire dependence must be on their frail boat. Still till the last moment they were unwilling to leave the once stout ship which had so long been their home.

"We must go, my lads," exclaimed Devereux, with a sigh, as the flames, fanned by the wind, rapidly approached the quarter-deck. "One good thing is, that should she drive on shore, and the French be in the neighbourhood, they will not benefit by her."

"Hurrah! one cheer for the old barkie before we leave her!" cried Reuben Cole, as they launched the boat on to the ice. "Another good is, that not another mortal man will set his foot on her deck after us."

"Hurrah! hurrah! hurrah!" they shouted, as they ran the boat over the ice.

They did not leave the ship a moment too soon, for scarcely had they got their boat into the water to the leeward of the floe, than the fore-mast, already a pyramid of fire, fell with a loud crash on the ice.

"There is something more coming, and the further off we are, the better," cried Devereux. "I should have thought of that before. Give way, lads; the fire will soon reach the magazine."

So long as the boat was under the lee of the floe she made tolerably fine weather of it; but as she increased her distance, the seas came rolling up after her, threatening every instant to engulph her. A mast had been stepped, and a sail got ready for hoisting. This was now run up, and assisted her greatly.

Devereux steered, and even he could scarcely keep his eyes from the burning ship. A cry from his companions made him for an instant turn his head. There was a thundering deep report; and as he looked for an instant, the whole ship seemed, with her remaining masts and spars one mass of flame, to be lifted bodily up out of her icy cradle into the air. Up, up it went, and then, splitting into ten thousand fragments, down it came hissing and crashing, some into the foaming sea, and others on to the ice, where they continued to burn brilliantly. There was no cheering this time. Paul felt more inclined to cry, as he witnessed the fate of the gallant frigate.

"If the wreckers on shore were expecting a prize, they'll be mistaken," observed Reuben, when all had been silent for some time.

They had enough to do to look after their own safety. It was already dusk. Masses of ice were floating about, not very thickly, but thick enough to make it a matter of difficulty to avoid them. The land was flat, and they were nearer to it than they supposed. A point appeared on the right. If they could get round it without being swamped, they would be in smooth water. They gave the point a sufficient berth. A heavy sea came rolling by them; luffing up, they ran in, and in another minute found themselves standing up a river of some size in perfectly smooth water. The weather was very cold, and they were anxious to get on shore as soon as possible. The further up they went, however, the more likely they were, they thought, to find satisfactory shelter, for as yet no houses of any sort could be seen. Shelter, however, must, if possible, be found, for although they had provisions, the weather was too cold to allow them to remain out, if it could be helped. They stood on for nearly half an hour, when a light was seen glimmering on the opposite shore. They steered towards it, fortunately lowering the sail when at some distance from it, for before the boat had lost way, her stem struck against the ice which fringed the bank, and very nearly stove in her bow. Searching about, however, they at length found a landing-place, and with hearts thankful for their escape sprang on shore. That they might not be a burden to the people whose hospitality they intended to seek, they loaded themselves, not only with the valuables they had rescued from the wreck, but with a good supply of provisions. They proceeded, therefore, boldly along a tolerable road in the direction of the light, or rather lights, for several appeared as they advanced.

"Oh, depend on it we shall have a cordial reception," said O'Grady. "Very likely that is some fat old Burgomaster's country residence, and he is giving a ball, or an entertainment of some sort, for which we shall come in."

"As likely it is a flour-mill, and those lights we see are from its windows," remarked Devereux.

"We shall soon settle the point, for we shall be up to the place directly," said Paul. "The lights are lower than I at first thought, and appear to be in the windows of several houses. Hark! I hear the tramp of horses coming along the road."

"Qui va la?" shouted a voice, in sharp, stern accents. "Stand and declare yourselves!"

"We are in for it," whispered O'Grady. "What can the fellows be?"

"French dragoons, I am afraid," answered Paul, "There is no use attempting to deceive them. They ask who we are."

"Gerrard, you speak French better than I do; tell them," said Devereux.

"Naval officers who have lost their ship, and are seeking for shelter this bitter cold night," shouted Paul.

"Come then with us," exclaimed the sergeant in command of the patrol, riding up. "Your story, friends, may or may not be true. If you are spies, the consequences may be unpleasant."

Escorted by the horsemen, they were conducted to the building they had seen. It appeared to be a large country house. All the outhouses and lower rooms were converted into stables, little trouble having been taken to remove rich Brussels carpets or valuable furniture. They were led upstairs to a large room, where several officers were seated at supper, and were announced as prisoners just captured on the road, reporting themselves as naval officers.

"A likely story," observed the commanding officer—a general apparently by his uniform. "What have you to say for yourselves?"

"That our tale is true," answered Devereux. "Any person on the coast must have seen our ship burning. If you will send, you can ascertain the truth of that part of our account."

"It is a considerable distance from the coast, and we cannot spare men to send," said the general, gruffly.

"The boat by which we landed will be found at the bank of the river," observed Paul, quietly.

"Very likely, but that will only prove that you landed from some ship off the coast," exclaimed the general, in an angry tone. "You were found prowling about my head-quarters, the act of spies, and as spies you will be treated. If your story is not authenticated, you will be shot at sunrise."

"Say, rather, brutally murdered!" said Devereux, indignantly. "I call all here to witness that I state that I am a British officer, that these are my subordinates, that all I have said is true, and that we landed here not knowing that the French were occupying the country."

The general, once well known for his atrocious cruelties, had made a signal to the guard to lead away the prisoners, when a young man entered the room dressed in the uniform of an hussar. Paul looked at him very hard, struck by his strong likeness to Alphonse Montauban.

"What!" exclaimed the new comer, springing forward, and taking Paul's hand, "Is it possible?"

His voice made Devereux and O'Grady turn their heads; and in spite of the astonished and angry looks of the general and some of his officers, he grasped their hands; then turning to the general, he cried out—

"What have these officers done? They appear to be treated as criminals. I know them well. They are old friends, who, when I was their prisoner, treated me with kindness, sympathy, and generosity. I will answer for it that whatever account they have given of themselves is the true one."

"That alters the case, my dear Count," said the general, in a blander tone than he had as yet used. "If they really have been wrecked, although we must consider them as prisoners, they shall receive all courtesy at our hands, and be exchanged as soon as possible."

Of course Devereux again gave an account of their adventures, on the truth of which Alphonse staked his honour.

"Very well; then if they will pass their parole, they shall be committed to your charge, Count," said the general, with a more courteous glance at the English officers than he had hitherto bestowed.

All arrangements having been made, the prisoners accompanied Alphonse to his quarters, where, with the aid of the provisions they had brought, an ample repast was soon spread before them. Of course they were all eager to know how Alphonse had happened so opportunely to make his appearance. He briefly told them that his father, who was no other than the old gentleman in the chateau whom Paul and O'Grady had known as *Mon Oncle*, was the Count de Montauban, and that his title having been restored by the Emperor, he had, on his death, succeeded to it; that having left the marine, of which his experiences had made him heartily sick, he had entered the army, and had rapidly risen to the command of a troop in a light cavalry regiment. His corps belonged to a division of the army which for some strategical object had been pushed forward, but was expected quickly to retreat, when he thought it very possible that the general would set them at liberty.

The old friends spent a very pleasant evening, much pleasanter, O'Grady remarked, for his part, than if he had expected to be taken out to be shot the next morning as a spy. He asked, not without a blush, increased when he saw Paul's laughing eye fixed on him, after Rosalie.

"Oh, my dear cousin is well, and merry as ever, if I may judge by her letters, for she writes constantly to me; indeed, I may confess that our parents have arranged an affair between us which we neither of us shall be loath to carry out. When I saw her, she laughed a great deal at the attempts of my young Irish friend, as she called you, O'Grady, to learn French, and said that she was afraid she would have had to give you up as a hopeless case."

W. H. G. Kingston

Poor Paddy made an hysterical attempt to join the laugh of his companions against himself, and it was observed that he never again, at least not for some years, spoke about his dear little Rosalie.

After a detention of some weeks, the whole party were, as Alphonse had anticipated they would be, released, and having ample funds which the young Count pressed on them, they made their way without difficulty to Cuxhaven, which place of course the captain and officers and crew of the lost frigate had long since left. They succeeded, however, without much delay in getting over to England. Mary recovered her health, and on Devereux becoming a commander, they were married. O'Grady married one of her younger sisters a few years afterwards, and when peace came, paid a very pleasant visit to his old friends the Count and Countess Montauban.

Paul rose to the top of his profession, and used to take great delight in narrating to his grandchildren his adventures when he was a cabin-boy. To one of these grandchildren I am indebted for this history.

# ABOUT THE AUTHOR

**William Henry Giles Kingston** (1814 - 1880), writer of tales for boys, born in London, but spent much of his youth in Oporto, where his father was a merchant.

His first book, The Circassian Chief, appeared in 1844. His first book for boys, Peter the Whaler, was published in 1851, and had such success that he retired from business and devoted himself entirely to the production of this kind of literature, in which his popularity was deservedly great; and during 30 years he wrote upwards of 130 tales, including The Three Midshipmen (1862), The Three Lieutenants (1874), The Three Commanders (1875), The Three Admirals (1877), Digby Heathcote, etc.

He also conducted various papers, including The Colonist, and Colonial Magazine and East India Review. He was also interested in emigration, volunteering, and various philanthropic schemes. For services in negotiating a commercial treaty with Portugal he received a Portuguese knighthood, and for his literary labours a Government pension.

# Choose from Thousands of 1stWorldLibrary Classics By

| | | |
|---|---|---|
| A. M. Barnard | Booth Tarkington | Edward Everett Hale |
| Ada Leverson | Boyd Cable | Edward J. O'Biren |
| Adolphus William Ward | Bram Stoker | Edward S. Ellis |
| Aesop | C. Collodi | Edwin L. Arnold |
| Agatha Christie | C. E. Orr | Eleanor Atkins |
| Alexander Aaronsohn | C. M. Ingleby | Eleanor Hallowell Abbott |
| Alexander Kielland | Carolyn Wells | Eliot Gregory |
| Alexandre Dumas | Catherine Parr Traill | Elizabeth Gaskell |
| Alfred Gatty | Charles A. Eastman | Elizabeth McCracken |
| Alfred Ollivant | Charles Amory Beach | Elizabeth Von Arnim |
| Alice Duer Miller | Charles Dickens | Ellem Key |
| Alice Turner Curtis | Charles Dudley Warner | Emerson Hough |
| Alice Dunbar | Charles Farrar Browne | Emilie F. Carlen |
| Allen Chapman | Charles Ives | Emily Bronte |
| Alleyne Ireland | Charles Kingsley | Emily Dickinson |
| Ambrose Bierce | Charles Klein | Enid Bagnold |
| Amelia E. Barr | Charles Hanson Towne | Enilor Macartney Lane |
| Amory H. Bradford | Charles Lathrop Pack | Erasmus W. Jones |
| Andrew Lang | Charles Romyn Dake | Ernie Howard Pie |
| Andrew McFarland Davis | Charles Whibley | Ethel May Dell |
| Andy Adams | Charles Willing Beale | Ethel Turner |
| Angela Brazil | Charlotte M. Braeme | Ethel Watts Mumford |
| Anna Alice Chapin | Charlotte M. Yonge | Eugene Sue |
| Anna Sewell | Charlotte Perkins Stetson | Eugenie Foa |
| Annie Besant | Clair W. Hayes | Eugene Wood |
| Annie Hamilton Donnell | Clarence Day Jr. | Eustace Hale Ball |
| Annie Payson Call | Clarence E. Mulford | Evelyn Everett-green |
| Annie Roe Carr | Clemence Housman | Everard Cotes |
| Annonaymous | Confucius | F. H. Cheley |
| Anton Chekhov | Coningsby Dawson | F. J. Cross |
| Archibald Lee Fletcher | Cornelis DeWitt Wilcox | F. Marion Crawford |
| Arnold Bennett | Cyril Burleigh | Fannie E. Newberry |
| Arthur C. Benson | D. H. Lawrence | Federick Austin Ogg |
| Arthur Conan Doyle | Daniel Defoe | Ferdinand Ossendowski |
| Arthur M. Winfield | David Garnett | Fergus Hume |
| Arthur Ransome | Dinah Craik | Florence A. Kilpatrick |
| Arthur Schnitzler | Don Carlos Janes | Fremont B. Deering |
| Arthur Train | Donald Keyhoe | Francis Bacon |
| Atticus | Dorothy Kilner | Francis Darwin |
| B.H. Baden-Powell | Dougan Clark | Frances Hodgson Burnett |
| B. M. Bower | Douglas Fairbanks | Frances Parkinson Keyes |
| B. C. Chatterjee | E. Nesbit | Frank Gee Patchin |
| Baroness Emmuska Orczy | E. P. Roe | Frank Harris |
| Baroness Orczy | E. Phillips Oppenheim | Frank Jewett Mather |
| Basil King | E. S. Brooks | Frank L. Packard |
| Bayard Taylor | Earl Barnes | Frank V. Webster |
| Ben Macomber | Edgar Rice Burroughs | Frederic Stewart Isham |
| Bertha Muzzy Bower | Edith Van Dyne | Frederick Trevor Hill |
| Bjornstjerne Bjornson | Edith Wharton | Frederick Winslow Taylor |

Friedrich Kerst
Friedrich Nietzsche
Fyodor Dostoyevsky
G.A. Henty
G.K. Chesterton
Gabrielle E. Jackson
Garrett P. Serviss
Gaston Leroux
George A. Warren
George Ade
Geroge Bernard Shaw
George Cary Eggleston
George Durston
George Ebers
George Eliot
George Gissing
George MacDonald
George Meredith
George Orwell
George Sylvester Viereck
George Tucker
George W. Cable
George Wharton James
Gertrude Atherton
Gordon Casserly
Grace E. King
Grace Gallatin
Grace Greenwood
Grant Allen
Guillermo A. Sherwell
Gulielma Zollinger
Gustav Flaubert
H. A. Cody
H. B. Irving
H.C. Bailey
H. G. Wells
H. H. Munro
H. Irving Hancock
H. R. Naylor
H. Rider Haggard
H. W. C. Davis
Haldeman Julius
Hall Caine
Hamilton Wright Mabie
Hans Christian Andersen
Harold Avery
Harold McGrath
Harriet Beecher Stowe
Harry Castlemon
Harry Coghill
Harry Houidini

Hayden Carruth
Helent Hunt Jackson
Helen Nicolay
Hendrik Conscience
Hendy David Thoreau
Henri Barbusse
Henrik Ibsen
Henry Adams
Henry Ford
Henry Frost
Henry James
Henry Jones Ford
Henry Seton Merriman
Henry W Longfellow
Herbert A. Giles
Herbert Carter
Herbert N. Casson
Herman Hesse
Hildegard G. Frey
Homer
Honore De Balzac
Horace B. Day
Horace Walpole
Horatio Alger Jr.
Howard Pyle
Howard R. Garis
Hugh Lofting
Hugh Walpole
Humphry Ward
Ian Maclaren
Inez Haynes Gillmore
Irving Bacheller
Isabel Cecilia Williams
Isabel Hornibrook
Israel Abrahams
Ivan Turgenev
J.G.Austin
J. Henri Fabre
J. M. Barrie
J. M. Walsh
J. Macdonald Oxley
J. R. Miller
J. S. Fletcher
J. S. Knowles
J. Storer Clouston
J. W. Duffield
Jack London
Jacob Abbott
James Allen
James Andrews
James Baldwin

James Branch Cabell
James DeMille
James Joyce
James Lane Allen
James Lane Allen
James Oliver Curwood
James Oppenheim
James Otis
James R. Driscoll
Jane Abbott
Jane Austen
Jane L. Stewart
Janet Aldridge
Jens Peter Jacobsen
Jerome K. Jerome
Jessie Graham Flower
John Buchan
John Burroughs
John Cournos
John F. Kennedy
John Gay
John Glasworthy
John Habberton
John Joy Bell
John Kendrick Bangs
John Milton
John Philip Sousa
John Taintor Foote
Jonas Lauritz Idemil Lie
Jonathan Swift
Joseph A. Altsheler
Joseph Carey
Joseph Conrad
Joseph E. Badger Jr
Joseph Hergesheimer
Joseph Jacobs
Jules Vernes
Julian Hawthrone
Julie A Lippmann
Justin Huntly McCarthy
Kakuzo Okakura
Karle Wilson Baker
Kate Chopin
Kenneth Grahame
Kenneth McGaffey
Kate Langley Bosher
Kate Langley Bosher
Katherine Cecil Thurston
Katherine Stokes
L. A. Abbot
L. T. Meade

L. Frank Baum
Latta Griswold
Laura Dent Crane
Laura Lee Hope
Laurence Housman
Lawrence Beasley
Leo Tolstoy
Leonid Andreyev
Lewis Carroll
Lewis Sperry Chafer
Lilian Bell
Lloyd Osbourne
Louis Hughes
Louis Joseph Vance
Louis Tracy
Louisa May Alcott
Lucy Fitch Perkins
Lucy Maud Montgomery
Luther Benson
Lydia Miller Middleton
Lyndon Orr
M. Corvus
M. H. Adams
Margaret E. Sangster
Margret Howth
Margaret Vandercook
Margaret W. Hungerford
Margret Penrose
Maria Edgeworth
Maria Thompson Daviess
Mariano Azuela
Marion Polk Angellotti
Mark Overton
Mark Twain
Mary Austin
Mary Catherine Crowley
Mary Cole
Mary Hastings Bradley
Mary Roberts Rinehart
Mary Rowlandson
M. Wollstonecraft Shelley
Maud Lindsay
Max Beerbohm
Myra Kelly
Nathaniel Hawthrone
Nicolo Machiavelli
O. F. Walton
Oscar Wilde

Owen Johnson
P.G. Wodehouse
Paul and Mabel Thorne
Paul G. Tomlinson
Paul Severing
Percy Brebner
Percy Keese Fitzhugh
Peter B. Kyne
Plato
Quincy Allen
R. Derby Holmes
R. L. Stevenson
R. S. Ball
Rabindranath Tagore
Rahul Alvares
Ralph Bonehill
Ralph Henry Barbour
Ralph Victor
Ralph Waldo Emmerson
Rene Descartes
Ray Cummings
Rex Beach
Rex E. Beach
Richard Harding Davis
Richard Jefferies
Richard Le Gallienne
Robert Barr
Robert Frost
Robert Gordon Anderson
Robert L. Drake
Robert Lansing
Robert Lynd
Robert Michael Ballantyne
Robert W. Chambers
Rosa Nouchette Carey
Rudyard Kipling
Saint Augustine
Samuel B. Allison
Samuel Hopkins Adams
Sarah Bernhardt
Sarah C. Hallowell
Selma Lagerlof
Sherwood Anderson
Sigmund Freud
Standish O'Grady
Stanley Weyman
Stella Benson
Stella M. Francis

Stephen Crane
Stewart Edward White
Stijn Streuvels
Swami Abhedananda
Swami Parmananda
T. S. Ackland
T. S. Arthur
The Princess Der Ling
Thomas A. Janvier
Thomas A Kempis
Thomas Anderton
Thomas Bailey Aldrich
Thomas Bulfinch
Thomas De Quincey
Thomas Dixon
Thomas H. Huxley
Thomas Hardy
Thomas More
Thornton W. Burgess
U. S. Grant
Upton Sinclair
Valentine Williams
Various Authors
Vaughan Kester
Victor Appleton
Victor G. Durham
Victoria Cross
Virginia Woolf
Wadsworth Camp
Walter Camp
Walter Scott
Washington Irving
Wilbur Lawton
Wilkie Collins
Willa Cather
Willard F. Baker
William Dean Howells
William le Queux
W. Makepeace Thackeray
William W. Walter
William Shakespeare
Winston Churchill
Yei Theodora Ozaki
Yogi Ramacharaka
Young E. Allison
Zane Grey